Deutsch: ZWEITE STUFE

**A Second-Level
Course
in
German**

Gerald E. Logan

Deutsch: ZWEITE STUFE

A Second-Level Course in German

For English-speaking students who want to continue developing communication skills in German.

This book is designed to follow *Deutsch: Kernstufe*

NEWBURY HOUSE PUBLISHERS, Inc.
Rowley, Massachusetts

Library of Congress Cataloging in Publication Data

Logan, Gerald E.
   Deutsch, zweite Stufe.

   SUMMARY: A textbook of German grammar for second-year students in high school and college.
   1. German language--Grammar--1950-   [1. German language--Grammar] I. Title.
PF3111.L68   438'.2'421   76-51773
ISBN 0-88377-063-6

Photographs on pp. 28, 46, 217 are by *David Braswell.*

All other photographs are by the courtesy of *German Information Center,* 410 Park Avenue, New York City.

Book design by *Janina Grzedzielska.*

NEWBURY HOUSE PUBLISHERS, Inc.

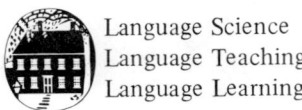
Language Science
Language Teaching
Language Learning

68 Middle Road, Rowley, Massachusetts 01969

Copyright © 1977 by Newbury House Publishers, Inc. All rights reserved. No part of this book may be reproduced or transmitted in any form or by any means, electronic or mechanical, including photocopying, recording, or by any information storage and retrieval system, without permission in writing from the Publisher.

First printing: March 1977
Printed in the U.S.A.

PREFACE

Deutsch: ZWEITE STUFE and its precursor, *Deutsch: KERNSTUFE,* are based on a learning rationale gained from long teaching experience. This rationale has been shaped pragmatically—by those techniques and activities which effected the desired results in students. Teachers—and students—may, of course, differ about the results that are desired. In most cases, however, we have found that a common goal is the ability of people to communicate (especially orally) as soon as possible in the second language, and to refine this ability in subsequent work.

Specific rationale for the approach in our courses has been outlined in detail in the *Teacher's Manual* for *Deutsch: KERNSTUFE* and the *Teacher's Guide* for *German Conversational Practice* (both published by Newbury House Publishers).

We would like to urge interested teachers to acquaint themselves with this rationale and to read Professor Pit Corder's *Introducing Applied Linguistics.* (Corder is Professor of Applied Linguistics and Head of the Department of Linguistics at the University of Edinburgh in Scotland. The paperbound edition of his book is distributed by Penguin Books.) His is an eminently sensible and practical book.

It is very important that teachers contemplating using *Deutsch: ZWEITE STUFE* consult the *Teacher's Manual,* which is available from the publisher. In addition to a brief rationale, there are details for planning the second-level course, answers for the practice tests, and a series of tests with answers for the "test lessons" in the text. There is also a list of lessons and sections which have been recorded (available from the publisher) or can be recorded by the teacher.

G. E. L.

TABLE OF CONTENTS

Erster Teil 1-59
   Thema: Krieg
   New Grammar: *Plurals; Imperative Forms*
   (See page 2 for the details of the contents in this part.)

Zweiter Teil 61-118
   Thema: Der Rhein
   New Grammar: *Narrative Past*
   (See page 62 for the details of the contents in this part.)

Dritter Teil 119-179
   Thema: Die Liebe
   New Grammar: *Past Perfect Tense; Perfect Tenses of the Modals; Subjunctive; Conditional Sentences*
   (See page 120 for the details of the contents in this part.)

Vierter Teil 181-238
   Thema: Fantasiewelt
   New Grammar: *Relative Pronouns; Pronoun Agreement; "da" and "wo" compounds*
   (See page 182 for the details of the contents in this part.)

Complement 239-284
   New Grammar: *Passive; Comparison of Adjectives; Ordinals/Fractions; Present Participles; Genitive; Reflexives; Time Phrases; Indirect Discourse; Wishes; Negation; Words often Confused; Some Common Idioms*
   (See page 241 for the details of the contents and for the lesson numbers.)

Vocabularies
   English-German 287-295
   German-English 297-307

Deutsch: ZWEITE STUFE

ERSTER TEIL

Das Thema: KRIEG

"Den Sohn. Und den Mann. Und in der Mitte den General. Und dann liest sie die Briefe, die der General schrieb. 1917. Für Deutschland. —— 1940. Für Deutschland. —— Mehr liest die Mutter nicht. Ihre Augen sind ganz rot. Sind so rot."

Lessons 1-4	4
Ein Lied: "Sag mir, wo die Blumen sind!"	
Lessons 5-7	13
Die deutsche Sprache: Wiederholung (Verbformen)	
Lessons 9-14	22
Die deutsche Sprache: Etwas Neues (Mehrzahl und Befehlsform)	
Lessons 17-22	40
Zum Lesen: "Die lange lange Straße lang" (eine Geschichte)	
"September" (ein Gedicht)	

Test Lessons
    Lesson 8   22
    Lessons 15-16   36

"Wann wird man je verstehen?"

Deutsch: ZWEITE STUFE

"Sag mir, wo die Mädchen sind!"

LESSON 1

A. **Your objectives:** To be able to read (or sing) the first three verses of the song in Section C while looking at the text—with pronunciation and intonation which would be readily understood by a native speaker of German (your teacher will be the judge); to demonstrate your understanding of any line, phrase, or word in the song by being able to give English (or German, if so directed by your teacher) equivalents; and to be able to write the three verses without error if they are dictated to you in German.

B. **How to get there:** Listen to the recording of the song several times. Then study the text, using the English equivalents where necessary, until you feel that you have the meaning clear in your mind. Listen again to the recording while looking at the text. If the meaning "comes through" with no trouble, try listening without looking at the text. You understand it if you know the meaning of everything you are hearing without having to refer to any vocabulary lists or translations. Keep going back to the text until you have reached this level of comprehension.

Check to see if you can explain any words or phrases in the text (in English—or German, if so directed).

Lesson 1

Practice writing any new words. Do a final check by having someone read the lines from the song to you while you write them as a dictation (there is no need to keep writing those lines which repeat), or by playing the recording, a line at a time, pausing to write each line as a dictation. Practice writing any words you miss until you can do a dictation with no errors.

C. **What to learn:**   *SAG MIR,[1] WO DIE BLUMEN SIND!

Sag mir, wo die Blumen sind!
Wo sind sie geblieben?[2]
Sag mir, wo die Blumen sind!
Was ist gescheh'n?[3]
Sag mir, wo die Blumen sind!
Mädchen pflückten[4] sie geschwind.[5]
Wann wird[6] man je[7] versteh'n?
Wann wird man je versteh'n?

Sag mir, wo die Mädchen sind!
Wo sind sie geblieben?
Sag mir, wo die Mädchen sind!
Was ist gescheh'n?
Sag mir, wo die Mädchen sind!
Männer[8] nahmen[9] sie geschwind.
Wann wird man je versteh'n?
Wann wird man je versteh'n?

Sag mir, wo die Männer sind!
Wo sind sie geblieben?
Sag mir, wo die Männer sind!
Was ist gescheh'n?
Sag mir, wo die Männer sind!
Zogen fort,[10] der Krieg[11] beginnt.
Wann wird man je versteh'n?
Wann wird man je versteh'n?

*WHERE HAVE ALL THE FLOWERS GONE? (Sag' mir, wo die Blumen sind). By Pete Seeger. © Copyright 1961, 1962 by FALL RIVER MUSIC INC. All Rights Reserved. Used by Permission.

German sheet music published by Essex Musikvertrieb GmbH, Drususgasse 7-11, Cologne 1, Germany. Recorded in German by Marlene Dietrich, Electrola E 22 180; Lolita, Polydor 24 964; Lys Assia, Telefunken UX 5125.

1 tell me	4 picked, plucked	7 ever	10 moved out; marched on
2 What has become of them?	5 quickly	8 men	
3 (has) happened	6 will (*future*)	9 took	11 the war

D. **Analysis or explanations:**   The forms **pflückten**, **nahmen**, and **zogen fort** are "simple past" forms of **pflücken**, **nehmen**, and **fortziehen**, respectively. You will learn more about these forms and how to use them yourself in German when you reach Lesson 30.

E. **Practice:** Repeat the lines of the song several times, trying to imitate the model on the recording as closely as possible for pronunciation and intonation.

F. **Evaluation:** When you can carry out all the activities specified in Section A, report for evaluation. Your "test" for any lesson in *Deutsch: Zweite Stufe* will always include *all* the activities in the *objectives,* exactly as outlined.

LESSON 2

A. **Your objectives:** To demonstrate the same mastery of the last three verses of the song (in Section C below) as you were expected to do in Lesson 1 (see Section A of Lesson 1); and, in addition, to be able to answer the 15 questions in Section E below in oral and written German when you see or hear the questions in German.

B. **How to get there:** Follow the same procedure for mastery of the three verses as directed in Lesson 1.

"Blumen blüh'n im Sommerwind."

Lesson 2

When preparing to answer the questions in Section E, be certain you *understand* the question and the answer and are not simply memorizing. If you have to memorize which answers go with particular questions, without really understanding the question and the reason for the answer, something is wrong with your learning procedure. If you continue this way, you are "setting yourself up" for serious difficulties later. Consult your teacher.

C. What to learn: Sag' mir, wo die Blumen sind* (continued)

Sag, wo die Soldaten[1] sind!
Wo sind sie geblieben?
Sag, wo die Soldaten sind!
Was ist gescheh'n?
Sag, wo die Soldaten sind!
Über Gräbern[2] weht[3] der Wind.
Wann wird man je versteh'n?
Wann wird man je versteh'n?

Sag mir, wo die Gräber sind!
Wo sind sie geblieben?
Sag mir, wo die Gräber sind!
Was ist gescheh'n?
Sag mir, wo die Gräber sind!
Blumen blüh'n[4] im Sommerwind.
Wann wird man je versteh'n?
Wann wird man je versteh'n?

Sag mir, wo die Blumen sind!
Wo sind sie geblieben?
Sag mir, wo die Blumen sind!
Was ist gescheh'n?
Sag mir, wo die Blumen sind!
Mädchen pflückten sie geschwind.
Wann wird man je versteh'n?
Wann wird man je versteh'n?

*(See page 5.)

1 soldiers
2 graves
3 to blow; drift
4 to bloom

D. Analysis or explanations:

You will notice that several plural forms of nouns appear in the song. In Lesson 3 you will learn the singular forms of these particular words.

In Lesson 9 we will begin to analyze plurals in German, to learn the plural forms of all nouns which appeared in *Deutsch: Kernstufe,* and to learn how to communicate in German with the subject, object, and "other" forms in the plural.

Deutsch: ZWEITE STUFE

Der Krieg in Deutschland. 1944.

E. **Practice:** When you have mastered the song as directed in the objectives for Lessons 1 and 2, you should be ready to answer the following questions:

Antworten Sie, bitte! (mit einem Wort)

1.	Was haben die Mädchen gepflückt?	Blumen
2.	Wer hat die Blumen gepflückt?	Mädchen
3.	Wer nahm die Mädchen?	Männer
4.	Wie nahmen sie die Mädchen?	geschwind
5.	Was machten die Männer dann?	zogen fort
6.	Was beginnt?	Krieg
7.	Was sind die Männer im Krieg?	Soldaten
8.	Worüber weht der Wind?	Gräbern
9.	Was macht der Wind?	weht
10.	Was machen die Blumen im Sommerwind?	blühen

Antworten Sie mit einem Satz!

11.	Wo sind die Blumen?	Mädchen haben sie gepflückt.
12.	Wo sind die Mädchen?	Männer haben sie genommen.
13.	Wo sind die Männer?	Sie sind fortgezogen/im Krieg.
14.	Was weht wo?	Der Wind weht über Gräbern.
15.	Was blüht wo?	Blumen blühen im Sommerwind.

F. **Evaluation:** When you have mastered the three verses as directed in Section A, and when you are able to answer all the questions in Section E, report for evaluation.

LESSON 3

A. **Your objectives:** To give the German, both orally and in writing, of all words or phrases in the song in Lessons 1 and 2 when given the English equivalents as cues. The German must include:

1. the correct article (**der, die,** or **das**) of all nouns;
2. the plural form of all nouns;
3. the infinitive and past participle of all irregular verbs, plus the third person singular, present tense form, *if* it has a stem change.

All of these forms can be found in Section C of this lesson.

B.	**How to get there:**	Use the English in the left-hand column as your cue. Practice saying (use recordings, if necessary) and then writing the German forms.
C.	**What to learn:**			

to stay	bleiben		ist geblieben
to bloom	blühen		
to move on	fortziehen		ist fortgezogen
to happen	geschehen	geschieht	ist geschehen
to take	nehmen	nimmt	genommen
to pick	pflücken		
to blow	wehen		
to understand	verstehen		verstanden
to become	werden	wird	ist geworden
to say, tell	sagen		
flower	die Blume		die Blumen
grave	das Grab		die Gräber
war	der Krieg		die Kriege
girl	das Mädchen		die Mädchen
man	der Mann		die Männer
soldier	der Soldat		die Soldaten
summer	der Sommer		die Sommer
wind	der Wind		die Winde
"one"	man		
ever	je		
quickly	geschwind		

D. **Analysis or explanation:**

Notice that the plural forms of nouns in German *all* have the article **die**. Therefore there is no need to memorize the plural article for each noun.

The verb **werden** is also used as the auxiliary verb of the *future tense* in German: **Er wird verstehen** = *He will understand.* You do not normally use **werden** to indicate the future unless you want to emphasize the fact that you are talking about the future, or it might be misunderstood that you are referring to the future. In both German and English a present tense form is usually sufficient to indicate the future: **Er fährt morgen nach Köln.** = *He's driving to Cologne tomorrow.*

Lesson 4

E. Practice: See Section B above.

F. Evaluation: When you can say and write the forms specified in Section A, report for evaluation.

LESSON 4

A. Your objectives: To be able to complete—as a review—the self-test in Section E, both orally and in written German.

B. How to get there: On a separate piece of paper, write out any exercises called for. Look up (in Lessons 1-4) any answers you don't know or are not 100% sure of. Learn these.

Then see if you can do the test again without error—or at least those parts you were uncertain about.

C. What to learn: Review any C sections in Lessons 1-4 which you find necessary.

D. Analysis or explanations: Review any D sections in Lessons 1-4 which you find necessary.

E. Practice: SELF-TEST
1. Write the lines from the song as a dictation. Use a recording or have someone read the text to you.
2. Answer the following questions concerning the song. Write the answers in German, using short, but complete, sentences.

    a. Was weht über Gräbern?
    b. Wo sind die Soldaten?
    c. Wer hat die Blumen gepflückt?
    d. Wie haben die Männer die Mädchen genommen?
    e. Sag mir, wo die Männer sind!
    f. Wissen wir, wann man je verstehen wird?

3. Give the German for each of the following English words. Include the articles and the plural forms of all nouns,

12   Deutsch: ZWEITE STUFE

"Sag mir, wo die Männer sind!"

the infinitives and past participles of *all* verbs, and the third person forms of those verbs which have "changed stems" in the third person, present tense.

to pick	soldier
flower	to stay
to bloom	to happen
to take	summer
girl	war
wind	to move on
to blow	to say
grave	quickly
to understand	"one"
man	ever

F. Evaluation: When you can do the self-test without referring to any written answers, you are ready to report for evaluation.

LESSON 5

A. Your objectives: To be able to do the exercises in Section E orally and in writing with no errors.

B. How to get there: Study Section D carefully. Then learn any of the forms in Section C you don't know. Then practice doing Section E orally and in writing until you can do it easily without having to refer to anything other than the cues.

C. What to learn: Following is a summary of the verb forms you will need to know in order to complete this lesson:

INFINITIVE	3rd PERSON (if irregular)
sagen	
nehmen	nimmt
werden	wird
sein	ist
dürfen	darf
müssen	muß
können	kann
wollen	will

Be certain to study Section D for a complete explanation of the forms and their uses!

D. Analysis or explanations:

To refresh your memory—

1. Verbs normally have the following endings in the present tense:

ich	gehe		wir	gehen
du	gehst		ihr	geht
er	geht		sie, Sie	gehen

But don't forget that some verbs "change stems" in the singular:

ich	nehme		wir	nehmen
du	**nimm**st		ihr	nehmt
er	**nimm**t		sie, Sie	nehmen

2. The modal auxiliaries follow a somewhat different pattern than most verbs in their singular forms:

	können	müssen	dürfen	wollen	sollen	mögen
ich, er, sie es	kann	muß	darf	will	soll	mag
du	kannst	mußt	darfst	willst	sollst	magst
wir, sie, Sie	können	müssen	dürfen	wollen	sollen	mögen
ihr	könnt	müßt	dürft	wollt	sollt	mögt

Remember when using the modals that the main verb remains in the infinitive position at the end:

Du **darfst** nicht mehr hier **spielen**!

3. The present perfect tense: If a verb is not one of the irregular ones whose past participle you have memorized, its past participle is formed—most commonly—by prefixing a **ge-** and adding a **-t**:

wohnen	**ge**wohn**t**
spielen	**ge**spiel**t**
blühen	**ge**blüh**t**

If the verb is an irregular one, however, you should already have memorized the past participle (or know where to look it up quickly):

nehmen	**genommen**
sehen	**gesehen**
finden	**gefunden**

Remember that certain verbs in German use **ist** (or some other form of **sein**) as the auxiliary in the present perfect tense:

He ate (or has eaten) in Berlin.   Er **hat** in Berlin gegessen.
BUT:
He stayed (has stayed) in Berlin.   Er **ist** in Berlin geblieben.

You should memorize the **ist** along with the past participles which require its use.

Lesson 5

"Sie sind in Berlin geblieben."

Check to see if you still remember the forms of the auxiliaries **sein** and **haben**:

	sein	haben
ich	bin	habe
du	bist	hast
er, sie, es	ist	hat
wir, sie, Sie	sind	haben
ihr	seid	habt

E. **Practice:** Give all the forms asked for, in the present tense, for the following verbs:

	sagen	nehmen	werden	sein
ich	_____	_____	_____	_____
wir	_____	_____	_____	_____
er	_____	_____	_____	_____
du	_____	_____	_____	_____
ihr	_____	_____	_____	_____

	dürfen	müssen	können	wollen
ich	_____	_____	_____	_____
ihr	_____	_____	_____	_____
sie (*plural*)	_____	_____	_____	_____
sie (*singular*)	_____	_____	_____	_____
du	_____	_____	_____	_____

F. **Evaluation:** When you are able to do Section E as directed in the objectives (Section A), report for evaluation.

LESSON 6

A. **Your objectives:** To be able to produce in oral and written German the sentences in Section E below when given only the English directions as cues.

Lesson 6

B. **How to get there:** Look at the right-hand column only when you have difficulty, and as a key to check your responses. (Recordings are available for checking pronunciation and intonation.)

When you can do all the sentences readily without having to refer to the answers, you have met the objectives.

C. **What to learn:** There is no new vocabulary in this section. If you have forgotten any of the words or forms of Lessons 1-5, refer to the respective C sections.

D. **Analysis or explanations:** In Lesson 5 we reviewed three points about German verbs. In this lesson we shall review two more, then practice these points in Section E below.

4. The point to remember about subordinate, or dependent, clauses is the *position* of the verb form which is "normally" adjacent to the subject:

    Ich **gehe** durch den Wald.
    BUT:
    ... weil ich durch den Wald **gehe**.

    Ich **will** durch den Wald gehen.
    BUT:
    ... weil ich durch den Wald gehen **will**.

    Ich **bin** durch den Wald gegangen.
    BUT:
    ... weil ich durch den Wald gegangen **bin**.

5. Many verbs have "separable" prefixes, usually in the form of prepositions such as **auf-**, **an-**, **mit-**, etc. Remember that the prefix stays at the end of the statement, even if the verb with which it is associated is not at the end:

    den Wolf **auf**schneiden
    Ich schneide den Wolf **auf**.
    ... weil ich den Wolf **auf**schneide.
    Ich will den Wolf **auf**schneiden.
    Wer hat den Wolf **auf**geschnitten?

E. Practice: 1. Using the phrase **auch über Gräbern wehen**, tell me that

1. the wind is doing this: Der Wind weht auch über Gräbern.
2. the wind can do this: Der Wind kann auch über Gräbern wehen.
3. the wind has done this: Der Wind hat auch über Gräbern geweht.
4. you know that the wind is doing this: Ich weiß, daß der Wind auch über Gräbern weht.
5. you know that the wind has done this: Ich weiß, daß der Wind auch über Gräbern geweht hat.

2. Using the phrase **im Sommerwind blühen**, how would you say in German that

6. the flowers are doing this?   Die Blumen blühen im Sommerwind.
7. the flowers will (*future*) do this?   Die Blumen werden im Sommerwind blühen.
8. the flowers have done this?   Die Blumen haben im Sommerwind geblüht.
9. it is beautiful the way (*wie*) the flowers do this?   Es ist schön, wie die Blumen im Sommerwind blühen.
10. it is sad how quickly the flowers have done this?   Es ist traurig, wie geschwind die Blumen im Sommerwind geblüht haben.

3. Using the phrase **geschwind fortziehen**, how does one express in German that

11. the soldiers are doing this?   Die Soldaten ziehen geschwind fort.
12. the soldiers must do this?   Die Soldaten müssen geschwind fortziehen.
13. the soldiers have done this?   Die Soldaten sind geschwind fortgezogen.
14. he doesn't understand why they're doing this?   Ich verstehe nicht, warum die Soldaten geschwind fortziehen.
15. we are sad when they have done this?   Wir sind traurig, wenn die Soldaten geschwind fortgezogen sind.

F. Evaluation: Report for evaluation when you can do the sentences in Section E without hesitation.

Lesson 6

"Über Gräbern weht der Wind."

LESSON 7

A. Your objectives: To be able to perform the directed expressions in Section E in oral and written German without hesitation and without reference to any "answers." No errors.

B. How to get there: Follow the same procedure indicated in Section B of Lesson 6.

C. What to learn: There is no new material in this lesson.

D. Analysis or explanations: Review Section D of Lessons 5 and 6 if necessary.

E. Practice:

1. Using the phrase **die Mädchen nicht verstehen**

   a. How would you say that this is the case with you?
   b. How would you tell me that this is the case with me?
   c. How would you tell a friend that this is what he wants?
   d. How would you tell several friends that they can do this?
   e. How would you tell me that Hans did this?
   f. How would you tell me that "they" did this?
   g. How would you translate into English each of the German sentences resulting from the above exercises?

   ANTWORTEN:
   a. Ich verstehe die Mädchen nicht.
   b. Sie verstehen die Mädchen nicht.
   c. Du willst die Mädchen nicht verstehen.
   d. Ihr könnt die Mädchen nicht verstehen.
   e. Hans hat die Mädchen nicht verstanden.
   f. Sie haben die Mädchen nicht verstanden.
   g. English translations of the above six sentences:
   (1) I don't understand the girls.
   (2) You don't understand the girls.
   (3) You don't want to understand the girls.
   (4) You can't understand the girls.
   (5) Hans didn't understand the girls.
   (6) They didn't understand the girls.

Lesson 7

2. Using the phrases **die schönen Blumen pflücken, den Pelz abnehmen,** and **spät nach Hause kommen**

   a. Say that you are doing each of the above.
   b. Tell a friend that he may do each of the above.
   c. Say that all of us (we) have done the above.
   d. Say that you know that I did the first activity above.
   e. Tell your friends that you are laughing because they must do the second activity above.
   f. Tell your friend that his mother wants to know why he did the third activity above.

   ANTWORTEN:
   a. Ich pflücke die schönen Blumen.
      Ich nehme den Pelz ab.
      Ich komme spät nach Hause.
   b. Du darfst die schönen Blumen pflücken.
      Du darfst den Pelz abnehmen.
      Du darfst spät nach Hause kommen.
   c. Wir haben die schönen Blumen gepflückt.
      Wir haben den Pelz abgenommen.
      Wir sind spät nach Hause gekommen.
   d. Ich weiß, daß Sie die schönen Blumen gepflückt haben.
   e. Ich lache, weil ihr den Pelz abnehmen müßt.
   f. Deine Mutter will wissen, warum du spät nach Hause gekommen bist.

F. Evaluation: Refer to Section A.

Berlin nach dem Krieg. 1945.

LESSON 8

A.	Your objectives:	To pass the review test on Lessons 1-7 with at least 90% accuracy.
B.	How to get there:	Make certain you can do all the E sections in Lessons 1-7.
C.	What to learn:	Review the C sections in Lessons 1-7.
D.	Analysis or explanations:	Review the D sections in Lessons 1-7.
E.	Practice:	See Section B above, and practice any exercises which cause you difficulty.
F.	Evaluation:	When you are confident that you have mastered all of the material reviewed in Lessons 1-7, report to the teacher and ask for the Lesson 8 test.

LESSON 9

A.	Your objectives:	To be able to give the German equivalents, orally and written, of all nouns listed in Section E below when given the English as cues; and to be able to give the German plural forms (listed in Section C), orally and written, of any of these same nouns.
B.	How to get there:	Memorize the plural forms of the nouns in Section C. *Check Section D first*! You will note that all the nouns, except for three, follow a common pattern in forming the plural. Then practice the English-German exercises in Section E. If you have any difficulty, use Section C as a "key." The English in Section E and the German forms in Section C are sequentially arranged.

Lesson 9

C. What to learn:

SINGULAR	PLURAL
die Abfahrt	die Abfahrten
die Aktentasche	die Aktentaschen
die Antwort	die Antworten
die Arbeit	die Arbeiten
die Bewegung	die Bewegungen
die Blume	die Blumen
die Dame	die Damen
die Ecke	die Ecken
	die Eltern
die Familie	die Familien
die Flasche	die Flaschen
die Fahrkarte	die Fahrkarten
die Frau	die Frauen
*die Freundin	die Freundinnen
die Gabel	die Gabeln
die Gepäckaufgabe	die Gepäckaufgaben
die Hoffnung	die Hoffnungen
die Haube	die Hauben
*die Hand	die Hände
die Hausaufgabe	die Hausaufgaben
*die Jugend	(no plural)
die Kartoffel	die Kartoffeln

D. Analysis or explanations:

MEHRZAHL (plural)

We are often inclined to believe that forming plurals in English is simple: "Just add an 's'." But what are the plurals of *man, woman, ox, child, goose, mouse, deer, fish, leaf*? It becomes clear that although most plurals are formed by adding "s," many are formed by changing the vowel sound, adding other endings, or by doing nothing at all.

German forms the plural in various ways too. Notice the plurals of the words used in the song of this unit:

die Blume	die Blumen
das Grab	die Gräber
das Mädchen	die **Mädchen**
der Mann	die **Männer**
der Soldat	die Soldaten

Notice also that the article for *all* plural forms is **die**! It makes no difference whether the singular was a **der**, **die**, or **das** word, the plural is always **die**.

We can rely heavily on certain patterns in learning the plural forms. For instance, most **die** words form their plurals by adding an **-n** (or **-en** if the word doesn't already end in an -e).

Since all the words listed in Section C of this lesson are **die** words, all you really need to do to learn the plurals is to learn the *exceptions*—those marked with an *!

E. **Practice:** Give the German singular form and then the plural form—first orally, then written—using the English equivalent as a cue. Section C can serve as your key.

departure	ticket
briefcase	woman; wife
answer	girl friend
work	fork
movement	baggage claim
flower	hope
lady	hood, cape
corner	hand
parents	homework
family	youth (young people)
bottle	potato

F. **Evaluation:** When you can give the German forms as directed, orally and written, for the English nouns listed in Section E, you are ready to report for evaluation.

LESSON 10

A. **Your objectives:** See Lesson 9.

B. **How to get there:** See Lesson 9.

Lesson 10

C. What to learn: Following is a continuation (begun in Lesson 9) of the plural forms of **die** (feminine) words which appeared in *Deutsch: Kernstufe:*

SINGULAR	PLURAL	SINGULAR	PLURAL
die Katze	die Katzen	die Speise	die Speisen
die Klinke	die Klinken	die Stunde	die Stunden
die Kleidung		die Stube	die Stuben
die Klasse	die Klassen	die Straßenbahn	die Straßenbahnen
	die Leute	die Sperre	die Sperren
die Mannschaft	die Mannschaften	die Tomate	die Tomaten
die Musik		die Tür	die Türen
*die Mutter	die Mütter	die Uhr	die Uhren
*die Nacht	die Nächte	die Universität	die Universitäten
die Post	die Posten	die Wanderung	die Wanderungen
die Rechnung	die Rechnungen	die Woche	die Wochen
die Schildkröte	die Schildkröten	*die Wurst	die Würste
die Schere	die Scheren	die Weile	die Weilen
die Schulter	die Schultern	die Zeit	die Zeiten
die Schule	die Schulen	die Zeitung	die Zeitungen
die Straße	die Straßen	die Zensur	die Zensuren
die Suppe	die Suppen	die Zwiebel	die Zwiebeln

D. Analysis or explanations: Note that only three words (*) deviate from the usual pattern of forming plurals of feminine words.

Note also that **die Leute** is already plural, and that **die Musik** has no plural. **Die Kleidung** is not normally used in the plural form, since it represents a "plural" idea: "garments" or "clothing." To represent a single article of clothing, one would use the word **Kleidungsstück**.

E. Practice: Give the German singular and plural forms of the following nouns, orally and written, using the English equivalents below as cues. Section C can serve as a key for checking your accuracy.

cat	food
door handle	hour
clothing	room
class	streetcar
people	gate, barrier
team	tomato

music	door
mother	clock
night	university
post office	hike
bill	week
turtle	sausage
scissors	while (short time)
shoulder	time
school	newspaper
street	grade, mark (report card)
soup	onion

(NOTE: The list of words above and in Lesson 9 does not contain *all* the feminine words which appeared in *Deutsch: Kernstufe,* since these words follow a definite pattern. If the student or teacher desires a complete list, especially as a vocabulary review, the vocabulary listing at the end of *Deutsch: Kernstufe* can be consulted.)

F. **Evaluation:** When you can perform the objectives as stated, you are ready for evaluation.

LESSON 11

A. **Your objectives:** To be able to do the exercises in Section E in German, orally and written, without error.

B. **How to get there:** Study Section D carefully; then practice Section E to the point of fluency.

C. **What to learn:** The exercises in Section E below require your knowledge of plural forms already learned. However, a careful study of the material in Section D is essential if you are to employ these plural forms properly.

Lesson 11

D. Analysis or explanations:

Since all plurals have the article **die** in the basic form, we do not have to be as concerned about endings as we were with the three separate forms (**der, die,** and **das**) in the singular. However, we can't treat the plural **die** exactly as we did the singular. Using the plural represents a change from the original basic forms, and you have probably realized by now that whenever a change from the basic article form occurs, the adjective endings change too.

The plural form of **der Mann** is **die Männer.** Let's see what happens to the plural form of this noun when it is used in different ways in sentences as a noun phrase:

SUBJECT (Nominative)	OBJECT (Accusative)	"OTHER" (Dative)
die al**ten** Männer	**die** al**ten** Männer	**den** al**ten** Männer**n**

We see that the subject and the object ("target") forms follow the same pattern: **-e, -en**. The dative form has an **-en, -en, -n** pattern.

Examples of sentences in the plural:

Die al**ten** Männer sind nicht mehr hier.
Kein**e** al**ten** Männer sind hier.

Hast du **die** al**ten** Männer gesehen?
Ich habe kein**e** al**ten** Männer gesehen.

Sie geben **den** al**ten** Männer**n** Kartoffelsuppe.
Warum will sie kein**en** al**ten** Männer**n** Suppe geben?

E. Practice:

1. If the plural form of **das kleine Kind** is **die kleinen Kinder,** what is the plural form of this phrase under the following conditions?

   a. It is the subject: **die kleinen Kinder**
   b. It is the object: **die kleinen Kinder**
   c. It serves some other function: **den kleinen Kindern**

2. What would be the *plural* forms of the following noun phrases if they were used to fill in the blanks in the sentences below? (To avoid difficulty later, DON'T JUST MEMORIZE answers! KNOW WHY, or consult your teacher!)

The noun phrases: **die nette Mutter**
der alte Mann
das junge Mädchen

a. _____ sind hier. die netten Mütter
die alten Männer
die jungen Mädchen

b. Kannst du _____ sehen? die netten Mütter
die alten Männer
die jungen Mädchen

c. Es ist hinter _____. den netten Müttern
den alten Männern
den jungen Mädchen

d. Das gefällt _____ nicht. den netten Müttern
den alten Männern
den jungen Mädchen

e. Wo sind _____ ? die netten Mütter
die alten Männer
die jungen Mädchen

F. Evaluation: When you can read each of the sentences above, filling in each of the blanks readily with the proper form of each of the noun phrases, both orally and then written; and when you can also do part 1 of Section E according to the directions, you are ready for evaluation.

LESSON 12

A. **Your objectives:** To be able to do the drills in Section E in oral and written German without hesitation and without error.

B. **How to get there:** Follow the directions in each section of the drills. Cover up the right-hand column while looking at (or listening to) the cues at the left. Then check your answer. Repeat the drills several times if you make an error in any sentence.

C. **What to learn:** The drills in Section E are based mainly on the plural forms you learned in Lessons 9 and 10.

D. **Analysis or explanations:** Don't forget that when you use plural forms as the subject in a sentence, or when you change the subject in a sentence to the plural form, *the personal verb must also be in the plural form.*

E. **Practice:**

1. Change the following sentences to plural forms:

a. Die Blume blüht.	Die Blumen blühen.
b. Das Mädchen pflückt die Blume.	Die Mädchen pflücken die Blumen.
c. Der Mann ist geblieben.	Die Männer sind geblieben.
d. Der Soldat ist fortgezogen.	Die Soldaten sind fortgezogen.
e. Das Grab hat Blumen.	Die Gräber haben Blumen.
f. Die Frau geht nach Hause.	Die Frauen gehen nach Hause.
g. Weil die Straßenbahn langsam fährt.	Weil die Straßenbahnen langsam fahren.
h. Die Gitarre macht schöne Musik.	Die Gitarren machen schöne Musik.
i. Die Katze hat nichts gefunden.	Die Katzen haben nichts gefunden.
j. Wo ist sie geblieben?	Wo sind sie geblieben?

2. Using the German phrase **die Blumen nehmen**, express in German that the subjects are carrying out the activity indicated in the phrase:

a. the girls	**Die Mädchen nehmen die Blumen.**
b. the men	**Die Männer nehmen die Blumen.**
c. the soldiers	**Die Soldaten nehmen die Blumen.**
d. the people	**Die Leute nehmen die Blumen.**
e. the parents	**Die Eltern nehmen die Blumen.**

30	Deutsch: ZWEITE STUFE

"Was machen die Soldaten?"

3. Using the phrase **zu Hause bleiben**, express in German that

a. the women are doing this:	Die Frauen bleiben zu Hause.
b. the soldiers want to do this:	Die Soldaten wollen zu Hause bleiben.
c. the men have done this:	Die Männer sind zu Hause geblieben.
d. the girls have to do this:	Die Mädchen müssen zu Hause bleiben.
e. you know that the soldiers want to do this:	Ich weiß, daß die Soldaten zu Hause bleiben wollen.

4. Using the phrase **die Blumen vergessen**, ask in German if

a. the girls are doing this:	Vergessen die Mädchen die Blumen?
b. the ladies have done this:	Haben die Frauen die Blumen vergessen?

Lesson 12 31

"Wissen Sie, daß die Männer die Blumen vergessen haben?"

c. I know why the men have done this: **Wissen Sie, warum die Männer die Blumen vergessen haben?**

d. the soldiers can do this: **Können die Soldaten die Blumen vergessen?**

e. the girls understand why the men have to do this: **Verstehen die Mädchen, warum die Männer die Blumen vergessen müssen?**

F. Evaluation: When you can do Section E readily and without error, report for evaluation.

LESSON 13

A. Your objectives: To be able to perform the exercises in Section E in oral and written German, fluently and without error.

B. How to get there: Study Section D carefully; then practice Section E as usual.

C. What to learn: There are no new terms in this lesson. The new structure is explained in Section D.

D. Analysis or explanations:

COMMAND FORMS

Command, or imperative, forms in German are based on the second person forms. This should be expected, since you are addressing another person directly when issuing a command.

To address a person you normally address as **du**, use the command form consisting of the *second person stem* (familiar) of the verb—with no ending (although you may sometimes hear or see an **-e**). Drop any of the umlauts which are added to certain verbs in the second and third persons singular. (Any exceptions to this general pattern will be explained later as particular problems arise.)

EXAMPLES:

INFINITIVE	SECOND PERSON (du)	COMMAND FORM
kommen	**Komm**st du?	**Komm** mit!
gehen	**Geh**st du?	**Geh** nach Hause!
lesen	**Lies**t du?	**Lies** das Buch!
vergessen	Du **vergiß**t das.	**Vergiß** das nicht!
fahren	**Fähr**st du?	**Fahr** langsam! (*not* **fähr**)
fallen	Du **fäll**st!	**Fall** nicht! (*not* **fäll**)

Note that all commands written in German are followed by an exclamation mark (!).

If you are addressing more than one person with the familiar form, just use the verb form you have learned previously (the form with "you-all," **ihr**):

Kommt mit!
Geht nach Hause!

Lesson 13

       Lest das Buch!
       Vergeßt das nicht!
       Fahrt langsam!
       Fallt nicht!

If the command is given to persons with whom you are on a formal basis, use the form already learned, including the pronoun **Sie**:

       Kommen Sie mit!
       Gehen Sie nach Hause!
       Lesen Sie das Buch!
       Vergessen Sie das nicht!
       Fahren Sie langsam!
       Fallen Sie nicht!

The verb "to be," **sein**, does not follow this general pattern:

INFINITIVE	SECOND PERSON FORMS	COMMAND FORMS
sein	Du **bist** nicht still.	**Sei** still!
	Ihr **seid** zu laut.	**Seid** nicht so laut!
	Sie **sind** wild.	**Seien** Sie nicht so wild!

E. Practice: How would you say each of the activities listed below as a command a) to a friend, b) to several family members, c) "formally"?

1. nach Hause gehen
    a. Geh nach Hause!
    b. Geht nach Hause!
    c. Gehen Sie nach Hause!

2. die Blumen pflücken
    a. Pflück die Blumen!
    b. Pflückt die Blumen!
    c. Pflücken Sie die Blumen!

3. heute zu Hause bleiben
    a. Bleib heute zu Hause!
    b. Bleibt heute zu Hause!
    c. Bleiben Sie heute zu Hause!

4. nicht mit dem VW fahren
    a. Fahr nicht mit dem VW!
    b. Fahrt nicht mit dem VW!
    c. Fahren Sie nicht mit dem VW!

5. jetzt gut zuhören
    a. Hör jetzt gut zu!
    b. Hört jetzt gut zu!
    c. Hören Sie jetzt gut zu!

"Hören Sie jetzt gut zu!"

6.	mein Buch nicht nehmen	a. Nimm mein Buch nicht!
		b. Nehmt mein Buch nicht!
		c. Nehmen Sie mein Buch nicht!
7.	nicht so dumm aussehen	a. Sieh nicht so dumm aus!
		b. Seht nicht so dumm aus!
		c. Sehen Sie nicht so dumm aus!
8.	um zwölf Uhr hier sein	a. Sei um zwölf Uhr hier!
		b. Seid um zwölf Uhr hier!
		c. Seien Sie um zwölf Uhr hier!

F. Evaluation: When you can perform the objectives in Section A concerning this lesson, report for evaluation.

LESSON 14
Review of Lessons 9-13

A. Your objectives: To be able to do the review exercises in Section E in oral and written German with no errors.

B. How to get there: Use Section E as a "diagnostic test," that is, do it first. Then check it with the teacher's key or have it checked. Review any sections which give you difficulty (part 1 of the test is based on Lessons 9 and 10; part 2 is based on Lessons 11 and 12; part 3 is based on Lesson 13).

C. What to learn: Review material in Section C of previous lessons as necessary, as revealed by your performance on the test in Section E.

D. Analysis or explanations: Review as necessary.

E. Practice:

1. What are the singular and plural forms in German of the following nouns?

answer	mother
flower	night
corner	school
family	street
bottle	soup
ticket	hour
woman	streetcar
girl friend	door
fork	clock
hand	week
potato	sausage
cat	time
class	newspaper

2. a) Use the plural of **die kleine Flasche** in the blanks of the following sentences:

_____ sind auf dem Tisch.
✯Die Milch ist in _____.
Wer hat _____ zerbrochen?
Hinter _____ sind die Pillen.
Wo sind _____?

b) Change the following sentences to the plural:

Die alte Mutter ist schwach.
Siehst du die graue Schildkröte?
Die Wurst kocht schon.
Sie stehen an der Ecke.

3. a) Give the command form of **in den See springen** if you are

talking to a friend,
addressing someone formally,
talking to friends

b) How would you do the following in German?

1. Order me to play the guitar.
2. Order your friend to do the same.
3. Order your friends to do so.
4. Order your brother to go home.
5. Order your sisters to stay home.
6. Command a stranger to listen to you
   (**mir zuhören**)

F. Evaluation: When you think you can do the test in Section E with no errors, report for testing. Keep repeating the test until you make no errors.

LESSON 15
Comprehensive Review Self-Test

A. Your objectives: To be able to do the "practice test" in Section E in oral and written German with at least 90% accuracy.

Lesson 15

B. **How to get there:** Follow the directions given in Section B of Lesson 14.

C. **What to learn:** Review.

D. **Analysis or explanations:** Review.

E. **Practice:** SELF-TEST
1. What do the following words or phrases mean?

    a. Wo sind sie geblieben?
    b. Mädchen pflückten sie geschwind.
    c. Wann wird man je verstehen?
    d. Männer nahmen sie geschwind.
    e. Zogen fort, der Krieg beginnt.
    f. Über Gräbern weht der Wind.
    g. Blumen blüh'n im Sommerwind.

2. Give the German for the following:

    a. to stay (infinitive and past participle)
    b. to move on (infinitive and past participle)
    c. to take (infinitive; 3rd person, present tense; and past participle)
    d. to understand (infinitive and past participle)
    e. to become (infinitive; 3rd person, present; past participle)
    f. flower (singular and plural)
    g. girl (singular and plural)
    h. man (singular and plural)
    i. soldier (singular and plural)
    j. quickly

3. Using the idea **sie geschwind pflücken**, how would you say that

    a. the girls are doing this?
    b. the girls can do this?
    c. the girls have done this?
    d. you know that the girls are doing this?
    e. you know that the girls have done this?

4. Give the singular and the plural forms in German of the following nouns:

    a. flower   f. youth
    b. girl friend   g. mother
    c. family   h. cat
    d. had   i. night
    e. potato   j. sausage

5. What are the plural forms of **die heiße Wurst** which would complete the following statements correctly?

    a. _____ sind da drüben.
    b. Wer hat _____ gegessen?
    c. Was ist das hinter _____ ?
    d. Wo sind _____ ?
    e. Zuviel Salz ist in _____ .

6. Change the following sentences (all nouns and verbs) to the plural:

    a. Die Straßenbahn fährt heute nicht.
    b. Das Mädchen nimmt die Blume mit.
    c. Der junge Mann gibt dem schönen Mädchen etwas.
    d. Die kleine Katze springt aus der Tür.
    e. Der treue Soldat geht in den Krieg.

7. Give the three possible command forms for the following phrases:

    a. nach Hause gehen
    b. nichts nehmen   (Give 3 forms for *each*!)
    c. langsam fahren

8. How would you say

    a. the little girls are not here?
    b. you can see the big bottles?
    c. they are under the old newspapers?
    d. "Eat the soup!" to your friend?
    e. "Eat the soup!" to several friends?
    f. "Eat the soup!" to your teacher?

F.	Evaluation:	If you can do the Self-Test without reference to any notes or previous lessons, and score 90% or better, you are ready to go on to Lesson 16. (Check your answers, or have them checked, against the key.)

If you did not score at least 90%, review carefully any of the lessons containing material you missed. Then repeat the test. (NOT ADVISABLE: To simply memorize the material in this test rather than to do a review!) |

LESSON 16

A.	Your objectives:	To pass the "unit" test based on Lessons 1-15 with at least 90% accuracy.
B.	How to get there:	Use the practice test in Lesson 15 as a guide for reviewing any lessons or sections which cause difficulty.
C.	What to learn:	Review.
D.	Analysis or explanations:	Review.
E.	Practice:	Review.
F.	Evaluation:	If you can do all sections of Lesson 15 without difficulty, report for testing.

Deutsch: ZWEITE STUFE

LESSON 17

A. Your objectives: To master the first part of the reading selection (which continues through Lesson 20) as evidenced by your ability to read it out loud with acceptable (to your teacher) pronunciation and intonation; and to be able to give the meanings of any sentences or individual vocabulary words (in English or German, whichever your teacher directs) requested.

B. How to get there:
1. Listen to the tape of the story once or twice, so that the overall "picture" of what's going on is clear to you.
2. Then read the story carefully, referring to the vocabulary when necessary, so that you understand every sentence.
3. Make a vocabulary study list (German-English) and learn the words you don't know well.
4. Then read the story again to see if you can now understand everything without having to refer to a vocabulary list or to "translation." Go over the story until you can do this.

C. What to learn: (Be sure to refer to Section D before beginning!)

DIE LANGE LANGE STRAßE LANG*[1]
Wolfgang Borchert

Links zwei drei vier links zwei drei vier links zwei weiter,[2] Fischer![3] drei vier links zwei vorwärts,[4] Fischer! schneidig,[5] Fischer! drei vier atme,[6] Fischer! weiter, Fischer, immer weiter zickezacke[7] zwei drei vier schneidig ist die Infantrie zickezackejuppheidi schneidig ist die Infantrie die Infantrie . . .

5   Ich bin unterwegs.[8] Zweimal hab ich schon gelegen.[9] Ich will zur Straßenbahn. Ich muß mit.[10] Zweimal hab ich schon gelegen. Ich hab Hunger. Aber mit muß ich. Muß. Ich muß zur Straßenbahn. Zweimal hab ich schon drei vier links zwei drei vier aber mit muß ich drei vier zickezacke zacke drei vier juppheidi ist die Infantrie die Infantrie fantrie fantrie . . .

10   57 haben sie bei Woronesch[11] begraben.[12] 57, die hatten keine Ahnung,[13] vorher[14] nicht und nachher[15] nicht. Vorher haben sie noch gesungen. Zickezackejuppheidi. Und einer hat nach Haus geschrieben: —dann kaufen wir uns ein

Lesson 17

"Die lange lange Straße lang."

Grammophon. Aber dann haben viertausend Meter weiter ab die Andern[16] auf Befehl[17] auf einen Knopf[18] gedrückt. Dann haben sie 57 bei Woronesch begraben.
15 Vorher haben sie noch gesungen. Hinterher[15] haben sie nichts mehr gesagt. 9 Autoschlosser,[19] 2 Gärtner, 5 Beamte,[20] 6 Verkäufer, 1 Friseur,[21] 17 Bauern,[22] 2 Lehrer, 1 Pastor, 6 Arbeiter, 1 Musiker, 7 Schuljungen. 7 Schuljungen. Die haben sie bei Woronesch begraben. Sie hatten keine Ahnung. 57.

*Reprinted by permission of Rowohlt Verlag.
From DRAUSSEN VOR DER TÜR UND AUSGEWÄHLTE ERZÄHLUNGEN by Wolfgang Borchert. Copyright Rowohlt Verlag GmbH, 1949

1	along (from **entlang**)	10	(ride) along
2	farther; "keep going"	11	(name of a city in Russia)
3	(the lieutenant's last name)	12	buried
4	forward	13	idea; premonition
5	sharp(ly)	14	beforehand; in advance
6	breathe	15	afterwards
7	"zigzag" (**zickezacke** and **juppheidi** are mainly "sing-song" syllables like "hickory-dickory-dock" or "eenie-meenie-minie-mo," etc.)	16	others (meaning the enemy)
		17	on command
		18	button (to set off artillery)
		19	auto mechanics
8	underway	20	public officials
9	to have lain ill or wounded in bed or in the hospital	21	barber
		22	farmers

Deutsch: ZWEITE STUFE

D. **Analysis or explanations:**

To get the feeling of what's going on here, you have to picture a soldier marching home from war. The ingrained military part of him keeps commanding and domineering the new "civilian" role. He even keeps counting cadence as he walks along, marching himself along to a military "sing-song" rhythm. War memories keep intruding. And he has the nagging worry, Can Lieutenant Fischer ever be just plain Mr. Fischer again, or has the war experience ruined that hope forever?

As you read along, you might ask yourself what some of the symbols stand for—the long long road, the yellow streetcar, etc.

Since we are supposed to be inside Fischer's mind, we often get somewhat disconnected, random thoughts—often expressed in choppy, incomplete sentences. If this style gives you some difficulty at first, even after reading the story

"2 Lehrer. 7 Schuljungen."

Lesson 18

several times, have the teacher or another student (who has already mastered this lesson) go through the first couple of paragraphs with you.

Here are a few notes on some of the expressions in Section C which may help you:

line 5 **Ich will zur Straßenbahn. Ich muß mit.**: The infinitives which go with the modals in these two sentences are "understood" to be there at the end. In the first sentence you feel **gehen**, and in the second, **fahren**. (**Ich will zur Straßenbahn gehen. Ich muß mitfahren.**) Native speakers of German often leave off this final infinitive when it is obvious what it must be.

line 7 **Zweimal hab ich schon drei vier . . .**: Here, after **schon**, the marching command starts breaking in again and interrupting his chain of thought. This occurs periodically.

line 10 **57 haben sie . . .**: The number refers to 57 soldiers in Fischer's military unit.

line 12 **Und einer** refers to **ein Soldat**.

line 13 **die Andern** is the subject of this rather long sentence. What is the verb? What did "the others" (the enemy) do? (**haben . . . gedrückt**)

E. **Practice:** See Section B above.

F. **Evaluation:** When you can read the story aloud readily, and when you can explain all the words or explain what's going on in any particular passage, you are ready to be evaluated.

LESSON 18
Die lange lange Straße lang (continued)

A. **Your objectives:** See Lesson 17, Section A.

B. **How to get there:** See Lesson 17, Section B.

"Nur daß die Straße so grau ist."

C.   What to learn: (There are helpful notes in Section D. Get acquainted with the material in that section before beginning to read.)

Und mich haben sie vergessen. Ich war noch nicht ganz tot. Juppheidi. Ich war noch ein bißchen lebendig.[23] Aber die andern, die haben sie bei Woronesch begraben. 57. 57. Mach noch ne[24] Null dran.[25] 570. Noch ne Null und noch ne Null. 57 000. Und noch und noch. Und noch. 57 000 000. Die haben sie bei
5   Woronesch begraben. Sie hatten keine Ahnung. Sie wollten nicht. Das hatten sie gar nicht gewollt. Und vorher haben sie noch gesungen. Juppheidi. Nachher haben sie nichts mehr gesagt. Und der eine hat das Grammophon nicht gekauft. Sie haben ihn bei Woronesch und die andern 57 auch begraben. Nur ich, ich, ich war noch nicht ganz tot. Ich muß zur Straßenbahn. Die Straße ist grau. Aber die Straßenbahn ist
10   gelb. Ganz wunderhübsch gelb. Da muß ich mit. Nur daß die Straße so grau ist. So grau und so grau. Zweimal hab ich schon zickezacke vorwärts, Fischer! drei vier links zwei links zwei gelegen drei vier weiter, Fischer! Zickezacke juppheidi links zwei drei vier wenn nur der Hunger der elende[26] Hunger immer der elende links zwei drei vier links zwei links zwei links zwei . . .

Lesson 18

15   Eben[27] hat einer zu mir gesagt: Guten Tag, Herr Fischer. Bin ich Herr Fischer? Kann ich Herr Fischer sein, einfach[28] wieder Herr Fischer? Ich war doch Leutnant Fischer. Kann ich denn wieder Herr Fischer sein? Bin ich Herr Fischer? Guten Tag, hat der gesagt. Aber der weiß nicht, daß ich Leutnant Fischer war. Einen guten Tag hat er gewünscht[29] — für Leutnant Fischer gibt es[30] keine guten
20   Tage mehr. Das hat er nicht gewußt.

23	alive	27	just now
24	e**i**ne	28	simply
25	**dranmachen** = add	29	wished
26	miserable	30	**es gibt** = there are

D. Analysis or explanations:

Notes concerning the text:

line 2   die anderen, **die** . . .: The repeated article here serves as an "emphatic" pronoun. In English we would use *them* or *those*. (**Sie** is the subject of this clause!)

line 4   The adding of zeroes to the number 57 is meant to show how insignificant the number of dead is to most people. 57 or 57,000,000 — who cares really?

line 5   Sie **wollten** nicht. (**Wollten** is the past of **wollen**.): The infinitive to be understood is "to die" or "to be buried" (**sterben** or **begraben werden**).

line 10   **Wunderhübsch** = "wonderfully pretty"

line 15   **einer** = "one" ("a man")

line 18   **der** is used here as the masculine pronoun, instead of **er**, as it often is in German.

E. Practice: See Section B of Lesson 17.

F. Evaluation: When you can read any part of the story aloud with proper pronunciation and intonation and can explain all the words or passages in the story, you are ready to report for evaluation.

"Das kleine Mädchen geht nebenan."

LESSON 19
Die lange lange Straße lang (continued)

A. **Your objectives:** See Lesson 17, Section A.

B. **How to get there:** See Lesson 17, Section B.

C. **What to learn:** (Be sure to refer to the notes in Section D.)

Und Herr Fischer geht die Straße lang. Die lange Straße lang. Die ist grau. Er will zur Straßenbahn. Die ist gelb. So wunderhübsch gelb. Links zwei, Herr Fischer. Links zwei drei vier. Herr Fischer hat Hunger. Er hält nicht mehr Schritt.[3][1] Er will doch noch mit, denn die Straßenbahn ist so wunderhübsch gelb in dem Grau.
5 Zweimal hat Herr Fischer schon gelegen. Aber Leutnant Fischer kommandiert: Links zwei drei vier vorwärts, Herr Fischer! Weiter, Herr Fischer! Schneidig, Herr Fischer, kommandiert Leutnant Fischer. Und Herr Fischer marschiert die graue Straße lang, die graue graue lange Straße lang.

Lesson 19

      Das kleine Mädchen hat Beine,[32] die sind wie[33] Finger so dünn.[34] Wie
10 Finger im Winter. So dünn und so rot und so blau und so dünn. Links zwei drei vier
machen die Beine. Das kleine Mädchen sagt immerzu und Herr Fischer marschiert
nebenan das sagt immerzu: Lieber Gott,[35] gib mir Suppe. Lieber Gott, gib mir
Suppe. Ein Löffelchen nur. Ein Löffelchen nur. Ein Löffelchen nur. Die Mutter hat
Haare,[36] die sind schon tot. Lange schon tot. Die Mutter sagt: Der liebe Gott kann
15 dir keine Suppe geben, er kann es doch nicht. Warum kann der liebe Gott mir keine
Suppe geben? Er hat doch keinen Löffel. Den hat er nicht. Das kleine Mädchen
geht auf seinen[37] Fingerbeinen, den dünnen blauen Winterbeinen, neben der
Mutter. Herr Fischer geht nebenan. Von der Mutter sind die Haare schon tot. Sie
sind schon ganz fremd um den Kopf. Und das kleine Mädchen tanzt rundherum[38]
20 um die Mutter herum um Herrn Fischer herum rundherum: Er hat ja keinen Löffel.
Er hat ja keinen Löffel. Er hat ja keinen nicht mal einen hat ja keinen Löffel. So
tanzt das kleine Mädchen rundherum. Und Herr Fischer marschiert hinteran.[39]
Aber Leutnant Fischer kommandiert: Links zwei juppvorbei schneidig, Herr
Fischer, links zwei und das kleine Mädchen singt dabei.[40] Er hat ja keinen Löffel.
25 Er hat ja keinen Löffel. Er hat ja keinen Löffel. Und zweimal hat Herr Fischer
schon gelegen. Vor[41] Hunger gelegen. Er hat ja keinen Löffel. Und der andere
kommandiert: Juppheidi juppheidi die Infantrie die Infantrie die Infantrie . . .
      57 kommen jede Nacht nach Deutschland. 9 Autoschlosser, 2 Gärtner, 5
Beamte, 6 Verkäufer, 1 Friseur, 17 Bauren, 2 Lehrer, 1 Pastor, 6 Arbeiter, 1
30 Musiker, 7 Schuljungen. 57 kommen jede Nacht an mein Bett, 57 fragen jede
Nacht: Wo ist deine Kompanie? Bei Woronesch, sag ich dann. Begraben, sag ich
dann. Bei Woronesch begraben. 57 fragen Mann für Mann: Warum? Und 57mal
bleib ich stumm.[42]
      57 gehen nachts zu ihrem Vater. 57 und Leutnant Fischer. Leutnant Fischer
35 bin ich. 57 fragen nachts ihren Vater: Vater, warum? Und der Vater bleibt 57mal
stumm. Und er friert[43] in seinem Hemd.[44] Aber er kommt mit.
      Aber ein Fenster[45] weiter sitzt eine Mutter. Die hat drei Bilder[46] vor sich.[47]
Drei Männer in Uniform. Links steht ihr Mann.[48] Rechts steht ihr Sohn.[49] Links
steht ihr Mann. Rechts steht ihr Sohn. Und in der Mitte steht der General.

31	**schritthalten** = to keep in step	41	because of
32	legs	42	silent
33	like, as	43	freezes; shivers
34	thin	44	shirt
35	**Lieber Gott** = dear God	45	window
36	hair	46	pictures
37	her	47	**vor sich** = in front of herself
38	round about	48	husband
39	behind	49	son
40	at the same time		

48   Deutsch: ZWEITE STUFE

"Aber ein Fenster weiter sitzt eine Mutter."

"Und in der Mitte—der General."

Lesson 19

D. Analysis or explanations:

line 2   **Die** ist gelb: Equivalent to English "it." The **die** refers to **die Straßenbahn.**

line 3   **Er will . . . mit.** Understood: mit**gehen.**

line 11   **Sagt immerzu** = keeps on talking

line 12   **nebenan** = next to him

line 13   **Löffelchen** (diminutive of **Löffel**: "little spoon")

line 16   **Den** hat er nicht (again, an article used as a pronoun; **den Löffel** is understood)

line 17   **Fingerbeinen** = "finger-like legs"

line 18   **Von der Mutter sind die Haare** = The mother's hair is . . .

line 21   **nicht mal einen** = "not even one"

line 28   **jede** = every

line 32   **Mann für Mann** = "one after another"

line 34   **nachts** = at night; nights

line 37   **weiter** = farther

E. Practice: See Lesson 17, Section B.

F. Evaluation: When you can read every passage aloud with proper intonation and pronunciation, and when you can explain every word or passage (see Lesson 17, Section A), you are ready for evaluation.

LESSON 20
Die lange lange Straße lang (concluded)

A. **Your objectives:**   See Lesson 17, Section A.

B. **How to get there:**   See Lesson 17, Section B.

C. **What to learn:**   (Notes in Section D.)

Den General von ihrem Mann und ihrem Sohn. Und wenn die Mutter abends zu Bett geht, dann stellt[50] sie die Bilder, daß sie sie sieht, wenn sie liegt. Den Sohn. Und den Mann. Und in der Mitte den General. Und dann liest sie die Briefe,[51] die der General schrieb.[52] 1917. Für Deutschland. —steht auf dem einen. 1940. Für
5 Deutschland. —steht auf dem anderen. Mehr liest die Mutter nicht. Ihre Augen sind ganz rot. Sind so rot.

"Ich komme die Straße und den Hunger nicht entlang."

Lesson 20

Aber ich bin über.[53] Juppheidi. Für Deutschland. Ich bin noch unterwegs. Zur Straßenbahn. Zweimal hab ich schon gelegen. Wegen[54] dem Hunger. Juppheidi. Aber ich muß hin. Der Leutnant kommandiert. Ich bin schon unterwegs. Schon lange lange unterwegs.

Nur ich. Ich bin noch unterwegs. Noch immer unterwegs. Schon lange, so lang schon lang schon unterwegs. Die Straße ist lang. Ich komm die Straße und den Hunger nicht entlang. Sie sind beide[55] so lang.

Ein Mensch[56] läuft durch die Straße. Die lange lange Straße lang. Er hat Angst. Er läuft mit seiner Angst durch die Welt. Der Mensch bin ich. Ich bin 25. Und ich bin unterwegs. Bin lange schon und immer noch unterwegs. Ich will zur Straßenbahn. Ich muß mit der Straßenbahn, denn alle sind hinter mir her.[57] Sind furchtbar[58] hinter mir her. Ein Mensch läuft, läuft mit seiner Angst durch die Straße. Der Mensch bin ich. Ein Mensch läuft vor dem Schreien[59] davon.[60] Der Mensch bin ich. Ein Mensch glaubt an[61] Tomaten und Tabak. Der Mensch bin ich. Ein Mensch springt auf die Straßenbahn, die gelbe gute Straßenbahn. Der Mensch bin ich.

Wohin fahren wir denn? frag ich den Schaffner.[62] Da gibt er mir ein hoffnungsgrünes[63] Billet.[64] Bezahlen[65] müssen wir alle, sagt er und hält seine Hand auf. Und ich gebe ihm 57 Mann. Aber wohin fahren wir denn? frag ich die andern. Wir müssen doch wissen: Wohin? Da sagt einer: Das wissen wir auch nicht.

"Und keiner weiß: wohin."

Das weiß keine Sau.⁶⁶ Und alle nicken mit dem Kopf und grummeln:⁶⁷ Das weiß keine Sau. Aber wir fahren. Tingeltangel, macht die Klingel⁶⁸ der Straßenbahn und keiner weiß wohin. Aber alle fahren mit. Und der Schaffner macht ein
30 unbegreifliches⁶⁹ Gesicht. Es ist ein uralter⁷⁰ Schaffner mit zehntausend Falten.⁷¹ Man kann nicht erkennen, ob es ein böser oder ein guter Schaffner ist. Aber alle bezahlen bei ihm. Und alle fahren mit. Und keiner weiß: wohin? Tingeltangel, macht die Klingel der Straßenbahn. Und keiner weiß: wohin? Und alle fahren: mit. Und keiner weiß ... und keiner weiß ... und keiner weiß ...

50	puts	61	believes in
51	letters	62	conductor
52	wrote	63	"hope-green"
53	left over	64	ticket
54	because of	65	pay
55	both	66	sow (pig)
56	human being, person	67	grumble
57	behind me (chasing after me)	68	bell
58	terribly	69	incomprehensible
59	screaming	70	ancient
60	away from	71	wrinkles

D. Analysis or explanations:

line 1   **von ihrem Mann** = of her husband

line 2   **liegt** (from **liegen** = to lie)

line 4   1917. **Für Deutschland ... 1940. Für Deutschland ...** (indicating that the father and son died "for Germany" during each of the world wars, respectively.)

line 4½ **steht** = is written

line 9   **hin** = a prefix which usually accompanies **gehen** or other verbs of locomotion and means "to there" or "to that place." It could be used here in another sense, meaning "to death."

line 12 **Ich komm ... nicht entlang** = I never get to the end of ...

E. Practice: See Lesson 17, Section B.

F. Evaluation: Same as previous 3 lessons.

LESSON 21

A. Your objectives: To be able to answer the questions in Section E about the story in Lessons 17-20 orally in German, and to be able to give English equivalents for the German words in Section C.

B. How to get there: Check the new words which appeared in the story by going down the left-hand column in Section C. Learn any you miss or don't know.

Review the story by reading it once more rapidly. Then try to answer the questions in Section E. If you can't answer these without looking at the answers or referring again to the story, you haven't become familiar enough with the text and you should go over it again.

C. What to learn:

lang	along	rundherum	all around
weiter	farther	hinteran	behind (them)
vorwärts	forward	dabei	in addition; in accompaniment
schneidig	sharp		
atmen	breathe	jede	every
unterwegs	underway	stumm	silent
gelegen	to have been in the hospital	frieren	to freeze; shiver
		das Hemd	shirt
begraben	buried	das Fenster	window
die Ahnung	idea; premonition	das Bild	picture
vorher	beforehand	vor sich	in front of one
nachher	afterwards	der Sohn	son
die Andern	the others	der Mann	husband; man
der Befehl	command	stellen	to put
der Knopf	button	liegen	to lie
hinterher	afterwards	der Brief	letter
der Autoschlosser	mechanic	schrieb	wrote
der Beamte	civil servant	über	left over; over; above
der Friseur	barber	wegen	on account of
der Bauer	farmer	beide	both
lebendig	alive	der Mensch	human being, person
dranmachen	to add	furchtbar	terribly
elend	miserable	das Schreien	screaming

"Vater. Warum?"
Und der Vater bleibt stumm.

eben	just now	das Billet	ticket
einfach	simply	bezahlen	to pay
wünschen	to wish	die Sau	sow (pig)
es gibt	there is/are	grummeln	grumble
schritthalten	to keep in step; to keep up with	die Klingel	bell
		unbegreiflich	incomprehensible
das Bein	leg	uralt	ancient
dünn	thin	die Falten	wrinkles

D. Analysis or explanations:

Wolfgang Borchert died on November 20, 1947, at the age of twenty-six. He was a book dealer and then an actor until 1941, when he was sent to the eastern front (Russia). Letters he had written which were critical of the state got him eight months imprisonment in a military jail in Nürnberg, where he became very ill with jaundice and diphtheria. He was sentenced to death, but then sent to the eastern front again. But because of his health he was released. He read poetry in cabarets in Hamburg, but could not keep his political opinions quiet and ended up in a prison again, this time in Berlin. In 1945 he returned to the ruins of Hamburg,

Lesson 22

> chronically ill and feverish, a broken man. Friends got him to a sanitorium in Switzerland, but he had only two years left.
>
> His stories are not too difficult to read. The excerpts in Lessons 17-20 are as he wrote them. You may be interested in reading more. He has written many very powerful short stories.

E. **Practice:** FRAGEN:

1. Wie oft hat Fischer "gelegen"? Er hat schon **zweimal** gelegen.
2. Wohin will Fischer gehen? Er will **zur Straßenbahn.**
3. Was haben sie mit den 57 gemacht? Sie haben sie bei Woronesch **begraben.**
4. Warum haben die 57 nicht mehr gesungen? Sie waren **tot.**
5. Wer war nicht tot? **Fischer** war nicht tot.
6. Was will das kleine Mädchen tun? Sie will **Suppe essen.**
7. Wann kommen die 57 nach Deutschland? Sie kommen **jede Nacht** nach Deutschland.
8. Was hat die Mutter vor sich? Sie hat **drei Bilder** vor sich.
9. Warum sind die Augen der Mutter rot? **Sie hat geweint.**
10. Wer ist der Schaffner? ? ? ? ? ? (der Tod? Gott? das Leben? die Zeit?)

F. **Evaluation:** When you can answer the questions in Section E in German, and when you can give English equivalents for the German words in Section C, you are ready for evaluation.

LESSON 22

A. **Your objectives:** To pass the final test on *Die lange lange Straße lang* with at least 90% accuracy.

B. **How to get there:** Take the practice test in Section E without referring to any notes or answers. If you get at least 90% of the items correct (your teacher will check it or lend you the key), you are ready for the final test.
   If you don't get 90%, you need to review either the vocabulary (see Lesson 21, Section C) or the story itself.

C. **What to learn:** Review Lessons 17-21 if necessary.

D. **Analysis or explanations:** Review previous 5 lessons if necessary.

E. **Practice:** I. What do the following words or phrases mean?

1. Vorwärts, Fischer!
2. atmen
3. Ich bin lange unterwegs.
4. vorher
5. nachher
6. auf den Knopf drücken
7. die Bauern arbeiten
8. noch ne Null
9. Er hat eben gesagt—
10. Er will mit.
11. dünn wie Finger
12. rundherum
13. stumm
14. frieren
15. der Brief
16. davonlaufen
17. der Schaffner
18. die Klingel klingelt
19. mit zehntausend Falten
20. keiner weiß wohin

II. Complete the sentences below with words chosen from the right-hand column. There are exactly enough words, and none is used twice.

1. Die Straßenbahn ist _____ .
2. Die Anderen haben auf einen _____ gedrückt.
3. 57 haben sie bei Woronesch _____ .
4. Ich war noch nicht ganz _____ .
5. Für Leutnant Fischer gibt es keine guten _____ mehr.
6. Links, zwei, drei, _____ .
7. Das kleine Mädchen hat _____ ,
8. die sind wie Finger so _____ .
9. Der liebe Gott hat keinen _____ .
10. Ein Mensch läuft durch die _____ .
11. Wir wissen nicht, _____ wir fahren.
12. Die Straße ist so lang und _____ .

grau ✓
Tage ✓
gelb ✓
vier ✓
Löffel ✓
wohin ✓
Knopf ✓
Straße ✓
begraben ✓
Beine ✓
tot ✓
dünn ✓

F. **Evaluation:** If you had no difficulty with the practice test, you are ready to take the final test on the story. If you did have difficulty, review where necessary before taking the final.

Lesson 22

Berlin. Nach dem Krieg.

OPTIONAL LESSON
(for extra credit)

A. Your objectives: To be able to read the poem "September" out loud with acceptable (to your teacher) intonation and pronunciation; and to be able to explain the meaning of any words or passages (in German or English, as directed) required.

B. How to get there: Go through the poem carefully, and in each sentence or clause underline the subject once and the verb or action twice. Understanding *who* or *what is doing what* should give you a solid beginning for understanding the poem.

C. What to learn:

SEPTEMBER*
Hermann Hesse

Der Garten trauert,[1]
kühl sinkt in die Blumen der Regen.[2]
Der Sommer schauert[3]
still seinem Ende entgegen.[4]

Golden tropft[5] Blatt um Blatt[6]
nieder vom hohen[7] Akazienbaum.
Sommer lächelt[8] erstaunt[9] und matt[10]
in den sterbenden[11] Gartenraum.

Lange noch bei den Rosen
bleibt er stehen, sehnt[12] sich nach Ruh.[13]
Langsam tut[14] er die großen
müdgewordenen Augen zu.

*Reprinted courtesy of SUHRKAMP VERLAG, Frankfurt, Germany.

1	to mourn; grieve	8	smile
2	rain	9	astonished
3	shiver; shower	10	exhausted
4	toward	11	dying
5	trickle down; drip	12	to long for
6	leaf after leaf	13	peace; rest
7	high; tall	14	to close

D. Analysis or explanations:

There are two problems you may have:

1. What is the subject in the second line of the poem?
2. What does the **er** stand for in the second and third lines of the last stanza?

Optional Lesson

ANSWERS:
1. der Regen
2. der Sommer

Notice that **müdgewordenen** is a compound word (an adjective here) made up of **müde** (*tired*) and the past participle **geworden** (*have become*). In English we would probably have to render this as a relative clause ("closes his big eyes, which have become tired").

Two other poems with similar themes which you might enjoy are *Herbsttag* by Rainer Maria Rilke and *Ballade des äusseren Lebens* by Hugo von Hofmannsthal.

E. Practice: Listen to the recorded version of the poem several times. Practice reading it aloud yourself several times—after you are sure you understand it.

F. Evaluation: You will be evaluated according to the objectives in Section A.

"Lange noch bei den Rosen bleibt er stehen, sehnt sich nach Ruh."

ZWEITER TEIL

Das Thema: DER RHEIN (Lieder und Legenden)

"Ich hab' den Vater Rhein in seinem Bett geseh'n!
Ja, der hat's wunderschön!
Der braucht nie aufzustehen!
Und rechts und links vom Bett,
Da steht der beste Wein!
Ach, wäre ich doch nur der alte Vater Rhein!"

Lessons 23-25   64
    Zwei Lieder: Ich hab' den Vater Rhein in seinem Bett geseh'n!
                   Der treue Husar

Lessons 26-29   70
    Die deutsche Sprache: Wiederholung (Adjektivendungen,
                            Pronomen und **das** Wörter)

Lessons 30, 33-35   81
    Die deutsche Sprache: Etwas Neues (die Imperfektform der
                            schwachen Verben: "simple past"
                            form of regular verbs)

Lessons 36-39   97
    Die deutsche Sprache: Etwas Neues (die Imperfektform der
                            starken Verben: "simple past" form
                            of irregular verbs)

Lessons 40-43   105
    Etwas zum Lesen: Eine Geschichte: "Jung-Siegfried"
                      Ein Gedicht: "Die Lorelei" (Optional)

Test Lessons
    Lesson 31   85
    Lesson 32   87
    Lesson 44   114
    Lesson 45   118

"Ich hab' den Vater Rhein in seinem Bett geseh'n!"

Deutsch: ZWEITE STUFE

LESSON 23

A. Your objectives: To be able to read the song in Section C out loud with acceptable pronunciation, and to be able to explain the meaning (in German or English, whichever your teacher directs) of all the words or passages in the song.

B. How to get there: Listen to the recorded version of the song several times while looking at the printed version. Say or sing the words along with the recording until you feel you can duplicate the pronunciation and intonation.

    Also make certain you understand the meaning of every sentence. Refer to the vocabulary list provided when necessary.

C. What to learn: In September und Oktober findet man in Deutschland sehr viele Feste.[1] Es gibt das Oktoberfest in München und Weinfeste am Rhein und an der Mosel. Wenn die Deutschen ein Fest haben, singen sie gern. Es folgen ("there follow") zwei Lieder[2] – "Festlieder."

ICH HAB' DEN VATER RHEIN IN SEINEM BETT GESEH'N!*

1. Ich hatte[3] was[4] getrunken,
   es war wohl[5] ein sehr guter Wein!
   Denn[6] ich bin umgesunken,[7]
   und unten[8] am[9] Rhein schlief ich ein.[10]
   Da lag[11] ich, und plötzlich,[12] ja, wen[13] sah[14] ich da!
   Ich rieb[15] mir die Augen.[16] Wißt Ihr, wen ich sah?

[Students or teachers may want to enjoy recordings of this popular Rhine song. Records which have appeared:
  Dietmar Kivel und Orchester Will Glahé/ DECCA; Willy Schneider/ POLYDOR;
  Kurt-Adolf Thelen/ PHILIPS]
*Walzerlied (A Walz)
Text: Heinz Korn – Musik: Heinz Korn, Toni Steingass
Copyright MCMLX des Liedertextes bei Edition Supra
Will Glahé K. G. Köln
Reprinted with the friendly permission of the original publishers and the composer, Heinz Korn.

Lesson 23

REFRAIN:
Ich hab' den Vater Rhein in seinem Bett geseh'n.
Ja, der[17] hat's wunderschön![18] Der braucht[19] nie[20] aufzusteh'n![21]
Und rechts und links vom Bett, da steht der beste Wein!
Ach, wäre ich doch nur[22] der alte Vater Rhein!

1	festivals	12	suddenly
2	songs	13	whom
3	had	14	saw
4	something	15	rubbed
5	probably	16	**mir die Augen** = my eyes
6	because, for	17	he
7	collapsed	18	especially wonderful
8	down there	19	need, have to
9	by the	20	never
10	I fell asleep	21	to get up
11	lay	22	**wäre ich doch nur** = if only I were

OPTIONAL (second verse)
2. Wenn früh der Wecker[1] läutet,[2]
schrillt[3] er wie verrückt[4] durch das Haus.
Ich weiß, was das bedeutet:[5]
ich muß aus den Federn[6] heraus.[7]
"Was soll das,"[8] so ruf' ich, "ich bin das jetzt satt![9]
Ich kenne da jemand,[10] der's[11] viel besser hat!"

Ich hab' den Vater Rhein in seinem Bett geseh'n . . .

1	alarm clock	7	(understood: **herausspringen**)
2	rings	8	"What's the use of this?"
3	sounds shrilly	9	full ("fed up with that")
4	crazy	10	someone
5	means	11	who ("who has it a lot better")
6	"feathers" (feather bed)		

D. Analysis or explanations:

The forms **hatte, war, schlief, lag, sah, rieb** are "simple past" or "narrative past" forms, corresponding to *had, was, slept, lay, saw, rubbed* in English (or, perhaps, more correctly, to *was having, was sleeping, was lying,* etc.). Their use and forms are explained in detail in Lessons 33 and 36.

It should be obvious that this song is a "personification" of the Rhine, "father Rhine." (We have songs in the United States personifying the Mississippi River, "Old Man River," for instance. We also refer to the bottom of a river as the river "bed.") The "wine on both sides of the river's bed" refers to the extensive vineyards on the steep banks and canyon walls along the Rhine river.

Many record albums exist containing songs about the Rhine—many of them "drinking songs." Ask your teacher if you might listen to others—if you enjoy them, that is.

E. **Practice:** Refer to Section B.

F. **Evaluation:** You will be evaluated according to the objectives stated in Section A.

LESSON 24

A. **Your objectives:** To be able to say and write the footnoted German words and phrases which appeared in the song in Lesson 23, when given English equivalents; and to be able to answer the questions in Section E (about the song in Lesson 23) in German.

B. **How to get there:** Use the English equivalents in Section C as cues, and keep "testing" yourself until you make no errors.

Then practice answering the questions in Section E with complete German sentences. If there are any answers you don't know, you aren't acquainted well enough with the text in Lesson 23. Refer back to the text of the song.

The answers are not provided for "blind" memorization, but for you to check the grammatical accuracy of your answers.

C. **What to learn:**

1.	festival	das **Fest**/die **Feste**
2.	song	das **Lied**/die **Lieder**
3.	he	**der** (see last note in D of Lesson 18)
4.	especially wonderful	**wunderschön**
5.	to need	**brauchen**
6.	never	**nie**

Lesson 24

Ein Festtag
in Deutschland.

7.	to get up	aufstehen/ist aufgestanden
8.	if only I were	wäre ich (doch) nur
9.	had	hatte (from haben)
10.	something	was (from etwas)
11.	probably	wohl
12.	because; for (in the sense of "because")	denn
13.	collapse	umsinken/ist umgesunken
14.	down there	da unten
15.	by the	am (an/dem)
16.	fell asleep	schlief ein (from einschlafen)
17.	lay	lag (from legen)
18.	suddenly	plötzlich
19.	whom	wen (target form of wer)
20.	saw	sah (from sehen)
21.	rubbed	rieb (from reiben)
22.	my eyes (when indicating something done to them)	mir die Augen

D. **Analysis or explanations:** See Lesson 23.

E. **Practice:**

FRAGEN (Antworten Sie mit einem Satz!)

1. Wen hat der Sänger gesehen? (**Sänger** = singer)
2. Wo hat er ihn gesehen?
3. Was braucht er nie zu tun?
4. Was steht neben seinem Bett?
5. Was will der Sänger sein?
6. Was hatte er wohl getrunken?
7. Was ist dann geschehen?
8. Was machte er, nachdem (*after*) er umgesunken ist?
9. Was machte er, weil er nicht glaubte, was er sah?
10. Und wen hat er gesehen?

ANTWORTEN:
1. Er hat den **Vater Rhein** gesehen.
2. Er hat ihn **in seinem Bett** gesehen.
3. Er braucht nie **aufzustehen.**
4. **Der beste Wein** steht neben seinem Bett.
5. Er will der alte **Vater Rhein** sein.
6. Er hatte wohl **einen sehr guten Wein** getrunken.
7. Er **ist umgesunken.**
8. Er **schlief ein.**
9. Er **rieb** sich **die Augen.**
10. Er hat den **Vater Rhein** gesehen.

F. **Evaluation:** Refer back to Section A.

LESSON 25

A. **Your objectives:** To be able to read the song in Section C out loud with proper pronunciation and intonation; to be able to explain the meaning of any words or passages requested; and to be able to say and write the German for the 8 words or phrases in the footnotes when given English equivalents.

Lesson 25

B. **The way to get there:**   Follow the same procedure as outlined in Lessons 23 and 24.

C. **What to learn:**

DER TREUE HUSAR[1]

Es war einmal[2] ein treuer Husar,
Der liebt'[3] sein Mädel[4] ein ganzes[5] Jahr,[6]
Ein ganzes Jahr und noch viel mehr,[7]
Die Liebe nahm kein Ende mehr.[8]
Ein ganzes Jahr und noch viel mehr.
Die Liebe nahm kein Ende mehr.

1 hussar (*was a class of light-armed cavalrymen in Europe with quite vivid uniforms*)
2 there was once
3 loved (past form of **lieben**)
4 form of **das Mädchen**
5 whole
6 year
7 even longer
8 never ended (**nahm** is the past form of **nehmen** = to take)

Er liebt' sein Mädel ein ganzes Jahr.

D.	Analysis or explanations:	Again, the grammatical feature in this song is the past tense (as opposed to the present perfect tense): **war, liebte, nahm** (*was, loved, took*).
E.	Practice:	Can you give the German for the new words in the song when you are given the English equivalents?

there was once	**es war einmal**
hussar	**der Husar**
loved	**liebte**
girl	**das Mädel**
whole	**ganz**
year	**das Jahr**
still longer (or more)	**noch viel mehr**
took	**nahm**
end	**das Ende**
never ended	**nahm kein Ende mehr**

F.	Evaluation:	Refer to Section A.

LESSON 26
Adjektivendungen (Adjektivdeklination)

A.	Your objectives:	To be able to demonstrate your knowledge of the forms which noun phrases can take (the forms are summarized in Section C), by being able to perform the exercises in Section E correctly and without hesitation.
B.	The way to get there:	Review the forms in Section C, which you have practiced extensively in Lessons 50-96 of *Deutsch: Kernstufe.* Review their use in Section D. Then practice the drills in Section E. If you miss any of them, be certain to refer back to Sections C and D to determine *why*. Continue drilling until you can do all the exercises fluently and with no errors.
C.	What to learn:	The forms of noun phrases (the endings of the articles and adjectives):

Lesson 26

	der words	**das** words	**die** words
Nominative or "subject" forms	der --e --- ein --er ---	das --e --- ein --es ---	die --e --- eine -- e ---
Accusative or "target" forms	den --en --- einen --en ---	(no change)	(no change)
Dative or "other" forms	dem --en --- einem --en ---		der --en --- einer --en ---

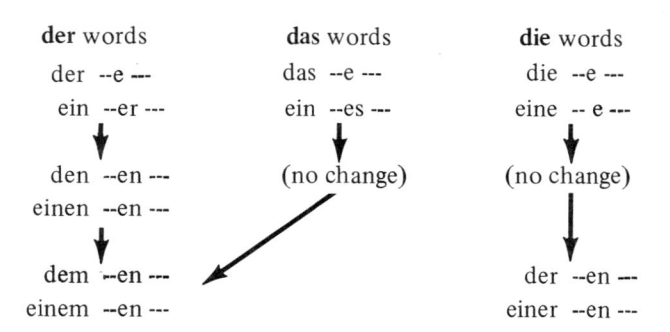

D. Analysis or explanations:

REMEMBER: The "basic form" is used when the phrase functions as the subject of a sentence. It is also used *after* such verbs as **sein** (*to be*) and **werden** (*to become*), since these verbs have no objects or targets (no *activity* is directed at the phrase). The technical grammatical term for this "subject" situation is the *nominative case.*

The "target" form is the form used when the phrase serves as the *object* of some activity (an action was done to or directed at or toward the phrase under question). We need to be "sensitized" to this situation only when we are dealing with a **der** word, since **die** and **das** words do not have special forms in this case. The technical grammatical term for this situation is the *accusative case.*

An "other" form is used when the phrase is neither a subject nor a target. This use usually "boils down" to serving a "to whom" (indirect object) or a "where at" function. We are usually expressing *relationship* between this phrase and the subject or object in the sentence. The technical grammatical term for this situation is the *dative case.*

E. Practice:

Practice the following drills. Remember that you can't use the correct form unless you know or feel that the phrase under question is functioning as a subject, an object, or "other."

How would you say in German

1. **das Bett/groß**

    a. that the object in 1 above is here?   **Das große Bett ist hier.**
    b. that you see this object?   **Ich sehe das große Bett.**
    c. that you are in it?   **Ich bin in dem großen Bett.**
    d. that you are jumping into it?   **Ich springe in das große Bett.**
    e. that you are under it?   **Ich bin unter dem großen Bett.**

Köln am Rhein.

Lesson 26

2. die Blume/gelb

   a. that the object in 2 above is beautiful? Die gelbe Blume ist schön.
   b. that you have picked it? Ich habe die gelbe Blume gepflückt.
   c. that you are next to (*neben*) it? Ich bin neben der gelben Blume.
   d. that you are giving Hans the object? Ich gebe Hans die gelbe Blume.
   e. that a bee (*eine Biene*) is on it? Eine Biene ist (sitzt) auf der gelben Blume.

Sagen Sie auf Deutsch

3. der Rhein/alt

   a. that the river mentioned above is long! Der alte Rhein ist lang.
   b. that you are on (*auf*) it! (in a boat, for instance) Ich bin auf dem alten Rhein.
   c. that you love it! Ich liebe den alten Rhein.
   d. that you want to see it! Ich will den alten Rhein sehen.
   e. that you are in it! Ich bin in dem alten Rhein.

4. ein Husar/treu

   a. that that is the above person! Das ist ein treuer Husar.
   b. that she's going with him! Sie geht mit einem treuen Husar.
   c. that she loves him! Sie liebt einen treuen Husar.
   d. that she gave it to him! Sie hat es einem treuen Husar gegeben.
   e. that *he* is really (*wirklich*) the above person! Er ist wirklich ein treuer Husar.

Fragen Sie ob (*ask if*)

5. sein Mädel/lieb

   a. that is the person above! Ist das sein liebes Mädel?
   b. he is buying her a flower! Kauft er seinem lieben Mädel eine Blume?
   c. I (your teacher) have seen her! Haben Sie sein liebes Mädel gesehen?
   d. he has forgotten her! Hat er sein liebes Mädel vergessen?
   e. he's telling that to her! Sagt er das seinem lieben Mädel?

F. **Evaluation:**   See Section A.

"Der Rhein ist sehr lang!"

LESSON 27
Pronomen

A. Your objectives: To be able to say and write the nominative (subject), accusative (target), and dative ("other") forms of the pronouns in German when given the English nominative form of each (as in Section C); and to be able to use these pronouns in each case, as demonstrated by your ability to do the exercises in Section E fluently without error.

B. How to get there: First, test your memory of the pronoun forms in Section C by referring only to the English and saying each of the three "cases" of each pronoun in turn. Note any that you miss and relearn them.

C. What to learn: Do you remember all of the pronoun forms? If not, learn those you have forgotten before trying to do the drills.

		SUBJECT	TARGET	"OTHER"
1.	I	ich	mich	mir
2.	you (*fam.*)	du	dich	dir
3.	he	er	ihn	ihm
4.	she	sie	sie	ihr
5.	it	es	es	ihm
6.	we	wir	uns	uns
7.	you (*fam. plural*)	ihr	euch	euch
8.	you (*formal*)	Sie	Sie	Ihnen
9.	they	sie	sie	ihnen

When you can recall all of them, test your spelling. Then do the drills in Section E, repeating as often as necessary until you can do them readily without mistakes.

D. Analysis or explanations: Note that these pronoun forms are used under exactly the same conditions as the noun phrases (review Section D of Lesson 26).

Note especially the parallels between previously learned noun phrses and the third person forms of pronouns:

Nominative	der	er	das	es	die	sie	die	sie
Accusative	den	ihn	das	es	die	sie	die	sie
Dative	dem	ihm	dem	ihm	der	ihr	den	ihnen

E. Practice: Referring to the English pronouns on page 75:

1. How would you say that each of the above is here?
2. How would you say that Gisela is buying each of the above a record (**eine Platte**)? (What form will you have to use, and *why*?)
3. How would you say that Mrs. Schmidt has seen each of the above? (What form, and why?)

ANTWORTEN:

1.
    a. Ich bin hier.
    b. Du bist hier.
    c. Er ist hier.
    d. Sie ist hier.
    e. Es ist hier.
    f. Wir sind hier.
    g. Ihr seid hier.
    h. Sie sind hier.
    i. Sie sind hier.

2.
    a. Gisela kauft mir eine Platte.
    b. Gisela kauft dir eine Platte.
    c. Gisela kauft ihm eine Platte.
    d. Gisela kauft ihr eine Platte.
    e. Gisela kauft ihm eine Platte.
    f. Gisela kauft uns eine Platte.
    g. Gisela kauft euch eine Platte.
    h. Gisela kauft Ihnen eine Platte.
    i. Gisela kauft ihnen eine Platte.

3.
    a. Frau Schmidt hat mich gesehen.
    b. Frau Schmidt hat dich gesehen.
    c. Frau Schmidt hat ihn gesehen.
    d. Frau Schmidt hat sie gesehen.
    e. Frau Schmidt hat es gesehen.
    f. Frau Schmidt hat uns gesehen.
    g. Frau Schmidt hat euch gesehen.
    h. Frau Schmidt hat Sie gesehen.
    i. Frau Schmidt hat sie gesehen.

F. Evaluation: Refer to Section A.

Ein kleines Haus in Bernkastel.

Lesson 28

LESSON 28

A. Your objectives: To be able to give the singular and plural forms of 48 neuter (**das**) nouns which you have learned previously (summarized in Section C).

B. How to get there: Using the English equivalents as your cues, try giving the singular form of each noun. Note those that you miss and relearn them.

Then study the summary of the plural forms in Section D before learning the plural forms of each individual noun.

"Das Eis schmeckt gut!"

C. What to learn: Following are most of the **das** words which occurred in *Deutsch: Kernstufe* and in this text up to this point. Their plurals are also listed. Be sure you know the meanings before learning the plurals.

eye	das Auge	die Augen
leg	das Bein	die Beine
bed	das Bett	die Betten
beer	das Bier	die Biere
picture	das Bild	die Bilder
bread	das Brot	die Brote
book	das Buch	die Bücher
thing	das Ding	die Dinge
village	das Dorf	die Dörfer
egg	das Ei	die Eier
ice	das Eis	

end	das Ende	die Enden
food	das Essen	
window	das Fenster	die Fenster
television	das Fernsehen	
building	das Gebäude	die Gebäude
money	das Geld	die Gelder
face	das Gesicht	die Gesichter
beverage; drink	das Getränk	die Getränke
gun	das Gewehr	die Gewehre
glass	das Glas	die Gläser
high school (college prep)	das Gymnasium	die Gymnasien
hair	das Haar	die Haare
chicken	das Hähnchen	die Hähnchen
house	das Haus	die Häuser
home	das Heim	die Heime
year	das Jahr	die Jahre
calf	das Kalb	die Kälber
cap; cape	das Käppchen	die Käppchen
child	das Kind	die Kinder
movie theater	das Kino	die Kinos
life	das Leben	die Leben
girl	das Mädchen, das Mädel	die Mädchen, die Mädel
time	das Mal	die Male
knife	das Messer	die Messer
ear	das Ohr	die Ohren
bicycle; wheel	das Rad	die Räder
restaurant	das Restaurant	die Restaurants
pig	das Schwein	die Schweine
cutlet; chop	das Schnitzel	die Schnitzel
steak	das Steak	die Steaks
piece	das Stück	die Stücke
animal	das Tier	die Tiere
birdie	das Vöglein	die Vöglein
weather	das Wetter	
word	das Wort	die Worte, die Wörter
room	das Zimmer	die Zimmer

D. Analysis or explanations: You should note that the plurals of these 48 nouns fall into 4 main groups: 14 of the nouns form their plural by adding an e; 10 nouns add er, and, in addition, the main vowel is umlauted if possible (ä, ö, ü); 5 add n or en; and 11 add

Lesson 29

nothing (and almost all of these have singular forms ending in **-el, -en,** or **-er**).

E. Practice: To master these nouns, practice saying the singular and plural of each noun in rapid succession with the articles.

    EXAMPLE:
      You see: *the book*
      You say: **das Buch; die Bücher**

F. Evaluation: You will be expected to give the singular and the plural forms (oral and/or written, as directed by your teacher), including the articles, when given the English equivalents as cues.

LESSON 29
Review

A. Your objectives: To be able to do the Self-Test in Section E quickly without errors.

B. How to get there: Look over the exercises in Section E. If you believe you can do them easily, try them. Then check the key (available from your teacher) to see if you made any errors.
    If you did make errors, or if you feel you aren't ready to try the self-test, review Lessons 26, 27, and 28.

C. What to learn: Review the C sections of Lessons 26-28, if necessary.

D. Analysis or explanations: Review the D sections of Lessons 26-28, if necessary.

E. **Practice:** 1. Can you readily complete (orally and in writing) the following statements with the proper German forms of the words or phrases indicated, without having to refer back to anything?

    a. _____ fährt zu schnell.
       der Mann/jung
       das Mädchen/schön
       die Straßenbahn/gelb

    b. Wer hat _____ gesehen?
       das Buch/neu
       die Blume/blau
       der Wagen/hellgrün
       er
       wir
       Sie
       ich
       es
       sie (*she*)
       du
       ihr

    c. Kauf _____ etwas!
       mein Kind/arm
       ich
       wir
       du
       ihr
       sie (they)
       deine Frau/nett
       Sie

2. Give the German singular and plural forms (orally and in writing) of each of the following nouns, without looking back at any of the lessons.

bicycle	hair	book
girl	glass	picture
child	egg	beer
year	village	bed
house	thing	eye

Lesson 30

Noch ein Fest.

F. **Evaluation:** Check your answers with the key. If you made no errors, go on to Lesson 30.

LESSON 30
Imperfektsformen

A. **Your objectives:** To demonstrate your mastery of the "simple past" tense forms by your ability to do the exercises in Section E readily and without error.

B. **How to get there:** Read the analysis of the imperfect tense in Section D, and study the actual forms of this tense in Section C. You will find also in Section C the regular (weak) verbs which are used in the Section E exercises. Then practice the exercises in Section E until you can do them without hesitation.

C. What to learn:

Review the following regular verbs which are used in the Section E exercises:

to do; make	machen
to knock	klopfen
•to live	wohnen
to buy	kaufen
to play	spielen
to snore	schnarchen
to look for	suchen
to laugh	lachen
to cry	weinen
to stare; gawk	gucken
to dance	tanzen
to get	holen
to wait	warten

Following are the forms for the imperfect or simple past tense of verbs in German (corresponding to the *-ed* past forms in English: play*ed,* knock*ed,* look*ed,* etc.)

Compare:

	PRESENT TENSE			PAST TENSE	
Infinitive	*Present Stem*		*Endings*	*Past Stem*	*Endings*
spielen	spiel-	ich	spiele	spielte	spielte
		du	spielst		spieltest
		er	spielt		spielte
		wir, sie	spielen		spielten
		ihr	spielt		spieltet

Notice that in the singular forms of this past tense only **du** effects an ending. This is parallel to what happens with the modals.

D. Analysis or explanations:

As we learned previously, most completed (perfected) actions are expressed in German with the perfect tense:

I found my book = **Ich habe mein Buch gefunden.**

There is, however, a simple past tense in German too. It occurs mostly in story-telling. When a German uses this tense, he has a feeling of being transported back to the time of the action, that is, being involved in an uncompleted (imperfected) action, much as we feel when we say "I *was doing* that." In general, we can say that the difference in English between *I drank the beer* (and that's why there isn't any now) and *I was drinking the beer* (at that time, when my mother came into the kitchen) is parallel to the difference in German between **Ich habe das Bier getrunken** and **Ich trank das Bier** (**trank** being the simple past form of **trinken**).

In both languages the first statement gives one a feeling of being psychologically in the present, concerned in some way about a previously completed activity. The second statement gives one the feeling of being back in the past, involved with the activity that was going on, and not yet completed, at that time.

As in English, we also have in German two ways of forming this past tense. If the verb is regular, or weak (*schwach*), both languages form the simple past by adding an ending. In English this is -*ed* (play*ed*, look*ed*, liv*ed*, laugh*ed*, etc.). In German the ending is **-te** (spiel**te**, schau**te**, wohn**te**, lach**te**). (Notice how some English words in the past approach this German form even in spelling: *made, slept, wept*; and how most words in the past in English approximate this German ending in their pronunciation.)

E. Practice: When you are certain that you know the verbs reviewed in Section C, do the following drills:

1. Ich machte das nicht.   Ich machte das nicht.
   a. (wir)   Wir machten das nicht.
   b. (ihr)   Ihr machtet das nicht.
   c. (Gisela)   Gisela machte das nicht.
   d. (du)   Du machtest das nicht.
   e. (Sie)   Sie machten das nicht.

2. Sie klopfte gerade an die Tür.   Sie klopfte gerade an die Tür.
   a. (du)   Du klopftest gerade an die Tür.
   b. (ihr)   Ihr klopftet gerade an die Tür.
   c. (ich)   Ich klopfte gerade an die Tür.

    d. (er)   Er klopfte gerade an die Tür.
    e. (Marie und Ernst)   Marie und Ernst klopften gerade an die Tür.
    f. (Erika und ich)   Erika und ich klopften gerade an die Tür.

3. Wir wohnten damals in Bad Boll.   Wir wohnten damals in Bad Boll.
    a. (Udo)   Udo wohnte damals in Bad Boll.
    b. (ich)   Ich wohnte damals in Bad Boll.
    c. (ihr)   Ihr wohntet damals in Bad Boll.
    d. (er)   Er wohnte damals in Bad Boll.
    e. (wir)   Wir wohnten damals in Bad Boll.
    f. (du)   Du wohntest damals in Bad Boll.

How would you say in German

    a. that you were buying a newspaper?   **Ich kaufte eine Zeitung.**
    b. that I was playing the guitar?   **Sie spielten die Gitarre.**
    c. that she was snoring loudly?   **Sie schnarchte laut.**
    d. that they were looking for me?   **Sie suchten Sie.**
    e. that you and Hans were looking in the mirror?   **Wir schauten in den Spiegel.**
    f. that you were laughing and crying?   **Ich lachte und weinte.**
    g. that I was looking through the door?   **Sie guckten durch die Tür.**
    h. that your mother was dancing in Berlin?   **Meine Mutter tanzte in Berlin.**
    i. that he was getting (*holen*) the menu?   **Er holte die Speisekarte.**
    j. to your friend that he was waiting in the room?   **Du wartetest in dem Zimmer.**

F. Evaluation: When you can do the exercises in Section E in German readily (orally and written), seeing or hearing only the left-hand column as a cue, you are ready for evaluation.

LESSON 31
Comprehensive Review Self-Test

A. **Your objectives:** To be able to pass the Self-Test with at least 90% accuracy (without referring to any notes or previous lessons while taking the test).

B. **How to get there:** Look over the exercises (Section E) of Lessons 17-30. Practice any which you feel unsure about. When confident that you are well prepared, you are ready to do the Self-Test in Section E of this lesson.

C. **What to learn:** Review.

D. **Analysis or explanations:** Review.

E. **Practice:**

1. What do the following words or phrases mean?

    a. atmen
    b. begraben
    c. vorher
    d. einfach
    e. es gibt

    f. das Bein
    g. dünn
    h. frieren
    i. das Fenster
    j. ihr Mann

2. How do you express the following in German?

    a. song (*singular and plural*)
    b. to need
    c. never
    d. to get up (*principal parts*)
    e. to collapse (*principal parts*)

    f. suddenly
    g. to rub
    h. there was once
    i. year
    j. end

3. Using the words or phrases

> der alte Mann
> die kleine Katze
> das freundliche Mädchen
> ich
> er

a. How would you say that each of the above is at home?
b. How would you say that Hans sees each of the above?
c. How would you say that Elke gives each of the above something?

4. Give the singular and plural forms of the following neuter nouns:

a. picture
b. book
c. egg
d. window
e. face

f. glass
g. house
h. child
i. girl
j. animal

5. How would you say that

a. you're knocking loudly?
b. you were knocking loudly?
c. they're playing over there?
d. they were playing over there?
e. he's waiting at home?

f. he was waiting at home?
g. I (your teacher) live in Germany?
h. I was living in Germany?
i. I lived (have lived) in Germany?
j. I want to live in Germany?

F. Evaluation: Check your answers (or have them checked) against the key. If you did 90% or better, review anything you may have missed, and then go on to Lesson 33.

If you did not score at least 90%, review as necessary (vocabulary? practice exercises? forms?). Then try the test again.

Lesson 32

"Gehen wir in eine Jugendherberge!"

LESSON 32
Lessons 17-31

A.	Your objectives:	To pass the review test as directed on the test, with at least 90% accuracy.
B.	How to get there:	Do not attempt to take the test unless you have passed all the self-tests in Lessons 17-31 with 90% or better, and have also reviewed any sections containing the type of material you missed.
C.	What to learn:	Review.
D.	Analysis or explanations:	Review.
E.	Practice:	Review.
F.	Evaluation:	Refer to Section B. When you are certain that you are ready, have the teacher administer the test.

LESSON 33

A. Your objectives: To be able to give the infinitive, the simple past stem, and the past participle of the weak (regular) verbs in Section C when given English equivalents as cues.

B. How to get there: Look at the English and make a quick check of how many of these verbs you still remember. *Learn* those you don't know!
Then refer to Section D for several explanations before practicing the exercises in Section E.

C. What to learn:

to fish	angeln
to breathe	atmen
to open (up)	aufmachen
to wake up	aufwachen
to order	bestellen
to pay	bezahlen
to bloom	blühen
to need	brauchen
to ask	fragen
to be happy	freuen (sich)
to feel	fühlen
to fill	füllen
to fear	fürchten
to believe	glauben
to look	gucken
to get (fetch)	holen
to hear	hören
to be interested	interessieren (sich)
to buy	kaufen
to knock	klopfen
to cost	kosten
to laugh	lachen
to put, lay	legen
to love	lieben
to make, do	machen

Lesson 33

D. Analysis or explanations: All the verbs form their past participles with a **ge-** prefix and a **-t** ending, except for

1. those with a separable prefix:

    aufgemacht
    aufgewacht

2. those with an inseparable prefix:

    bestellt
    bezahlt

3. and **interessieren:**

    interessiert

E. Practice: Refer to the English infinitives in Section B. Give, in order, the German infinitive, past stem, and past participle of each one.

Following are the answers to this exercise:

angeln	angelte	geangelt
atmen	atmete	geatmet
aufmachen	machte auf	aufgemacht
aufwachen	wachte auf	aufgewacht
bestellen	bestellte	bestellt
bezahlen	bezahlte	bezahlt
blühen	blühte	geblüht
brauchen	brauchte	gebraucht
fragen	fragte	gefragt
freuen	freute	gefreut
fühlen	fühlte	gefühlt
füllen	füllte	gefüllt
fürchten	fürchtete	gefürchtet
glauben	glaubte	geglaubt
gucken	guckte	geguckt
holen	holte	geholt
hören	hörte	gehört
interessieren	interessierte	interessiert
kaufen	kaufte	gekauft

klopfen	klopfte	geklopft
kosten	kostete	gekostet
lachen	lachte	gelacht
legen	legte	gelegt
lieben	liebte	geliebt
machen	machte	gemacht

F. Evaluation: Refer to Section A.

Interessierst du dich für Fachwerkhäuser?

LESSON 34

A. Your objectives: To be able to give the infinitive, the simple past stem, and the past participle of the weak verbs in Section C when given the English infinitives; and to be able to do fluently the exercise in Section E dealing with the negation of **müssen**.

B. How to get there: See Lesson 33, Section B.

C. What to learn:

to notice	merken
to grasp; pack	packen
to pick	pflücken
to talk	reden
to save a person	retten
to look	schauen
to give as a present	schenken
to taste	schmecken
to snore	schnarchen
to set; put	setzen
to play	spielen
to stare	starren
to put; stick	stecken
to look for; seek	suchen
to dance	tanzen
to dream	träumen
to sell	verkaufen
to swallow	verschlucken
to wait (for)	warten (auf)
to blow; drift	wehen
to cry	weinen
to wave	winken
to live	wohnen
to wonder	wundern (sich)
to pay	zahlen
to listen	zuhören

D. Analysis or explanations: The only past participles to beware of in the list in Section C are **zugehört, verkauft,** and **verschluckt.**

SPECIAL NOTE about **brauchen**:

We can usually negate verbs or phrases in German by adding **nicht** (or some other appropriate negative) at the proper place in the sentence. For example:

>Ich gehe in die Stadt.
>Ich gehe nicht in die Stadt.

With **müssen**, however, we do not end up with the negative idea we want if we do this. Even in English we have to do something else if we want to negate a certain aspect of the word "must."

I have to go and *I don't have to go* present no problem. They are the "opposites" we are looking for. But, if instead of using "have to" we use "must" to mean essentially the same thing, we then find that we can't get the effect we got above by simply adding a negative: *I must go* vs. *I must not go.* We find that in order to negate *I must go* in the way we did above, we have to change the statement to *I don't have to go* or *I don't need to go.*

In German **Ich muß gehen** presents exactly the same problem as does *I must go* in English. Here, too, in order to negate the idea and get the meaning we want, we have to change the verb. In German it is

>Ich **brauche nicht zu** gehen.

One line in the song in Lesson 23 is

>"Er braucht nie aufzustehen!"

What would be the positive statement of this idea?

>Er muß aufstehen.

E. Practice:

1. Give the German infinitives, past stems, and past participles for the English infinitives in Section C.

merken	merkte	gemerkt
packen	packte	gepackt
pflücken	pflückte	gepflückt
reden	redete	geredet

Lesson 35

retten	rettete	gerettet
schauen	schaute	geschaut
schenken	schenkte	geschenkt
schmecken	schmeckte	geschmeckt
schnarchen	schnarchte	geschnarcht
setzen	setzte	gesetzt
spielen	spielte	gespielt
starren	starrte	gestarrt
stecken	steckte	gesteckt
suchen	suchte	gesucht
tanzen	tanzte	getanzt
träumen	träumte	geträumt
verkaufen	verkaufte	verkauft
verschlucken	verschluckte	verschluckt
warten	wartete	gewartet
wehen	wehte	geweht
weinen	weinte	geweint
winken	winkte	gewinkt
wohnen	wohnte	gewohnt
wundern	wunderte	gewundert
zahlen	zahlte	gezahlt
zuhören	hörte zu	zugehört

2. Change the following to negative statements:

a. Er muß morgen zu Hause bleiben.   Er braucht morgen nicht zu Hause zu bleiben.
b. Wir müssen jetzt aufstehen.   Wir brauchen jetzt nicht aufzustehen.
c. Sie müssen die Tür aufmachen.   Sie brauchen die Tür nicht aufzumachen.
d. Muß Gisela zuhören?   Braucht Gisela nicht zuzuhören?
e. Warum müßt ihr hier sein?   Warum braucht ihr nicht hier zu sein?

F. Evaluation: Refer to Section A to determine whether you are ready for evaluation or not.

LESSON 35

A. Your objectives: To be able to do the exercises in Section E orally and in writing in German without errors.

94   Deutsch: ZWEITE STUFE

Schlafraum in einer Jugendherberge

B. How to get there: Follow the directions in Section E.

C. What to learn: This lesson contains no new material. It is designed to provide additional practice in using verb forms, especially in the narrative past.

D. Analysis or explanations: See Section D of Lesson 30 if necessary.

E. Practice: 1. Using the idea **das schöne Mädchen lieben**, how would you say that the following subjects do this?

                            a. ich   Ich liebe das schöne Mädchen.
                            b. wir   Wir lieben das schöne Mädchen.
                            c. du   Du liebst das schöne Mädchen.
                            d. ihr   Ihr liebt das schöne Mädchen.
                            e. er   Er liebt das schöne Mädchen.

                            2. How would you say that the above subjects *were doing* the activity mentioned? In other words, at some particular time in the past this *was* the case ("simple" past tense).

Lesson 35

a.	ich	Ich liebte das schöne Mädchen.
b.	wir	Wir liebten das schöne Mädchen.
c.	du	Du liebtest das schöne Mädchen.
d.	ihr	Ihr liebtet das schöne Mädchen.
e.	er	Er liebte das schöne Mädchen.

3. How would you say that the same subjects did (have done) this—that this was once the case but isn't now?

a.	ich	Ich habe das schöne Mädchen geliebt.
b.	wir	Wir haben das schöne Mädchen geliebt.
c.	du	Du hast das schöne Mädchen geliebt.
d.	ihr	Ihr habt das schöne Mädchen geliebt.
e.	er	Er hat das schöne Mädchen geliebt.

4. How would you say that each of the subjects want to do this?

a.	ich	Ich will das schöne Mädchen lieben.
b.	wir	Wir wollen das schöne Mädchen lieben.
c.	du	Du willst das schöne Mädchen lieben.
d.	ihr	Ihr wollt das schöne Mädchen lieben.
e.	er	Er will das schöne Mädchen lieben.

5. Say and write sentence *a.* in each of the four exercises above as it would appear in the statement **"Sie wissen, daß . . ."**

1a.	Sie wissen, daß ich das schöne Mädchen liebe.
2a.	Sie wissen, daß ich das schöne Mädchen liebte.
3a.	Sie wissen, daß ich das schöne Mädchen geliebt habe.
4a.	Sie wissen, daß ich das schöne Mädchen lieben will.

6. Using the idea **die Tür aufmachen**, how would you state that

a. you are doing this?	Ich mache die Tür auf.
b. he was doing this?	Er machte die Tür auf.
c. they did this?	Sie haben die Tür aufgemacht.
d. I may do this?	Sie dürfen die Tür aufmachen.
e. he knows that you were doing this?	Er weiß, daß ich die Tür aufmachte.

7. How would you say to a friend that

    a. he has to play soccer?   **Du mußt Fußball spielen!**
    b. he doesn't have to play football?   **Du brauchst nicht Fußball zu spielen.**
    c. he doesn't have to open the door?   **Du brauchst die Tür nicht aufzumachen.**
    d. he has to open the door?   **Du mußt die Tür aufmachen!**

F.   Evaluation: Refer to Section A to determine your readiness for evaluation.

Diese Fußballmannschaft hat gewonnen.

LESSON 36

A. Your objectives: To be able to give the principal parts of the 10 verbs in Section C in oral and written German when given the English infinitives as cues; and to be able to do the exercises in Section E fluently—all without error.

B. How to get there: First, study Section D; then memorize the principal parts of the verbs in Section C. Be sure to listen to the recordings, or to someone who knows German well, so that you will have a correct model for the pronunciation, especially of the new forms.

When you know the principal parts well, practice using them in Section E.

C. What to learn: (In the following four lessons we shall learn the principal parts of many of the more common strong, or irregular, verbs which we have had so far in *Deutsch: Kernstufe* and *Deutsch: Zweite Stufe*.)

		INFINITIVE FORM	PRESENT TENSE STEM CHANGE	IMPERFECT TENSE STEM	PAST PARTICIPLE
1.	to begin	anfangen	fängt an	fing an	angefangen
2.	to begin	beginnen		begann	begonnen
3.	to find	finden		fand	gefunden
4.	to win	gewinnen		gewann	gewonnen
5.	to read	lesen	liest	las	gelesen
6.	to take	nehmen	nimmt	nahm	genommen
7.	to write	schreiben		schrieb	geschrieben
8.	to sing	singen		sang	gesungen
9.	to see	sehen	sieht	sah	gesehen
10.	to drink	trinken		trank	getrunken

D. Analysis or explanations: If a verb is irregular (strong) we must learn the past stem, just as we would in English. One doesn't know that the past of *go* is *went,* of *think* is *thought,* of *cut* is *cut,* unless one has learned it through having heard or read it often.

While learning the past forms of the verbs we have had, we should also at the same time review the other forms of these verbs, and relearn any we have forgotten.

The different forms of a verb are usually referred to as the "principal parts" of the verb. If we know these principal parts, we can use the verb in all possible ways. For instance, if we are talking about the verb *to go* in English, we can not use it in all possible ways unless we know its two other principal parts in addition to the infinitive: *went* and *gone*.

The principal parts are thus

to go   went   gone

If we don't know these other parts, we might, as a child often does, use *to go* as a regular verb and say such things as "He goed home" or "They have already goed."

The principal parts in German must show us

1. the infinitive,
2. whether the stem changes in the present tense, second and third persons singular,
3. the "simple" past stem,
4. the past participle (and whether **ist**, or some form of it, is used as the auxiliary).

When we use these simple past forms, we add endings according to the same pattern that occurs with the weak verbs and with the modal auxiliaries; that is, in the singular only **du** effects an ending, and in the plural the endings are what we have come to expect from our very first lessons in German:

ich sang	wir, sie, Sie sang**en**
du sang**st**	ihr sang**t**

E. **Practice:**   Substitute the indicated subjects in the original sentences in each set of exercises below:

1. Er las ein neues Buch.   Er las eine neues Buch.
   a. (wir)   Wir lasen ein neues Buch.
   b. (du)   Du last ein neues Buch.
   c. (sie) (plural)   Sie lasen ein neues Buch.
   d. (Sie)   Sie lasen ein neues Buch.
   e. (sie) (singular)   Sie las ein neues Buch.
   f. (ihr)   Ihr last ein neues Buch.

Lesson 36

"Doch schriebst du diese Worte!"

2. Sie nahmen eine Flasche Wein.   Sie nahmen eine Flasche Wein.
   a. (er)   Er nahm eine Flasche Wein.
   b. (ich)   Ich nahm eine Flasche Wein.
   c. (wir)   Wir nahmen eine Flasche Wein.
   d. (du)   Du nahmst eine Flasche Wein.
   e. (ihr)   Ihr nahmt eine Flasche Wein.
   f. (Sie)   Sie nahmen eine Flasche Wein.

3. Schrieb sie die deutschen Wörter?   Schrieb sie die deutschen Wörter?
   a. (du)   Schriebst du die deutschen Wörter?
   b. (wir)   Schrieben wir die deutschen Wörter?
   c. (Sie)   Schrieben Sie die deutschen Wörter?
   d. (ich)   Schrieb ich die deutschen Wörter?
   e. (Hans)   Schrieb Hans die deutschen Wörter?
   f. (ihr)   Schriebt ihr die deutschen Wörter?

Substitute the indicated verbs in the original sentences. (Note that the tense is the narrative past.)

4. Der Mann las ein Buch.   Der Mann las ein Buch.
   a. (finden)   Der Mann fand ein Buch.
   b. (gewinnen)   Der Mann gewann ein Buch.
   c. (nehmen)   Der Mann nahm ein Buch.
   d. (sehen)   Der Mann sah ein Buch.
   e. (anfangen)   Der Mann fing ein Buch an.
   f. (beginnen)   Der Mann begann ein Buch.

5. Wir sahen nichts.   Wir sahen nichts.
   a. (trinken)   Wir tranken nichts.
   b. (singen)   Wir sangen nichts.
   c. (lesen)   Wir lasen nichts.
   d. (anfangen)   Wir fingen nichts an.
   e. (schreiben)   Wir schrieben nichts.
   f. (nehmen)   Wir nahmen nichts.

F. **Evaluation:** When you can give the principal parts of the 10 verbs in Section C in oral and written German when given the English infinitives as cues, and when you can do the exercises in Section E without error, you are ready for evaluation.

LESSON 37

A. **Your objectives:** See Lesson 36.

B. **How to get there:** Refer to Lesson 36.

C. **What to learn:**

11.	to eat	essen	ißt	aß	gegessen
12.	to give	geben	gibt	gab	gegeben
13.	to speak	sprechen	spricht	sprach	gesprochen

Lesson 37

14.	to stand	stehen		stand	gestanden
15.	to meet	treffen	trifft	traf	getroffen
16.	to stay	bleiben		blieb	geblieben (ist)
17.	to scream	schreien		schrie	geschri(e)en
18.	to climb	steigen		stieg	gestiegen (ist)
19.	to fall	fallen	fällt	fiel	gefallen (ist)
20.	to sleep	schlafen	schläft	schlief	geschlafen

D. Analysis or explanations: See Lesson 36. Also note the pattern of the vowel changes in many verbs as they form principal parts (similar to such a pattern in English as s*i*ng, s*a*ng, s*u*ng; dr*i*nk, dr*a*nk, dr*u*nk; s*i*nk, s*a*nk, s*u*nk; etc.):

essen	aß	
geben	gab	
sprechen	sprach	
stehen	stand	
treffen	traf	
bleiben	blieb	geblieben
schreien	schrie	geschrieen
steigen	stieg	gestiegen
fallen (fällt)	fiel	gefallen
schlafen (schläft)	schlief	geschlafen

Becoming aware of such patterns will make the learning of the principal parts much easier.

E. Practice:

1. Substitute the indicated subjects:

   Er aß Wurst mit Sauerkraut.   Er aß Wurst mit Sauerkraut.
   a. (wir)   Wir aßen Wurst mit Sauerkraut.
   b. (ich)   Ich aß Wurst mit Sauerkraut.
   c. (du)   Du aßest Wurst mit Sauerkraut.
   d. (Sie)   Sie aßen Wurst mit Sauerkraut.
   e. (ihr)   Ihr aßet Wurst mit Sauerkraut.

2. Substitute the indicated verb:

   Sie gaben so viel.   Sie gaben so viel.
   a. (essen)   Sie aßen so viel.
   b. (sprechen)   Sie sprachen so viel.
   c. (schreien)   Sie schrien so viel.

　　　　　　　　　　d. (steigen)　　　　　　Sie stiegen so viel.
　　　　　　　　　　e. (stehen)　　　　　　 Sie standen so viel.

　　　　　　　　3. Using the German phrase **miteinander sprechen,** how would you say that we (including you)

　a. were doing this?　　　　　　　　**Wir sprachen miteinander.**
　b. are doing this?　　　　　　　　　**Wir sprechen miteinander.**
　c. are permitted to do this?　　　　**Wir dürfen miteinander sprechen.**
　d. did (have done) this?　　　　　　**Wir haben miteinander gesprochen.**
　e. know that we were doing this?　**Wir wissen, daß wir miteinander sprachen.**

F.　Evaluation:　　　　　　When you can give the principal parts of the verbs and can do the exercises without error, you are ready for evaluation.

"Ich glaube nicht, daß das Boot in den See sank."

LESSON 38

A. Your objectives: See Lesson 36.

B. How to get there: See Lesson 36.

C. What to learn:

21.	to bring	bringen		brachte	gebracht
22.	to think	denken		dachte	gedacht
23.	to know	kennen		kannte	gekannt
24.	to drive	fahren	fährt	fuhr	gefahren (ist)
25.	to go, walk	gehen		ging	gegangen (ist)
26.	to come	kommen		kam	gekommen (ist)
27.	to run	laufen	läuft	lief	gelaufen (ist)
28.	to be	sein	ist	war	gewesen (ist)
29.	to sink	sinken		sank	gesunken (ist)
30.	to become	werden	wird	wurde	geworden (ist)

D. Analysis or explanations: See the previous two lessons.

E. Practice: 1. Substitute the verbs in the following sentence:

Ich ging damals sehr oft.   Ich ging damals sehr oft.
  a. fahren   Ich fuhr damals sehr oft.
  b. kommen   Ich kam damals sehr oft.
  c. laufen   Ich lief damals sehr oft.
  d. sein (add *da* to end)   Ich war damals sehr oft da.
  e. denken   Ich dachte damals sehr oft.

2. How would you ask a friend if

  a. he was becoming sick?   **Wurdest du krank?**
  b. he was bringing Gisela home?   **Brachtest du Gisela nach Hause?**
  c. he was driving a Volkswagen?   **Fuhrst du einen Volkswagen?**
  d. he was coming to school?   **Kamst du in die (zur) Schule?**
  e. he was in the restaurant?   **Warst du im Restaurant?**

3. Using the phrase **in den See sinken**, how would you say that

a. the boat (*das Boot*) is doing this?   Das Boot sinkt in den See.
b. it was doing this?   Das Boot sank in den See.
c. it did this?   Das Boot ist in den See gesunken.
d. it can't do this?   Das Boot kann nicht in den See sinken.
e. you don't believe that the boat was doing this?   Ich glaube nicht, daß das Boot in den See sank.

F. **Evaluation:** When you can give the principal parts of the 10 verbs in Section C while hearing or seeing only the English infinitives; and when you can do the exercises in Section E fluently, as directed, you are ready for evaluation.

LESSON 39

A. **Your objectives:** See Lesson 36.

B. **How to get there:** See Lesson 36.

C. **What to learn:**

31.	to have	haben	hat	hatte	gehabt
32.	to lie	liegen		lag	gelegen
33.	to call	rufen		rief	gerufen
34.	to shoot	schießen		schoß	geschossen
35.	to cut	schneiden		schnitt	geschnitten
36.	to sit	sitzen		saß	gesessen
37.	to carry	tragen	trägt	trug	getragen
38.	to do	tun		tat	getan
39.	to forget	vergessen	vergißt	vergaß	vergessen
40.	to know	wissen	weiß	wußte	gewußt

D. **Analysis or explanations:** See Lessons 36 and 37.

Lesson 40

E. **Practice:** 1. Substitute the given verb:

Ihr hattet damals nichts.   Ihr hattet damals nichts.
  a. schießen   Ihr schoßet[1] damals nichts.
  b. schneiden   Ihr schnittet damals nichts.
  c. tragen   Ihr trugt damals nichts.
  d. tun   Ihr tatet damals nichts.
  e. vergessen   Ihr vergaßet damals nichts.

[1] When the past stem ends with -t, -d, -ss, or -ß, or chs, an e is added between the stem and the ending.

2. How would you

  a. tell me I was lying on the sofa?   Du lagst auf dem Sofa. Sie lagen
  b. tell a friend he forgot the flowers?   Du vergaßest die Blumen.
  c. tell Hans and Gisela they were sitting   Ihr saßet hinter mir.
     behind you?
  d. tell me you were calling the children?   Ich rief die Kinder.
  e. tell me he wants to know what you were   Er will wissen, was ich schnitt.
     cutting?

F. **Evaluation:** When you can give the principal parts of the verbs in Section C while referring only to the English infinitives; and when you can do the exercises in Section E—all without error—you are ready for evaluation.

LESSON 40
Eine Geschichte

A. **Your objectives:** To be able to read the passage from the story in Section C out loud with pronunciation and intonation as close to that of your model as possible; and to be able to explain the meaning of any individual words or passages requested (in English or German, as directed by your teacher).

B. **How to get there:** Listen to the recording of the passage in Section C once or twice—until the general outline of what's going on is clear to you. Next, read the passage carefully to fill in the details, using the vocabulary at the end of the passage (or at the end of the book) when necessary.

Be certain to learn any words you have to look up!

Now go over the story at normal reading speed without referring to any vocabulary lists or notes. Repeat if necessary, until the meaning is clear without any pausing or translating.

C. **What to learn:** Es gibt viele Sagen (Legenden), die mit dem Rhein etwas zu tun haben. Sehr bekannt[1] sind die Geschichten[2] über die Nibelungen, Leute, die vor langer Zeit am Rhein wohnten. Der bekannteste Held[3] in diesen Sagen ist Siegfried. Es folgt[4] eine Geschichte über den jungen Siegfried:

"Am Rhein wohnte zu dieser Zeit ein König."

Lesson 40

JUNG-SIEGFRIED

Zu Xanten[5] am Niederrhein[6] wohnte zu dieser Zeit ein König,[7] der Siegmund hieß. Seine Frau, die Königin, hieß Sieglinde. Sie hatten ein Kind mit Namen Siegfried. Schon als kleiner Junge war er besonders stark[8] und tapfer.[9] Als er ein großer Junge war, war er sehr wild. Die Leute sagten dem König, er sollte Siegfried in die
5 Welt schicken.[10] Er konnte viel lernen, and dann wäre[11] er später ein besserer Junge. Siegfried war sehr froh. Er hatte schon lange andere Länder sehen wollen.

Also[12] ging Siegfried aus Xanten hinaus und in einen großen Wald hinein, wo tief unter einem Berg[13] sehr kleine Menschen, die Nibelungen, wohnten. Siegfried wußte es nicht, aber die Nibelungen hatten viel Gold und Silber und Juwelen,[14]
10 den Schatz[15] der Nibelungen, hier unter dem Berg.

Ein paar Tage lang wanderte Siegfried durch den dunklen Wald. Er aß Beeren und grüne Pflanzen, und trank das frische kalte Wasser, das er im Wald fand. Plötzlich[16] hörte er das "Kling-Klang" von Hämmern und wußte, daß das von einer Schmiede[17] kam. Fröhlich ging er in die kleine Hütte,[18] die unter einem großen
15 Eichenbaum stand, und fragte den Schmied, ob er nicht bei ihm schmieden lernen könnte. Der Schmied konnte immer einen willigen Jungen brauchen. Aber erst mußte Siegfried zeigen,[19] wie stark er war. Er nahm einen Hammer und schlug[20] auf das Eisen mit solcher Kraft,[21] daß der Hammer und das Eisen in tausend Stücke zerbrach.

1	well-known	8	strong	15	treasure
2	stories	9	brave	16	suddenly
3	hero	10	to send	17	blacksmith shop
4	there follows	11	would be	18	hut; cabin
5	at Xanten (a town)	12	therefore	19	to show
6	lower Rhine	13	mountain	20	beat
7	king	14	jewels	21	strength

D. Analysis or explanations: Relative pronouns in German are commonly just repetitions of the articles **der, die, das, den, dem,** etc. (In English, relative pronouns are usually forms of *who, which,* or, increasingly, *that*: "The man *who* is driving...," "The story *which* (or *that*) I heard....") Note the use of relative pronouns in Section C in lines 1 and 3 of the introduction, and line 1 of the story itself.

NOTES on the text:

line 6   **hatte ... sehen wollen** = had wanted to see

	line 8	**die Nibelungen**: Look up "Nibelungenlied" in a large encyclopaedia for interesting information.
	line 10	**der** Nibelungen = *of the* Nibelungs
	line 16	**könnte** = could
E.	Practice:	See Section B.
F.	Evaluation:	Refer to Section A.

LESSON 41

A.	Your objectives:	See Lesson 40.
B.	How to get there:	See Lesson 40.
C.	What to learn:	

JUNG-SIEGFRIED (continued)

Der Schmied hatte etwas Angst, weil Siegfried soviel Kraft hatte, aber er durfte bei dem Schmied bleiben. Er lernte gut, aber er kämpfte[22] immer mit den anderen Lehrlingen[23] und schlug sie so schwer, daß sie tagelang krank im Bett lagen. Also wollte der Schmied Siegfried endlich los werden.[24] Er schickte ihn in den Wald,
5 Kohlen[25] zu holen. Der Schmied wußte, daß dort ein großer böser Drache wohnte. Bevor Siegfried die Schmiede verließ, schmiedete er sich ein scharfes Schwert.[27] Dann lief er in den Wald.

". . . , daß dort ein großer böser Drache wohnte."

Lesson 41

      Bald sah er einen See, der von Seedrachen[28] wimmelte.[29] Er schnitt einem Drachen nach dem anderen den Kopf ab, aber es kamen immer mehr Drachen. Er
10 legte das Schwert beiseite,[30] holte viele Bäume und warf sie in den See. Dann zündete er sie an.[31] Das Wasser, das Drachenblut[32] und das Drachenfett[33] kochten zusammen, und ein bißchen von der Flüssigkeit[34] fiel auf Siegfrieds Hand. Er merkte, daß die Flüssigkeit bald hart wurde. Das Schwert konnte seine Hand nicht schneiden. Sie war so hart wie Drachenhaut![35] Jetzt hatte er einen Plan. Er
15 wartete, bis die Flüssigkeit kühler wurde, dann steckte er die Hand darin und begann, den Stoff über den ganzen Körper[36] zu schmieren. Aber da fiel ein Blatt von einem Lindenbaum auf seine Schulter, und die Haut wurde da nicht hart. Jetzt war Siegfried von keinem Schwert verwundbar,[37] außer[38] an der kleinen Stelle, wo das Lindenblatt gefallen war.

Ende

22	fought	28	sea dragons	34	liquid
23	apprentices	29	swarmed	35	dragon skin, hide
24	to get rid of	30	aside	36	body
25	coal	31	to light (**anzünden**)	37	vulnerable
26	dragon	32	dragon blood	38	except
27	sword	33	dragon fat		

      Es gibt andere Geschichten über Siegfried. Vielleicht wollen Sie sie lesen, besonders die Geschichte von Siegfrieds Tod, wo seine Frau einem Mann sagt, wie er die verwundbare Stelle an Siegfrieds Schulter finden könnte.

D. Analysis or explanations:

    line 6   **schmiedete er sich**: This is a reflexive phrase, the **sich** indicating he did this for *himself*. **Schmieden** means to forge, that is, to fashion out of metal. It is the activity that a **Schmied** (*blacksmith*) engages in.

    line 8   The **der** is another relative pronoun (see Section D of Lesson 40), which refers back to **See**: "a lake, which. . ."

    line 9   This first clause will make sense if you notice that the target or direct object in it is **den Kopf**: "He cut the head off one dragon after the other."

line 14   The pronoun **Sie** at the beginning of this line refers to *hand*. We would render it in English as *it,* since we don't usually refer to objects as having "gender."

line 19   The form **gefallen war** is the past perfect form *had fallen*. Compare this to **ist gefallen,** the present perfect form meaning *has fallen* or *fell*.

E. Practice: See Section B.

F. Evaluation: You will be evaluated exactly according to the objectives as stated in Section A.

Diese Helden kämpfen auf dem Fußballplatz.

LESSON 42

A. **Your objectives:** To be able to do the Self-Test in Section E orally and/or written (ask your teacher) with no errors.

B. **How to get there:** Follow the directions on the test.

C. **What to learn:** Review the story *Jung-Siegfried* and the new vocabulary words in it (Lessons 40-41), unless you are sure that you know it well enough already.

D. **Analysis or explanations:** See the D sections in Lessons 40-41.

E. **Practice:**

SELF-TEST
1. What do the following words mean? (If you have to look up any of them, you aren't really familiar enough with the story and its vocabulary!)

a.	Geschichte	f.	Schmied	k.	Kohle
b.	stark	g.	Schmiede	l.	Kopf
c.	Berg	h.	Hütte	m.	Haut
d.	Schatz	i.	zeigen	n.	Fett
e.	plötzlich	j.	Drache	o.	kämpfen

2. Pick appropriate words from the above list to complete the following sentences:

a. Unter einem _____ wohnten die Nibelungen.
b. Der Schmied arbeitete in einer kleinen _____ .
c. In dem Wald war ein großer böser _____ .
d. Siegfried schnitt den _____ von dem Drachen ab.
e. Wenn Sie viel Gold und Silber haben, haben Sie einen _____ .

3. Answer the following questions in German. Try using complete sentences, although your answer will be considered correct if it only contains the correct word or short phrase.

a. Wo wohnte Siegfried?
b. Wie hieß Siegfrieds Vater?
c. Was für ein Junge war Siegfried?

d. Wollte Siegfried in die Welt gehen?
e. Wo wohnten die Nibelungen?
f. Was hatten die Nibelungen da?
g. Was konnte Siegfried im Wald essen?
h. Wie zeigte Siegfried, daß er stark war?
i. Warum wollte der Schmied Siegfried los werden?
j. Was nahm Siegfried mit in den Wald?
k. Wo kochte Siegfried die Drachen?
l. Warum konnte kein Schwert Siegfrieds Hand schneiden?
m. Wo war Siegfrieds schwache Stelle?

4. Read the story out loud to test your pronunciation and intonation. You can do this in the following manner:

Play the recording, but read each sentence out loud *before* you hear it on the recording. This can be done by stopping the recording after each sentence, reading the *next* sentence aloud, then playing that sentence and comparing your pronunciation and intonation to the recording.

F. Evaluation: Check your answers against the key. Review if necessary.

LESSON 43
Ein Gedicht

This lesson is optional. Consult with your teacher about substituting some other type of assignment if you prefer.

A. Your objectives: To be able to read the poem (also a very famous song) in Section C with intonation and pronunciation as close to that of your model as possible; and to be able to explain (in German or in English, as directed by your teacher) the meaning of any words or longer passages requested.

B. How to get there: Listen to the recorded version while looking at the printed version. Do this as often as necessary until you understand everything well. Learn all new vocabulary (German to English). There are helpful notes in Section D.

Lesson 43

C. **What to learn:** Es folgt ein Gedicht von Heinrich Heine, *Die Lorelei.* Vielleicht haben Sie es schon in der Klasse als Lied gesungen. Es ist sehr berühmt. Man hört es, wenn man mit einem Schiff auf dem Rhein an dem Loreleifelsen[1] vorbeifährt. Dann singen viele Leute mit!

DIE LORELEI

Ich weiß nicht, was soll es bedeuten,[2]
Daß ich so traurig bin;
Ein Märchen[3] aus uralten Zeiten,
Das kommt mir nicht aus dem Sinn.[4]

5   Die Luft ist kühl und es dunkelt,
Und ruhig[5] fließt[6] der Rhein;
Der Gipfel[7] des Berges funkelt[8]
Im Abendsonnenschein.

Die schönste Jungfrau[9] sitzt
10   Dort oben[10] wunderbar,[11]
Ihr goldnes Geschmeide[12] blitzet,[13]
Sie kämmt[14] ihr goldenes Haar.

Sie kämmt es mit goldenem Kamme,
Und singt ein Lied dabei;
15   Das hat eine wundersame,[15]
Gewaltige[16] Melodei.

Den Schiffer[17] im kleinen Schiffe
Ergreift[18] es mit wildem Weh,[19]
Er schaut nicht die Felsenriffe,[20]
20   Er schaut nur hinauf in die Höh'.[21]

Ich glaube, die Wellen[22] verschlingen[23]
Am Ende Schiffer und Kahn,[24]
Und das hat mit ihrem Singen
Die Lorelei getan.

1 Lorelei cliff	9 maiden; virgin	17 skipper; sailor
2 to mean	10 up there	18 grips
3 fairy tale	11 wonderfully	19 longing
4 mind	12 trinkets	20 rocky reef
5 calmly	13 flash	21 heights
6 flows	14 combs	22 waves
7 peak	15 strange	23 swallow up
8 sparkles	16 powerful	24 boat

D. **Analysis or explanations:**

    line 4   "I can't get it out of my mind."

    line 7   **des** = of the

    line 14   **dabei** = in addition; in accompaniment

    line 17   Note that the *object* in this sentence is **den Schiffer**, and that the *subject* is **es** (referring to **das Lied**).

    line 24   **Die Lorelei** is the subject of this clause.

E. **Practice:**   See Section B.

F. **Evaluation:**   When you can carry out the objectives stated in Section A, you are ready for evaluation.

LESSON 44
Practice Test (Lessons 23-43)

A. **Your objectives:** To be able to do the practice test in this lesson with at least 90% accuracy, without having to memorize the specific items in the test (since the test contains only representative samples of a much larger amount of material which you are supposed to have learned).

B. **How to get there:** Review the sections listed in Section C to determine if you have forgotten anything. Make a list of—or mark lightly—anything you need to learn again, and then learn it.

C. **What to learn:** REVIEW: The practice test in Section E mainly contains vocabulary and structure, especially from Lessons 23-39. Check the following sections: 26C, 27C, 28C, 33C, 34C, 36C, 37C, 38C, 39C.

Lesson 44   115

Noch eine Jugendherberge (in Norddeutschland)

D. **Analysis or explanations:** See the D sections of any previous lessons you need to review.

E. **Practice:** PRACTICE TEST
1. Give the German equivalents of the following. Give both the singular and plural forms of the nouns, and the principal parts of the strong verbs:

    a. to get up
    b. to sink down
    c. to fall asleep
    d. to rub
    e. to love
    f. to lie
    g. I don't have to go
    h. never
    i. suddenly
    j. whole
    k. the year
    l. the song

2. What are the plurals of the following words? (If you can't do all of these correctly without looking up some of them, this should be an indication to you that you need to review the plurals.)

    a. das Auge   g. das Kind
    b. das Buch   h. das Messer
    c. das Ei   i. das Ohr
    d. das Fenster   j. das Restaurant
    e. das Glas   k. das Stück
    f. das Haus   l. das Zimmer

3. Give the simple past form of the following weak and strong verbs with the subjects indicated:

    suchen   **gehen**
    a. ich   f. ich
    b. du   g. du
    c. er   h. er
    d. wir   i. wir
    e. ihr   j. ihr

4. What are the principal parts of the following strong verbs? (If you can't do all of the verbs in this sample, this should be an indication to you that you need to review all the strong verbs!)

    a. essen   k. schneiden
    b. bleiben   l. schreiben
    c. fahren   m. sein
    d. geben   n. sehen
    e. gehen   o. sitzen
    f. kommen   p. sprechen
    g. lesen   q. tragen
    h. nehmen   r. treffen
    i. rufen   s. trinken
    j. schlafen   t. werden

5. How would you say that

    a. you were asking Waltraud?
    b. I was snoring loudly?

    c. he was crying alone?
    d. you and your friends (we) were crying together?
    e. (to friends) they were living in Berlin?
    f. they were listening well (*gut*)?
    g. you were staying at home?
    h. I was eating breaded veal cutlets?
    i. (to a friend) he was driving too fast?
    j. she was going around the corner?
    k. you-all were sleeping by the Rhine (*am Rhein*)?
    l. (to friends) they were singing beautifully?
    m. they were drinking beer?

6. Using the sentence components **wir/eine Klassenarbeit schreiben**, how would you say that the subject

    a. is carrying out the named activity?
    b. was doing this?
    c. ought to do this?
    d. did this?
    e. knows that you were doing this?

7. Using the sentence components **ich/in den kalten Rhein steigen**, how would you say that the subject

    a. did this?
    b. was doing this?
    c. is doing this?
    d. has to do this?
    e. has done this?
    f. doesn't understand why he must do this?

F. Evaluation: Check your answers, or have them checked, against the key. If you scored 90% or better, you should be ready to take the final unit test in Lesson 45. If you did not score 90%, or if you did poorly on any particular section of the test, review the appropriate lessons carefully before going on to the test.

LESSON 45

A. **Your objectives:** To pass the final unit test on Lessons 23-43 with a score of at least 90%.

B. **How to get there:** If you followed carefully the instructions for the practice test in Lesson 44, you should already be prepared.

C. **What to learn:** No new material.

D. **Analysis or explanations:** Given in Lessons 23-43.

E. **Practice:** Refer to Lesson 44.

F. **Evaluation:** Report to your teacher for test administration.

DRITTER TEIL

Das Thema: DIE LIEBE

"Blau ist ein Blümelein,
Das heißt Vergißnichtmein,
Dies Blümlein leg' ans Herz,
Und denk an mich!"

Lessons 46-49   122
    Ein Lied: "Ach, wie ist's möglich dann"
    Ein Lied: "Ich hätt' getanzt heut' Nacht"
Lessons 50-54   132
    Die deutsche Sprache: Wiederholung *und* Etwas Neues
        (Mehrzahl von "der" Wörtern und
        "ein" Wörtern)
Lessons 56-61   142
    Die deutsche Sprache: Etwas Neues (Plusquam-Perfekt,
    Perfekt der Modalverben,
    Konjunktiv)
Lessons 63-69   160
    Die deutsche Sprache: Etwas Neues (Konditionalsätze)

Test Lessons
    Lesson 55   140
    Lesson 62   159
    Lesson 70   176

"Und denk an mich!"

LESSON 46
Ein Lied: "Ach, wie ist's möglich dann"

A. **Your objectives:** To be able to read the song "Ach, wie ist's möglich dann" out loud with pronunciation and intonation as close to that of your model as possible; to be able to give the meaning of all words or passages (in German or English, whichever your teacher directs you to give); and to be able to answer the questions in Section E as directed there.

B. **How to get there:** Listen to the recorded version of the song while looking at the text in Section C. By referring to the vocabulary and the notes in Section D, you should be able to understand the song completely after listening to it several times.

Then practice imitating the pronunciation and intonation until you are satisfied that you are imitating the model as closely as possible.

Lastly check once more whether you know the meaning of the song—without reference to any vocabulary or notes. You should now be able to answer the questions in Section E.

C. **What to learn:** Das häufigste[1] Thema der Literatur und des Liedes[2] ist bestimmt[3] die Liebe. Das erste Lied unten wurde 1812 als Gedicht[4] geschrieben.[5] Es ist ein sehr sentimentalisches auf einem noch älteren[6] Volkslied basiertes Gedicht.

ACH, WIE IST'S MÖGLICH[7] DANN

    Ach, wie ist's möglich dann,
    Daß ich dich lassen[8] kann;
    Hab' dich von Herzen[9] lieb,[10]
    Das glaube mir!
5 Du hast die Seele[11] mein
    So ganz genommen ein,[12]
    Daß ich kein' Andre[13] lieb',
    Als[14] dich allein!

    Blau ist ein Blümelein,
10 Das heißt Vergißnichtmein,[15]
    Dies Blümlein leg' ans Herz,
    Und denk an mich!
    Stirbt[16] Blum' und Hoffnung[17] gleich[18]
    Wir sind an Liebe reich;[19]
15 Denn die stirbt nie[20] bei mir,
    Das glaube mir!

Lesson 46

Wär'[21] ich ein Vögelein,
Wollt'[22] ich bald bei dir sein,
Scheut'[23] Falk[24] und Habicht[25] nicht,
20   Flög' schnell zu dir.
Schöss'[26] mich ein Jäger tot,
Fiel'[27] ich in deinen Schoß;[28]
Säh'st[29] du mich traurig an,
24   Gern[30] stürb'[31] ich dann.

"Hab' dich von Herzen lieb."

1	frequent	12	to capture
2	song	13	no other
3	certainly	14	than
4	poem	15	forget-me-not
5	was written	16	to die
6	even older	17	hope
7	possible	18	although
8	leave	19	rich
9	heart	20	never
10	to love	21	were (if I were ...)
11	soul		

22   would want
23   would fear
24   falcon
25   hawk
26   if ... should shoot
27   would fall
28   lap
29   if you looked at ...
30   gladly
31   would die

D. **Analysis or explanations:**

footnote 1   **häufigste** is the superlative form of **häufig** meaning *the most frequent*

footnote 5   **wurde geschrieben** is the passive form of the verb (The passive is explained and practiced in Lessons C-1—C-8.)

footnote 6	The phrase **auf einem noch älteren Volkslied basiertes** would appear as a relative clause in English: *"(which is) based on an even older folk song."* The main clause in the sentence is **Es ist ein sehr sentimentalisches ... Gedicht**. The phrase, in German, is being used in this sentence as though it were an adjective phrase describing **Gedicht**. This is rarely done in English. It would be as if we took the sentence *The train, which was coming around the mountain, was late* and rendered it as *The coming-around-the-mountain train was late.*
line 5	**die Seele mein** is equivalent to **meine Seele**
line 6	**genommen ein** would normally be **eingenommen**
line 9	**Blümelein** is the diminutive form of **Blume**. (Both **-lein** and **-chen** are suffixes used in German to mean "little." In English we sometimes use the suffixes *-ette* and *-let* to do the same thing.)
line 13	"Although flower and hope may die"
lines 17-24	All verbs here are in the subjunctive or conditional form. These are commonly rendered in English by using "would" or "should" as auxiliaries, and introducing the clause with "if": "If I should die, ..." In German we can get this same feeling by using the special subjunctive forms you find here. (More about this in the coming grammar lessons in this unit.)
line 21	"If a hunter should shoot me dead"

E. Practice: Answer the following questions about the song in German. You should be able to answer in complete sentences, but at least include the italicized parts of the answers.

1. *Wer* muß *wen* lassen? — Ich muß *dich* lassen.
2. *Wie* lieb habe ich dich? — Ich habe dich *von Herzen* lieb.
3. *Was* hast du eingenommen? — Du hast *meine Seele* eingenommen.
4. Liebe ich auch *eine Andere*? — Ich liebe *keine Andere*.
5. *Welche Blume* ist blau? — Das *Vergißnichtmein* ist blau.
6. *Wohin* sollst du diese Blume legen? — Du sollst diese Blume *ans Herz* legen.
7. Können die Blume und Hoffnung sterben? — *Ja*, die Blume und Hoffnung können sterben.
8. Kann meine Liebe sterben? — Nein, die stirbt *nie* bei mir.

Lesson 46

"Du hast die Seele mein so ganz genommen ein, . . ."

9. Wenn (*if*) ich ein Vöglein wäre, was würde ich machen? Ich *wollte* bald *bei dir sein.*
  or
  Ich *flöge* schnell *zu dir.*
10. Würde ich Falk und Habicht scheuen? *Nein,* ich scheute sie nicht.
11. Wohin möchte ich fallen? Ich möchte *in deinen Schoß* fallen.
12. Wie würde ich gern sterben? Ich würde gern sterben, *wenn du mich traurig ansähest.*

F. **Evaluation:**   Refer to Section A.

"Ich hätt' getanzt heut' nacht!"

LESSON 47

A. **Your objectives:** See Lesson 46.

B. **How to get there:** See Lesson 46.

C. **What to learn:** Das zweite Lied ist Ihnen wahrscheinlich bekannt. Es ist aus der deutschen Übersetzung von *(version of) My Fair Lady.*

ICH HÄTT' GETANZT HEUT' NACHT*

Bett! Bett! Ich will noch nicht[1] ins Bett!
Wer legt sich hin,[2] der[3] so auf Wolken schwebt![4]
Schlaf! Schlaf! Ich däcḧt' nicht mal[5] an Schlaf,
Und wenn[6] ihr mir die Kronjuwelen gebt!

Lesson 47

5 Ich hätt'[7] getanzt heut' nacht,[8] die ganze Nacht heut' nacht, so gern und noch viel[9] mehr! Ich hätt' mir[10] viel erlaubt,[11] wovon ich sonst[12] geglaubt, daß das zu sündhaft[13] wär'! So war mir nie,[14] doch[15] wie[16] er dann auf einmal[17] den ersten[18] Schritt[19] mit mir gemacht. War mir so wunderbar, daß ich im Traum sogar[20] noch immer[21] tanz', tanz' tanz', heut' nacht!

*"I Could Have Danced All Night"
Copyright © 1956 by Alan Jay Lerner and Frederick Loewe, Chappell & Co., Inc., owner of publication and allied rights. Used by permission.

1	not yet	12	otherwise
2	to lie down	13	sinful
3	"when he"	14	I never felt like this before
4	to float	15	however
5	I wouldn't even think of	16	as, when
6	even if	17	suddenly
7	would (could) have	18	first
8	tonight	19	step
9	even more	20	even
10	myself	21	still keep on
11	allowed		

D. Analysis or explanations:

line 1   **gehen** can be understood as the infinitive after **ins Bett**

line 6   "I would have allowed myself much (would have dared to do many things), of which I normally believed that that would be too sinful."

line 7   **gemacht** can probably be rendered best in English by "took" (*took the first step*)

E. Practice: Answer the following questions about the song in Section C in German. You should be able to give answers in complete sentences; if not, try at least to give the italicized portions of the answers.

1. Warum will ich nicht ins Bett gehen?   *Ich schwebe auf Wolken.*
2. Würde ich schlafen, wenn du mir Geld gäbest?   *Nein,* auch nicht für die Kronjuwelen!

3.	Wie lange hätte ich heute nacht getanzt?	Ich hätt' *die ganze Nacht* getanzt—und noch viel mehr.
4.	Hat sie sich viel erlaubt?	*Nein, aber sie hätte* sich viel erlaubt.
5.	Wann war es ihr so wunderbar?	Wie er *den ersten Schritt* mit ihr gemacht hatte.
6.	Wie tanze ich noch immer?	Ich tanze *im Traum*.
7.	Hat sie die ganze Nacht getanzt?	*Nein, aber sie hätte* die ganze Nacht getanzt.

F. **Evaluation:** When you can (1) read the song out loud with proper pronunciation and intonation, (2) give the meaning of all words or passages in the song, and (3) answer all the questions in Section E, you are ready for evaluation.

"Daß ich im Traum sogar noch immer tanz', tanz', tanz' . . ."

LESSON 48

A. Your objectives: To demonstrate your knowledge of the vocabulary used in Lessons 46 and 47 by being able to give oral and written German forms when given the English equivalents as cues. For nouns you should give both the singular and plural forms; for verbs give the principal parts, including the subjunctive (see Section D for an explanation of how to form the subjunctive stem).

B. How to get there: Memorize any German forms in Section C which you don't know. Use the English equivalents as cues. Use the recorded materials to check on your pronunciation.

C. What to learn:

VERBS	INFINITIVE	3rd PERSON	PAST	P. PART.	SUBJUNCTIVE
to fall	fallen	fällt	fiel	ist gefallen	fiele
to fly	fliegen		flog	ist geflogen	flöge
to have	haben	hat	hatte	gehabt	hätte
to shoot	schießen		schoß	geschossen	schösse
to see	sehen	sieht	sah	gesehen	sähe
to be	sein	ist	war	ist gewesen	wäre
to die	sterben	stirbt	starb	ist gestorben	stürbe

NOUNS	SINGULAR	PLURAL
heart	das Herz	die Herzen
night	die Nacht	die Nächte
soul	die Seele	die Seelen
dream	der Traum	die Träume
cloud	die Wolke	die Wolken
the other (one)	die Andere	
	das Andere	die Anderen
	der Andere	

OTHER WORDS
tonight	heute nacht
possible	möglich
usually, normally, otherwise	sonst

D.	Analysis or explanations:	To form the subjunctive stem of most strong verbs, an **-e** is added to the simple past stem. *In addition,* the vowel is umlauted if possible (ä, ö, ü). The personal endings are the same as those added to the stem of weak verbs in the simple past (see Lesson 30). There is no difference between the simple past tense of most weak verbs and the subjunctive forms. Compare the *past* forms in the vocabulary in Section C with the subjunctive forms. You will see that the only exception to the rule given above is **starb/stürbe** (instead of the expected **stärbe**).
E.	Practice:	How would you say in German that

1. you're falling? — Ich falle.
2. you were falling? — Ich fiel.
3. you fell? — Ich bin gefallen.
4. he flew? — Er ist geflogen.
5. he would fly (subjunctive) — Er flöge. (Er würde fliegen.)
6. she sees that? — Sie sieht das.
7. she would shoot it? — Sie schösse es (würde es schießen).
8. had she known that, she would be here? — Hätte sie das gewußt, wäre sie hier. (variations possible)
9. they died? — Sie sind gestorben.
10. you would have danced? — Ich hätte getanzt.

F.	Evaluation:	When you can give all the forms requested in Section C, and can give the German sentences in Section E when given only the English directions as cues, you are ready for evaluation.

LESSON 49
Self-Test

A.	Your objectives:	To be able to do the Self-Test in Section E with at least 90% accuracy.
B.	How to get there:	Follow the directions in Section E.

Lesson 49

C. What to learn: Review of Lessons 46-48.

D. Analysis or explanations: See Lessons 46-48.

E. Practice:

1. Using the recordings as your model, write the verses of the songs in Lessons 46 and 47 as a dictation. Stop the recording after each line, write that line in German, then play the next line. (Or you may have someone read the texts to you line by line.)

2. Write out the answers to the questions in Section E of Lessons 46 and 47 without looking at the answers.

3. Explain (in English) the difference between the following pairs of sentences:

    Ich habe getanzt.   Ich hätte getanzt.
    Ich war reich.   Ich wäre reich.
    Ich flog schnell zu dir.   Ich flöge schnell zu dir.

4. Give the German for the following words. Also give the singular and plural of the nouns and the principal parts of the strong verbs:

    a. possible   f. tonight
    b. my soul   g. to die
    c. the other one   h. to fly
    d. cloud   i. to love
    e. the good dream   j. to shy away from; to fear

F. Evaluation: Check your answers with the key. If you had to look up anything in these samples, or if you made several errors, you probably haven't learned the material well enough to be ready for testing yet. Review.

    If you did well (90% or better), report to your teacher for a short test before going on to the next lesson.

Deutsch: ZWEITE STUFE

Gammler musizieren.

LESSON 50
Die deutsche Sprache: Wiederholung (Mehrzahl von "der" Wörtern und von "ein" Wörtern)

A. Your objectives: To be able to give the singular and plural forms in German of the 21 masculine words in Section C when given only English equivalents as cues; and to be able to do the drills in Section E as directed—all without error.

B. How to get there: Check your knowledge of the nouns in Section C. Relearn any singular forms you may have forgotten. Then learn the plurals. Note the patterns (see Section D). Use the recordings to perfect your pronunciation.

Then do the drills in Section E as directed. Use the recordings here also.

C. What to learn: Following are some of the more common masculine (**der**) words you have learned. Review any you may have forgotten; then learn the plurals of all of the words in the list.

Lesson 50

Kein Jäger, sondern
ein Schäfer mit seinem
treuen Hund.

worker	der Arbeiter, -	football	der Fußball, ⸚e
arm	der Arm, -e	hippie	der Gammler, -
platform	der Bahnsteig, -e	station (train)	der Bahnhof, ⸚e
official	der Beamte, -n	gentleman	der Herr, -en
goblet	der Becher, -	hunter	der Jäger, -
bite	der Bissen, -	jazz cellar	der Jazzkeller, -
bouquet	der Blumenstrauß, ⸚e	coffee	der Kaffee
oak tree	der Eichenbaum, ⸚e	calendar	der Kalender, -
fish	der Fisch, -e	comrade	der Kamerad, -en
friend	der Freund, -e	cheese	der Käse, -
barber	der Friseur, -e		

D. **Analysis or explanations:** Notice, again, that the plurals of these words fall into certain patterns. Nine of them add an **-e,** and all of these, except for **der Arm,** also umlaut the main vowel if possible (ä, ö, ü). Eight of the words have plurals which are the same as the singular. And, as we have observed previously, most of them are words which end in **-er, -en,** or **-el** in the singular. The rest of the words add **-en** in forming the plural.

E. **Practice:** Change the following sentences to the plural (change *all* the nouns). Don't forget to change the verb also, if the subject has been changed.

1. Der Arbeiter sieht den Kamerad. — Die Arbeiter sehen die Kameraden.
2. Der Gammler ging zum Friseur. — Die Gammler gingen zu den Friseuren.
3. Der Herr hat einen Blumenstrauß gebracht. — Die Herren haben Blumensträuße gebracht.
4. Der Bahnsteig ist da drüben. — Die Bahnsteige sind da drüben.
5. Der Jäger stand unter dem Eichenbaum. — Die Jäger standen unter den Eichenbäumen.
6. Der kleine Fisch schwimmt im Becher herum. — Die kleinen Fische schwimmen in den Bechern herum.
7. Wo ist der Bahnhof? — Wo sind die Bahnhöfe?
8. Der Freund hatte den Kalender. — Die Freunde hatten die Kalender.

F. **Evaluation:** Refer to Section A.

LESSON 51

A. **Your objectives:** To be able to give the German forms of the **ein** words when given the English as cues; and to be able to give the plural forms of the sentences in Section E. You should make no errors.

B. **How to get there:** Check your memory of the **ein** words in Section C. Memorize any you have forgotten (English to German).

Then refresh your memory of the plural forms, reviewed in Section D and first explained in detail in Lesson 11.

Finally, practice changing the sentences in Section E until you can do them fluently without error.

Lesson 52

C. What to learn: The **ein** words are:

a, an	ein	her	ihr
no, not a	kein	our	unser
my	mein	your (*fam. pl.*)	euer
your (*fam. sing.*)	dein	their	ihr
his	sein	your (formal)	**Ihr**

D. Analysis or explanations: When the **ein** words in Section C are used in the plural in noun phrases, the expected plural endings occur:

NOMINATIVE	ACCUSATIVE	DATIVE
die guten Freunde	die guten Freunde	den guten Freunden
meine guten Freunde	meine guten Freunde	meinen guten Freunden
ihre guten Freunde	ihre guten Freunde	ihren guten Freunden

E. Practice: Change the nouns to the plural:

1. Sein guter Kamerad ist gestorben. — Seine guten Kameraden sind gestorben.
2. Mein neuer Fußball hat viel gekostet. — Meine neuen Fußbälle haben viel gekostet.
3. Siehst du unsren großen Eichenbaum? — Siehst du unsre großen Eichenbäume?
4. Sie steigen auf ihren neuen Bahnsteig. — Sie steigen auf ihre neuen Bahnsteige.
5. Der Beamte trinkt aus eurem teuren Becher. — Die Beamten trinken aus euren teuren Bechern.
6. Ihr alter Kamerad bleibt bei keinem Arbeiter. — Ihre alten Kameraden bleiben bei keinen Arbeitern.
7. Dein schöner Blumenstrauß ist hier. — Deine schönen Blumensträuße sind hier.
8. Was machen Sie mit Ihrem bunten Kalender? — Was machen Sie mit Ihren bunten Kalendern?

F. Evaluation: Refer to Section A.

LESSON 52

A. Your objectives: To be able to give the singular and plural forms of the 22 masculine nouns in Section C in German, when given the English equivalents as cues; and to be able to give the German sentences according to the English directions in Section E. No errors.

B. How to get there: Follow the usual procedure for these types of exercises.

C. What to learn:

suitcase	der Koffer, -	mirror	der Spiegel, -
human	der Mensch, -en	rock	der Stein, -e
pancake	der Pfannkuchen, -	day	der Tag, -e
umbrella	der Regenschirm, -e	dance	der Tanz, ⸚e
juice	der Saft, ⸚e	tea	der Tee
salad	der Salat, -e	death	der Tod, -e
counter	der Schalter, -	forest	der Wald, ⸚er
ham	der Schinken, -	way	der Weg, -e
tail	der Schwanz, ⸚e	wine	der Wein, -e
lake	der See, -n	wolf	der Wolf, ⸚e
bacon	der Speck	train	der Zug, ⸚e

D. Analysis or explanations: Note the patterns of the nouns in Section C—the same patterns described in Section C of Lesson 50. In this group 5 nouns ending in **-en, -el,** and **-er** have no endings in the plural; 12 add **-e,** and most of these umlaut the main vowel if possible; 2 add **-n** or **-en. Der Wald** is the only noun which does not fall into one of the three major patterns of pluralization for masculine nouns.

E. Practice: How would you say in German that

1. your red suitcase is here? — **Mein roter Koffer ist hier.**
2. your red suitcases are here? — **Meine roten Koffer sind hier.**
3. you have no red suitcase? — **Ich habe keinen roten Koffer.**
4. you have no red suitcases? — **Ich habe keine roten Koffer.**
5. it is in her red suitcase? — **Es ist in ihrem roten Koffer.**
6. they are in her red suitcases? — **Sie sind in ihren roten Koffern.**
7. his good friends are here? — **Seine guten Freunde sind hier.**
8. their arms are tired? — **Ihre Arme sind müde.**
9. you see our beautiful lakes? — **Ich sehe Ihre schönen Seen.**
10. we see their long tails? — **Sie sehen ihre langen Schwänze.**
11. it is behind the oak trees? — **Es ist hinter den Eichenbäumen.**
12. he is buying the poor hippies cheese and wine? — **Er kauft den armen Gammlern Käse und Wein.**

F. Evaluation: Refer to Section A.

LESSON 53
Self-Test

A. Your objectives: To be able to do the Self-Test in Section E with at least 90% accuracy.

B. How to get there: Review any material in Lessons 50-52 which you feel unsure about. This Self-Test is only *a sampling of the material* involved; therefore, looking up and relearning only the material in the test is not sufficient preparation to insure your knowledge of what is being tested.

C. What to learn: Refer to Sections C and E of Lessons 50-52.

D. Analysis or explanations: See Section D in Lessons 50-52.

E. Practice:

SELF-TEST

1. Write the singular and plural forms of the following sampling of **der** words:

~~Arm~~ *Arm Arme* arm   forest *Wald, Wälder*
~~Blumenstrauß~~ *Blumensträuße* bouquet   train *Zug, Züge*
~~Freund~~ friend *Freunde*   human *Mensch, Menschen*
~~Bahnhof~~ train station *Bahnhöfe*   tree *Baum, Bäume*
~~Koffer~~ suitcase *Koffer*   mirror *Spiegel, Spiegel*

2. Give the German words for the following:

no (*adj.*) *kein*   your (*sing. fam.*) *dein*   his *sein*
our *unser*   your (*formal*) *Ihr*   a, an *ein*
her *ihr*   your (*fam. pl.*) *euer*
their *ihr*   my *mein*

3. Give the proper endings for *their beautiful forest* (**der Wald, ⸚er**) in German when it occurs in sentences which require the use of this phrase as follows:

a. subject (nominative) *der schöne Wald*
b. target (accusative) *den schönen Wald*
c. other (dative) *dem schönen Wald*
d. subject, plural *die schönen Wälder*
e. target, plural *die schönen Wälder*
f. other, plural *den schönen Wäldern*

4. Using the phrase **der Fußball/neu** (plural: **Fußbälle**), how would you say in German that

a. they have the new football?
b. they have the new footballs?
c. they have your new football?
d. they have your new footballs?
e. your new football is not here?
f. your new footballs are not here?
g. it (**es**) is behind the new football?
h. it is behind his new football?
i. it is behind his new footballs?
j. our new football is next to (**neben**) their new footballs?

F. Evaluation: After reviewing, do the Self-Test without referring to any of the lessons. Then check it or have it checked against the key.

If you do poorly on any part, review carefully the material involved. Then test yourself again by doing the entire section in the original lesson (50, 51, or 52) as a test.

If you did well, go on to Lesson 54.

Studenten protestieren in München.

LESSON 54
Review Self-Test (Lessons 46-53)

A. Your objectives: To be able to do the Self-Test in Section E without referring to any of the previous lessons while taking the test. Your score should be 90% or better.

B. How to get there: Go over Lessons 46-53 quickly. Stop and review if you think you may have forgotten any of the vocabulary or exercises.
When you feel that you know all the material previously learned and practiced, you should be ready to try the test.

C. What to learn: Review where necessary (see Section B).

D. Analysis or explanations: Review where necessary (see Section B).

E. Practice:

SELF-TEST

1. What do the following words or phrases mean?

   a. möglich — possible
   b. liebhaben — to love
   c. das Herz — the heart
   d. die Seele — the soul
   e. als — than, as
   f. Vergißnichtmein — forget-me-not
   g. sterben — to die
   h. die Hoffnung — the hope
   i. reich — rich
   j. wär' ich — if I were
   k. der Schoß — the lap
   l. Blümlein — (little) flowers
   m. noch nicht — not yet
   n. schweben — to float
   o. heute nacht — tonight
   p. sonst — otherwise
   q. sündhaft — sinful
   r. auf einmal — suddenly
   s. der Schritt — the step
   t. wunderbar — wonderful

2. How would you express the following in German? (Give all principal parts of any strong verbs, and the plurals of any nouns.)

   a. to fall — fallen, fällt, fiel, ist gefallen, fiele
   b. to fly — fliegen, flog, ist geflogen, flöge
   c. to have — haben, hat, hatte, gehabt, hätte
   d. to see — sehen, sieht, sah, gesehen, sähe
   e. to be — sein, ist, war, ist gewesen, wäre
   f. heart — das Herz, die Herzen
   g. soul — die Seele, die Seelen
   h. dream — der Traum, die Träume
   i. cloud — die Wolke, die Wolken
   j. possible — möglich

3. Give the singular and plural forms of the following masculine nouns:

a. arm *Arme Arme* f. gentleman *Herr, Herren*
b. bouquet *Strauss Sträusse* g. lake *See Seen*
c. oak tree *baum bäume* h. mirror *Spiegel Spiegel*
d. friend *Freund Freunde* i. day *Tag Tage*
e. football *Fussball Fussbälle* j. forest *Wald Wälder*

4. How would you say in German that

a. his old friend is here?
b. his old friends are here?
c. you see his old friend?
d. you see his old friends?
e. he's buying his old friend a beer?
f. he's buying his old friends a beer?

5. Give the German equivalents of

a. my arm *mein Arm* e. her mother *ihr Mutter*
b. my left (**link-**) arm *mein linker Arm* f. their new football
c. our team *unser Mannschaft* g. your (**du**) last (**letzt-**) day
d. our strong (**stark-**) team *unser starke Mannschaft*

F. Evaluation: Check answers (or have them checked) against the key. If you had less than 90% correct, review and repeat.

LESSON 55
Test

A. Your objectives: To be able to do the test covering Lessons 46-53 with at least 90% accuracy.

B. How to get there: You should be properly prepared if you have carefully evaluated the objectives in the lessons covered.

C. What to learn: See the C sections in Lessons 46-53 where necessary.

Lesson 55

D.	Analysis or explanations:	See the D sections in Lessons 46-53 where necessary.
E.	Practice:	The Self-Tests in Lessons 49 and 54 can serve as a quick check and extra practice.
F.	Evaluation:	Report to the teacher for the test when you believe you are ready. If you score less than 90%, you will be asked to review some more and to be tested again.

Und nochmal tanzen.

LESSON 56
Die deutsche Sprache: Etwas Neues (Plusquamperfekt, Perfekt der Modalverben, Konjunktiv)

A. Your objectives: To be able to do the exercises in Section E as directed, fluently and with no errors.

B. How to get there: Study carefully the explanation in Section D. Then check Section C to make sure you know the past forms of **haben** and **sein** well.

Then practice the exercises in Section E until you can do them readily.

C. What to learn: Following are the past forms of **sein** and **haben**, the two auxiliaries used in the perfect tenses:

	haben		sein
ich	**hatte**	ich	**war**
du	**hattest**	du	**warst**
er, sie, es	**hatte**	er, sie, es	**war**
wir, sie, Sie	**hatten**	wir, sie, Sie	**waren**
ihr	**hattet**	ihr	**wart**

D. Analysis or explanations:

THE PAST PERFECT TENSE

Whenever we say that by a certain time in the past we *had* done something, we are using the past perfect tense—meaning that an act was completed or "perfected" before some stated or implied time in the past:

> By midnight last night I *had finished* my homework.
> When the sun came through the window I realized we *had danced* all night.

The past perfect tense is quite parallel in form and in use when we compare English and German:

| I *had danced* all night. | Ich **hatte** die ganze Nacht **getanzt.** |
| I *had permitted* myself a great deal. | Ich **hatte** mir viel **erlaubt.** |

Lesson 56

But, of course, we must not forget that many German verbs use **sein** as the auxiliary in the perfect tenses. For these verbs the past perfect form will require the past tense of the auxiliary:

I *had walked* through the streets.   Ich **war** durch die Straßen **gegangen.**

They *had stayed* home.   Sie **waren** zu Hause **geblieben.**

E. Practice: 1. Substitute the subjects indicated:

Ich hatte die ganze Nacht getanzt.   Ich hatte die ganze Nacht getanzt.
- a. (wir)   Wir hatten die ganze Nacht getanzt.
- b. (ihr)   Ihr hattet die ganze Nacht getanzt.
- c. (du)   Du hattest die ganze Nacht getanzt.
- d. (er)   Er hatte die ganze Nacht getanzt.
- e. (Sie)   Sie hatten die ganze Nacht getanzt.

2. Substitute the subjects indicated:

Wir waren in den Wald gegangen.   Wir waren in den Wald gegangen.
- a. (du)   Du warst in den Wald gegangen.
- b. (Siegfried)   Siegfried war in den Wald gegangen.
- c. (Hans und Fritz)   Hans und Fritz waren in den Wald gegangen.
- d. (ihr)   Ihr wart in den Wald gegangen.
- e. (ich)   Ich war in den Wald gegangen.

3. Tell me that you had done the following:

- a. in Deutschland wohnen   Ich hatte in Deutschland gewohnt.
- b. das nicht verstehen   Ich hatte das nicht verstanden.
- c. die Blumen pflücken   Ich hatte die Blumen gepflückt.
- d. zu Hause bleiben   Ich war zu Hause geblieben.
- e. den Vater Rhein sehen   Ich hatte den Vater Rhein gesehen.
- f. etwas trinken   Ich hatte etwas getrunken.
- g. in den See fallen   Ich war in den See gefallen.
- h. spät nach Hause kommen   Ich war spät nach Hause gekommen.
- i. stark und tapfer sein   Ich war stark und tapfer gewesen.
- j. Gitarre spielen   Ich hatte Gitarre gespielt.

"Ich weiß, daß sie in den See gefallen waren."

4. Ask your friend if he had done each of the above:

   a. Hattest du in Deutschland gewohnt?
   b. Hattest du das nicht verstanden?
   c. Hattest du die Blumen gepflückt?
   d. Warst du zu Hause geblieben?
   e. Hattest du den Vater Rhein gesehen?
   f. Hattest du etwas getrunken?
   g. Warst du in den See gefallen?
   h. Warst du spät nach Hause gekommen?
   i. Warst du stark und tapfer gewesen?
   j. Hattest du Gitarre gespielt?

5. How would you say that you know that they had done each of the above?

   a. Ich weiß, daß sie in Deutschland gewohnt hatten.
   b. Ich weiß, daß sie das nicht verstanden hatten.
   c. Ich weiß, daß sie die Blumen gepflückt hatten.
   d. Ich weiß, daß sie zu Hause geblieben waren.
   e. Ich weiß, daß sie den Vater Rhein gesehen hatten.
   f. Ich weiß, daß sie etwas getrunken hatten.
   g. Ich weiß, daß sie in den See gefallen waren.
   h. Ich weiß, daß sie spät nach Hause gekommen waren.
   i. Ich weiß, daß sie stark und tapfer gewesen waren.
   j. Ich weiß, daß sie Gitarre gespielt hatten.

F. Evaluation: Refer to Section A.

LESSON 57

A. Your objectives: To be able to do the exercises in Section E as directed, fluently and with no errors.

B. How to get there: Memorize the four sentences in Section C. Study carefully Section D in which a new and unexpected word order sequence is presented.

Then practice the exercises in Section E.

C. What to learn: THE PERFECT TENSES OF THE MODAL AUXILIARIES

I want to see the Rhine.　　　　　Ich will den Rhein sehen.
I wanted to see the Rhine.　　　　Ich wollte den Rhein sehen.
　　　　　　　　　　　　　　　　Ich habe den Rhein sehen wollen.
I had wanted to see the Rhine.　　Ich hatte den Rhein sehen wollen.

D. Analysis or explanations:

Notice in the examples in Section C that in the perfect tenses involving the modal auxiliaries with another verb there is no real past participle form (no form with ge-). The natural tendency of languages toward simplicity has produced what is often called a "double infinitive" construction.

Another unexpected thing about the perfect tenses of the modals is the position of the auxiliary in a subordinate clause:

Es ist wahr, daß ich den Rhein sehen will.
Es ist wahr, daß ich den Rhein sehen wollte.
Es ist wahr, daß ich den Rhein **habe** sehen wollen.
Es ist wahr, daß ich den Rhein **hatte** sehen wollen.

We would expect the auxiliary to come last, based on our experience up to this point, but instead it comes before the "double infinitive." Usually it is placed immediately preceding the other verbs, but not always. When there is a prefix, or some other element that is so closely related to the verb that it is felt as part of this second "pole," the auxiliary precedes it. (We will indicate when this is necessary. Later you will learn how to determine this for yourself.)

E. Practice:

1. Using the verbal idea **die Straße entlang gehen,** say that

   a. you want to do this:　　　　　　Ich will die Straße entlang gehen.
   b. you were wanting to:　　　　　　Ich wollte die Straße entlang gehen.
   c. you wanted to do it:　　　　　　Ich habe die Straße entlang gehen wollen.
   d. you had wanted to:　　　　　　　Ich hatte die Straße entlang gehen wollen.

2. Using the idea **wie ein Vöglein fliegen,** how would you say that

   a. he can do this?　　　　　　　　　Er kann wie ein Vöglein fliegen.
   b. he was able to do this (at a certain time in the past)?　　Er konnte wie ein Vöglein fliegen.

Lesson 57

"Er hat wie ein Vöglein fliegen können."

c. he was able to do this (but no more)?   **Er hat wie ein Vöglein fliegen können.**
d. he had been able to?   **Er hatte wie ein Vöglein fliegen können.**

3. Using the idea **den Vogel tot schießen,** how would you say that I (your teacher)

a. must do this?   **Sie müssen den Vogel tot schießen.**
b. had to do this (then)?   **Sie mußten den Vogel tot schießen.**
c. had to do this (once)?   **Sie haben den Vogel tot schießen müssen.**
d. had had to do this?   **Sie hatten den Vogel tot schießen müssen.**

4. Using the idea **die ganze Nacht tanzen,** how would you tell Fritz that he

a. may do this?   **Du darfst die ganze Nacht tanzen.**
b. was being allowed to do this?   **Du durftest die ganze Nacht tanzen.**
c. was permitted to do this?   **Du hast die ganze Nacht tanzen dürfen.**

5. Using the idea **den Drachen töten**, how would you say that Siegfried

a. is supposed to do it?	**Siegfried soll den Drachen töten.**
b. was (then) under obligation to do this?	**Siegfried sollte den Drachen töten.**
c. was supposed to do this (but hasn't)?	**Siegfried hat den Drachen töten sollen.**
d. had been obligated to do this?	**Siegfried hatte den Drachen töten sollen.**

F. Evaluation: When you can do the exercises in Section E fluently and without error, orally and/or written (depending on whether or not both these skills are part of your objectives), you are ready for evaluation.

LESSON 58

A. Your objectives: To be able to do the exercises in Section E fluently and without error.

B. How to get there: Review Section D of Lesson 57; then practice Section E in this lesson.

C. What to learn: No new material.

D. Analysis or evaluations: Refer to Lesson 57.

E. Practice: The exercises here will be based on the ideas in Section E of Lesson 57. Therefore, have your book open to that section as well as to this page!

1. Referring to Section E of Lesson 57, express number 1, a-d, by beginning each sentence with "**Alle wissen, daß...**" The word **entlang** should be considered as part of the second pole. Therefore, in the perfect tenses the auxiliary will precede **entlang**.

Lesson 58

". . . , daß ich die Straße hatte entlang gehen wollen."

ANTWORTEN:
a. Alle wissen, daß ich die Straße entlang gehen will.
b. Alle wissen, daß ich die Straße entlang gehen wollte.
c. Alle wissen, daß ich die Straße habe entlang gehen wollen.
d. Alle wissen, daß ich die Straße hatte entlang gehen wollen.

2. Express number 2, a–d, beginning with **"Ich verstehe nicht, wie . . ."**

ANTWORTEN:
a. Ich verstehe nicht, wie er wie ein Vöglein fliegen kann.
b. Ich verstehe nicht, wie er wie ein Vöglein fliegen konnte.
c. Ich verstehe nicht, wie er wie ein Vöglein hat fliegen können.*
d. Ich verstehe nicht, wie er wie ein Vöglein hatte fliegen können.*

*If the phrase **wie ein Vöglein** is felt to be a predicate complement—much more closely bound to **fliegen** than, for instance, to **er**—the latter two sentences would be expressed with the **hat** and **hatte** appearing between **er** and **wie**.

3. Express number 3, a-d, beginning with **"Wir glauben nicht, daß . . ."** (**tot** should be considered as part of the verb, or predicate).

ANTWORTEN:
a. Wir glauben nicht, daß Sie den Vogel tot schießen müssen.
b. Wir glauben nicht, daß Sie den Vogel tot schießen mußten.
c. Wir glauben nicht, daß Sie den Vogel haben tot schießen müssen.
d. Wir glauben nicht, daß Sie den Vogel hatten tot schießen müssen.

4. Express number 4, a-d, beginning with **"Wir verstehen nicht, warum . . ."**

ANTWORTEN:
a. Wir verstehen nicht, warum du die ganze Nacht tanzen darfst.
b. Wir verstehen nicht, warum du die ganze Nacht tanzen durftest.
c. Wir verstehen nicht, warum du die ganze Nacht hast tanzen dürfen.
d. Wir verstehen nicht, warum du die ganze Nacht hattest tanzen dürfen.

5. Express number 5, a-d, beginning with **"Er liest gern, wo . . ."**

ANTWORTEN:
a. Er liest gern, wo Siegfried den Drachen töten soll.
b. Er liest gern, wo Siegfried den Drachen töten sollte.
c. Er liest gern, wo Siegfried den Drachen hat töten sollen.
d. Er liest gern, wo Siegfried den Drachen hatte töten sollen.

F. **Evaluation:** When you can do the exercises in Section E fluently, you are ready to be evaluated.

LESSON 59

A. **Your objectives:** To demonstrate your understanding of the subjunctive (after careful study of Section D!) by being able to do the exercises in Section E fluently and without error.

B. **How to get there:** Study Section D thoroughly! If you do the exercises in Section E as a memory exercise, without really understanding

Lesson 59 151

"Wenn ich das machen könnte, ..."

what you are doing or what the subjunctive is all about, you will surely have a great deal of difficulty in subsequent lessons!

When you understand Section D (ask for help if you don't), then go on to Section E.

C. **What to learn:** Refer to Section D.

D. **Analysis or explanations:** THE SUBJUNCTIVE
The subjunctive as a form is hardly recognized or considered as such by students in English any more. Have you ever stopped to think about statements such as the following in English?

> If I *had* a lot of money, I ...
> *Were* I only a little older, I would ...
> If I *went (were to go)* home now, my teacher would ...

"Wenn ich viel Geld hätte, ... "

These are remnants of the Germanic subjunctive forms.

In the first statement you are referring to the present time, yet you are using a "past" form, *had.* In the second statement you are also using a "past" form, but how do you explain the use of the normally plural form *were* with the singular pronoun *I*?

There is no point in going into a detailed analysis or into the historical development of these forms here. Let it suffice merely to bring to your attention that a "different" form, *based on the past tense forms,* is often used when we want to state *a condition contrary to what is actually the case.* When you hear the above statements, you know "I haven't got a lot of money" and that "I'm not as old as I need or want to be."

Such a use requires the subjunctive form in German also. (This is, however, not the only use for the subjunctive forms, as you will learn later.)

Before going any farther, let us consider how one forms the subjunctive of verbs in German in order to express what we wish were the case at the present time. The most commonly used forms of the subjunctive are based on the past tense forms, even though they refer to present conditions. If the verb is a "regular" or weak verb, there is usually no difference between the subjunctive form and the ordinary past. We recognize that it is subjunctive by the context in which it is used. Some examples of regular verbs in a "subjunctive" statement:

Wenn er jetzt die Gitarre spielte, ...   If he *were playing* the guitar now, ...
Wenn sie jetzt in den Spiegel schauten, ...   If they *were looking* into the mirror now, ...

But if the verb is an irregular verb, we must form the subjunctive by supplying a new stem. In general, this is done by adding an umlaut to the vowel in the past stem, if possible (ä, ö, ü), and also adding an **e**. To repeat: To form the subjunctive stem, *umlaut the past stem and add an* -e. (This is only for strong verbs!)

INFINITIVE	PAST STEM	SUBJUNCTIVE STEM
gehen	ging	**ginge**
sehen	sah	**sähe**
schießen	schoß	**schösse**
sein	war	**wäre**
haben	hatte	**hätte**
steigen	stieg	**stiege**

The personal endings then follow the usual pattern for the past tense:

ich ginge
du gingest
er, sie, es ginge

wir, sie, Sie gingen
ihr ginget

NOTE: Two verbs which we have learned as irregular verbs do not fit the pattern of subjunctive formation explained above:

kennen	kannte	**kennte**
sterben	starb	**stürbe**

Probably the most common use of the subjunctive is in "if" clauses when they express conditions "contrary to fact." Two positions of the personal verb in the subjunctive are possible in German, equivalent to what is *sometimes* possible in English:

If I had known, ...	**Wenn ich gewußt hätte,** ...
Had I known, ...	**Hätte ich gewußt,** ...
	Wenn sie hier wäre, ...
	Wenn ein Jäger den Wolf schösse, ...
	Schösse ein Jäger den Wolf, ...

E. Practice:

WARNING! Do not merely memorize these exercises without understanding them! Be certain you have studied Section D thoroughly first!

Express the following ideas as introductory "if" clauses in the subjunctive, with yourself as the subject. Use only the more common form, that is, the form beginning with **wenn**.

EXAMPLE: viel Geld haben   Wenn ich viel Geld hätte, ...

1. in Deutschland wohnen — Wenn ich in Deutschland wohnte, ...
2. die Gitarre gut spielen — Wenn ich die Gitarre gut spielte, ...
3. besser hören — Wenn ich besser hörte, ...
4. Filetsteak bestellen — Wenn ich Filetsteak bestellte, ...
5. so gut wie Udo Jürgens singen — Wenn ich so gut wie Udo Jürgens sänge, ...
6. morgen zu arbeiten anfangen — Wenn ich morgen zu arbeiten anfinge, ...
7. Schildkrötensuppe essen — Wenn ich Schildkrötensuppe äße, ...
8. den Wolf tot schießen — Wenn ich den Wolf tot schösse, ...

F. Evaluation: Refer to Section A.

LESSON 60

A. Your objectives: To demonstrate your knowledge of the present tense subjunctive forms of the modal auxiliaries (in Section C) by

Lesson 60

your ability to do the exercises in Section E fluently and without error.

B. How to get there: Memorize the subjunctive forms of the modals in Section C; then practice the exercises in Section E until you can do them fluently.

C. What to learn: Following are the subjunctive forms of the modals. Except for **sollen** and **wollen**, the modals follow the subjunctive pattern of the irregular verbs (that is, they add an umlaut to the past form and end with an **-e**).

INFINITIVE	PAST	SUBJUNCTIVE
dürfen	durfte	**dürfte**
können	konnte	**könnte**
müssen	mußte	**müßte**
mögen	mochte	**möchte**
sollen	sollte	**sollte**
wollen	wollte	**wollte**

D. Analysis or explanations: Refer to Lesson 59.

E. Practice: Continue the following sentences with "if" clauses, indicating that the idea expressed might be the opposite.

EXAMPLES:
Ich kann nicht nach Hause gehen, aber . . .   wenn ich nach Hause gehen könnte, . . .
Ich will das tun, aber . . .   wenn ich das nicht tun wollte, . . .

(Notice that negative statements must be changed to positive and vice versa.)

1. Ich darf das Lied nicht singen, aber . . .   wenn ich das Lied singen dürfte, . . .
2. Du kannst das Gedicht gut vorlesen, aber . . .   wenn du das Gedicht nicht gut vorlesen könntest, . .
3. Er braucht nicht zu gehen, aber . . .   wenn er gehen müßte, . . .
4. Ich mag das nicht, aber . . .   wenn ich das möchte, . . .
5. Wir sollen hier bleiben, aber, . . .   wenn wir nicht hier bleiben sollten, . . .
6. Ihr wollt nicht tanzen, aber . . .   wenn ihr tanzen wolltet, . . .
7. Sie dürfen nicht fahren, aber . . .   wenn sie fahren dürften, . . .

156 Deutsch: ZWEITE STUFE

    8. Hans kann gut schießen, aber . . .   wenn er nicht gut schießen könnte, . . .
    9. Du brauchst das nicht zu lernen, aber . . .   wenn du das lernen müßtest, . . .
   10. Die Kinder wollen Tee trinken, aber . . .   wenn die Kinder keinen Tee trinken wollten, . . .

(keinen)

F. Evaluation: Refer to Section A.

"Wenn du mich liebtest, . . ."

LESSON 61

A. Your objectives: To demonstrate your ability to use the subjunctive in past time by being able to do the exercises in Section E fluently and without error.

B. How to get there: Study Section D. When you have understood it, begin practicing Section E. Don't neglect to use the recordings for oral practice!

C. What to learn: Refer to Section D.

D. Analysis or explanations:

SUBJUNCTIVE REFERRING TO PAST TIME
If the "condition" refers to the past, both English and German use a form based on the past perfect forms (Lesson 56):

If I had seen that . . .	Wenn ich das gesehen hätte, . . .
Had I seen that . . .	Hätte ich das gesehen, . . .
If we had gone along . . .	Wenn wir mitgegangen wären, . . .
Had we gone along . . .	Wären wir mitgegangen, . . .

E. Practice:

1. Express the following ideas as conditional "if" clauses in the past. Use *they* as the subject (*"If they had . . ."*). For each idea give two answers, one for each of the possible word order patterns.

a. das nicht erlauben	Wenn sie das nicht erlaubt hätten, . . .
	Hätten sie das nicht erlaubt, . . .
b. mir den Schatz geben	Wenn sie mir den Schatz gegeben hätten, . . .
	Hätten sie mir den Schatz gegeben, . . .
c. die ganze Nacht tanzen	Wenn sie die ganze Nacht getanzt hätten, . . .
	Hätten sie die ganze Nacht getanzt, . . .
d. nicht so dumm sein	Wenn sie nicht so dumm gewesen wären, . . .
	Wären sie nicht so dumm gewesen, . . .
e. bis Mittag schlafen	Wenn sie bis Mittag geschlafen hätten, . . .
	Hätten sie bis Mittag geschlafen, . . .
f. auf das neue Rad steigen	Wenn sie auf das neue Rad gestiegen wären, . . .
	Wären sie auf das neue Rad gestiegen, . . .

g. nicht mit der Straßenbahn fahren

Wenn sie nicht mit der Straßenbahn gefahren wären, ...

Wären sie nicht mit der Straßenbahn gefahren, ...

h. den Drachen töten

Wenn sie den Drachen getötet hätten, ...

Hätten sie den Drachen getötet, ...

2. Give German equivalents of the following, beginning with **wenn**:

a. If I were living in Hamburg, ...   Wenn ich in Hamburg wohnte, ...
b. If I had lived in Regensburg, ...   Wenn ich in Regensburg gewohnt hätte, ...
c. If you were not so ill, ...   Wenn du nicht so krank wärest, ...
d. If you had not been so ill, ...   Wenn du nicht so krank gewesen wärest, ...
e. If Gisela were sitting here with me, ...   Wenn Gisela hier neben mir säße, ...
f. If Gisela had been sitting here with me, ...   Wenn Gisela hier neben mir gesessen hätte, ...
g. If we were driving to Munich, ...   Wenn wir nach München führen, ...
h. If we had driven to Munich, ...   Wenn wir nach München gefahren wären, ...
i. If you-all had believed us, ...   Wenn ihr uns geglaubt hättet, ...
j. If you-all believed us, ...   Wenn ihr uns glaubtet, ...
k. If they had given me the money yesterday, ...   Wenn sie mir gestern das Geld gegeben hätten, ...
l. If they were to give me the money today, ...   Wenn sie mir heute das Geld gäben, ...

F. Evaluation: Refer to Section A.

"Wenn es jetzt Weihnachtstag wäre, ..."

LESSON 62
Self-Test

A. Your objectives: To be able to do the Self-Test in Section E with at least 90% accuracy.

B. How to get there: If you have mastered the previous 6 lessons (56-61), you should be prepared to take the Self-Test already. If you are unsure of yourself, review any parts of Lessons 56-61 which you feel are necessary.

C. What to learn: Refer to any C sections of Lessons 56-61 for which you feel it is necessary.

D. Analysis or explanations: Refer to any D sections of Lessons 56-61 for which you feel it is necessary.

E. Practice: SELF-TEST

1. **die ganze Nacht tanzen**
   zu dir fliegen
   a. How would you say that you had done each of the above?
   b. How would you tell me that I had done each of the above?
   c. How would you say that he had done each of the above?

2. **in Deutschland wohnen**
   durch die Straßen gehen
   a. How would you say you want to do each of the above?
   b. How would you say that you wanted to do each of the above (present perfect tense)?
   c. How would you say that you had wanted to do each of the above?
   d. How would you say that I understand why you wanted to do each of the above activities?

3. What are the subjunctive "stems" of each of the following verbs?

gehen	sollen
sehen	dürfen
fliegen	kennen
sein	sterben
haben	wohnen

4. Fußball spielen
   den bösen Wolf sehen
   in den See fallen
   a. How would you begin a sentence with each of the above ideas, indicating that "if" you were to do each of the above, ... (that is, "If I played football, ...")?
   b. How would you do the same thing, but changing the time to the past ("If I had played football, ...")?

F. Evaluation: Check (or have checked) your answers against the key. If you did well (90% +), you are ready for the test on this section.

If you did not do 90%, review the necessary exercises before attempting the test which accompanies this lesson.

LESSON 63
Etwas Neues: Konditionalsätze

A. Your objectives: To demonstrate your ability to form "conditional" sentences in German by being able to do the exercises in Section E fluently and without error.

B. How to get there: Study Section D; then practice the exercises in Section E.

C. What to learn: No new material. Refer to Section D for new structure explanations.

D. Analysis or explanations:

CONDITIONAL SENTENCES

The "if" clauses explained and practiced in Lessons 59-61 are usually part of a complete "conditional sentence" if they are meant to convey conditions contrary to fact. Such a sentence contains the "condition" plus the "conclusion":

If I *had* a lot of money, I *would buy* a new car.
Wenn ich viel Geld **hätte**, **würde** ich einen neuen Wagen **kaufen**.

For conditions in the present or future, this **würde** construction in the conclusion clause is becoming very common

"Wenn ich viel Geld hätte, würde ich einen neuen Wagen kaufen!"

in spoken German. However, it is not used in place of the subjunctive form with **sein, haben,** or the modals.

E. Practice: 1. Using the **wenn** plus subjunctive construction in the first, or "conditional," clause, and the **würde** plus infinitive construction in the conclusion (except with **sein, haben,** and the modals), form conditional sentences with the following elements. Concentrate also on the meaning of what you are saying—not just on the form! (Note that answers *follow* the exercises below.)

EXAMPLES: (ich) (ein Jäger sein)   (den Wolf tot schießen)
Wenn ich ein Jäger **wäre, würde** ich den Wolf tot **schießen.**
(If I *were* a hunter, I *would shoot* the wolf dead.)

a. (ich) (dich lieb haben)   (immer bei dir sein)
b. (wir) (das nicht glauben)   (nicht mitgehen)
c. (du) (die ganze Nacht tanzen)   (ich) (mit dir tanzen)

d. (ihr) (die Wahrheit wissen)   (nicht in Berlin bleiben)
e. (Hans) (jetzt nach Hause gehen)   (seine Mutter) (ihn nicht erkennen) erkannt
f. (Sie) (nicht so viel Geld mitbringen)   (wir) (durch diese dunkle Straße gehen)
g. (ich) (in Deutschland wohnen)   (im Rhein schwimmen)
h. (du) (Gisela gut kennen)   (sie lieben)
i. (wir) (nicht so wild sein)   (mehr lernen)
j. (ihr) (täglich etwas früher aufstehen)   (den Sonnenaufgang sehen)

2. State that Hans would do the following if he were rich (**reich**):

a. nach Deutschland fahren
b. in einem großen Hause wohnen
c. nur in den besten Restaurants essen
d. den armen Leuten helfen
e. meiner Familie nichts geben

3. State that we would be rich if we did the following:

a. nicht immer so viel kaufen
b. oft zu Hause bleiben
c. nicht in den besten Restaurants essen
d. mehr arbeiten
e. unser Geld immer in die Bank stecken

4. How would you say in German

a. to me that I would run home if I saw a wolf?
b. to your friend that if he went home he could eat something?
c. that if you knew that you wouldn't ask?
d. about you and me that we could drive to Berlin if the car were not in the repair shop (**die Werkstatt**)?
e. to several friends that if they drank beer Gisela wouldn't be going along?

ANTWORTEN:
1. a. Wenn ich dich lieb hätte, wäre ich immer bei dir.
   b. Wenn wir das nicht glaubten, würden wir nicht mitgehen.
   c. Wenn du die ganze Nacht tanztest, würde ich mit dir tanzen.
   d. Wenn ihr die Wahrheit wüßtet, würdet ihr nicht in Berlin wohnen. bleiben
   e. Wenn Hans jetzt nach Hause ginge, würde seine Mutter ihn nicht erkennen.
   f. Wenn Sie nicht so viel Geld mitbrächten, würden wir durch diese dunkle Straße gehen.
   g. Wenn ich in Deutschland wohnte, würde ich im Rhein schwimmen.

"Hans würde nach Deutschland fliegen, wenn er reich wäre."

    h. Wenn du Gisela gut kenntest, würdest du sie lieben.
    i. Wenn wir nicht so wild wären, würden wir mehr lernen.
    j. Wenn ihr täglich etwas früher aufständet, würdet ihr den Sonnenaufgang sehen.

2. a. Wenn Hans reich wäre, würde er nach Deutschland fahren.
    b. Wenn Hans reich wäre, würde er in einem großen Haus wohnen.
    c. Wenn Hans reich wäre, würde er nur in den besten Restaurants essen.
    d. Wenn Hans reich wäre, würde er den armen Leuten helfen.
    e. Wenn Hans reich wäre, würde er meiner Familie nichts geben.

(Any of the above sentences could have been expressed with the clauses interchanged: **Hans würde nach Deutschland fahren, wenn er reich wäre.** The same order is possible with the sentences below.)

3. a. Wenn wir nicht immer so viel kauften, wären wir reich.
    b. Wenn wir oft zu Hause blieben, wären wir reich.
    c. Wenn wir nicht in den besten Restaurants äßen, wären wir reich.
    d. Wenn wir mehr arbeiteten, wären wir reich.
    e. Wenn wir unser Geld immer in die Bank steckten, wären wir reich.

4. a. Wenn Sie einen Wolf sähen, würden Sie nach Hause laufen.
    b. Wenn du nach Hause gingest, könntest du etwas essen.)

(It is unlikely that **würde** would be used with a modal. The subjunctive form of the modal is used.)

 c. Wenn ich das wüßte, würde ich nicht fragen.
 d. Wenn das Auto nicht in der Werkstatt wäre, könnten wir nach Berlin fahren.
 e. Wenn ihr Bier tränket, würde Gisela nicht mitgehen.

F. Evaluation: Refer to Section A.

LESSON 64

A. Your objectives: See Lesson 63.

B. How to get there: See Lesson 63.

C. What to learn: See Lesson 63.

D. Analysis or explanations: See Lesson 63.

E. Practice:

CONDITIONAL EXERCISES—continued
Following are some pairs of sentences stating the "facts" as they are. Put the sentences together as conditional sentences, indicating what the case would be if the opposite were true. *This will require changing negative statements to positive ones and vice versa.*

EXAMPLE: Sie hat Hans nicht gern. Sie geht nicht mit ihm ins Kino.
       Wenn sie Hans gern hätte, würde sie mit ihm ins Kino gehen.

 a. Ich bin kein Jäger. Ich schieße keine Tiere.
 b. Ich denke nicht an dich. Ich komme nicht nach Hause.
 c. Ich glaube dir nicht. Ich gehe nicht mit.
 d. Sie sieht nicht intelligent aus. Wir sprechen nicht mit ihr.
 e. Sie kommen nicht spät an. Wir brauchen nicht lange zu warten.
 f. Er trinkt kein Bier. Er fährt den Wagen.
 g. Wir verstehen Deutsch. Wir bleiben in Deutschland.
 h. Ihr redet nicht laut genug. Wir hören nicht zu.

Lesson 64 165

LINKS: Urlaub vom königlichen Alltagsbetrieb machen zur Zeit Silvia und Carl Gustaf. In Klosters, im Haus von Prinzessin Birgitta von Schweden, genießen sie unbeschwerte Ferientage

...enn wir Deutsch nicht verständen, ...wir nicht in Deutschland bleiben."

...ersuppe.

...e ich Tiere schießen.
...ich nach Hause kommen.
...mitgehen.
...rden wir mit ihr sprechen.
...wir lange warten.
...en Wagen nicht fahren.
...nden, würden wir nicht in Deutschland bleiben.
h. Wenn ihr laut genug redetet, würden wir zuhören.
i. Wenn du auf Gisela wartetest, würde ich nicht bleiben.
j. Wenn wir nicht krank wären, würden wir keine Hühnersuppe essen.

F. Evaluation: When you can perform the exercises in Section E fluently and with no errors, you are ready to be evaluated.

LESSON 65

A.	Your objectives:	To demonstrate your ability to use the conditional structure when referring to past time, as shown by your ability to do the exercises in Section E fluently without error.
B.	How to get there:	Study Section D carefully; then practice the exercises in Section E.
C.	What to learn:	Refer to Section D.
D.	Analysis or explanations:	CONDITIONAL SENTENCES (PAST TIME)

If we wish to express conditions in the past—expressing "what might have been"—we use the subjunctive form based on the *past perfect tense* as explained in Lesson 56. We use this form also in the conclusion. We do *not* use a form with **würde** when we are expressing conclusions in the past.

In fact, at this point it would be best never to use **würde** in the conclusion clause when we have **sein, haben**, the modals (as explained in Lesson 63), or, as now, any clauses in the past.

Wenn ich das **gewußt hätte, hätte** ich es dir **gesagt**.
(If I *had known* that, I *would have told* you.)

Wenn ich Hans **gesehen hätte, wäre** ich **mitgegangen**.
(If I *had seen* Hans, I *would have gone* along.)

Wenn wir in den See **gefallen wären, wärest** du böse **gewesen**?
(If we *had fallen* into the lake, *would* you *have been* angry?)

E. Practice:

1. Express the ten pairs of ideas in Lesson 63, Section E (number 1, a-j), as *conditional sentences in the past.*

ANTWORTEN:
a. Wenn ich dich lieb gehabt hätte, wäre ich immer bei dir gewesen.
b. Wenn wir das nicht geglaubt hätten, wären wir nicht mitgegangen.
c. Wenn du die ganze Nacht getanzt hättest, hätte ich mit dir getanzt.
d. Wenn ihr die Wahrheit gewußt hättet, wäret ihr nicht in Berlin geblieben.
e. Wenn Hans (jetzt) nach Hause gegangen wäre, hätte seine Mutter ihn nicht erkannt.

"Wenn ihr die Wahrheit gewußt hättet, wäret ihr nicht in Berlin geblieben."

    f. Wenn Sie nicht so viel Geld mitgebracht hätten, wären wir durch diese dunkle Straße gegangen.
    g. Wenn ich in Deutschland gewohnt hätte, hätte ich im Rhein geschwommen.
    h. Wenn du Gisela gut gekannt hättest, hättest du sie geliebt.
    i. Wenn ihr täglich etwas früher aufgestanden wäret, hättet ihr den Sonnenaufgang gesehen.

2. Express the ten sentences in Lesson 64, Section E, as conditional sentences in the past. (Don't forget to change positive statements to negative and vice versa.)

ANTWORTEN:
    a. Wenn ich Jäger gewesen wäre, hätte ich Tiere geschossen.
    b. Wenn ich an dich gedacht hätte, wäre ich nach Hause gekommen.
    c. Wenn ich dir geglaubt hätte, wäre ich mitgegangen.

d. Wenn sie intelligent ausgesehen hätte, hätten wir mit ihr gesprochen.
e. Wenn sie spät angekommen wären, hätten wir lange warten müssen.
f. Wenn er Bier getrunken hätte, hätte er den Wagen nicht gefahren.
g. Wenn wir Deutsch nicht verstanden hätten, wären wir nicht in Deutschland geblieben.
h. Wenn ihr laut genug geredet hättet, hätten wir zugehört.
i. Wenn du auf Gisela gewartet hättest, wäre ich nicht geblieben.
j. Wenn wir nicht krank gewesen wären, hätten wir keine Hühnersuppe gegessen.

3. State the following pairs of sentences as conditional sentences by beginning with **wenn**. (Negative clauses will have to be changed to positive ones.) All subjunctive statements in the past—no matter what type of past form they are derived from—are expressed by only *one* subjunctive form, as explained in Section D. (Note that answers follow exercise j.)

a. Er ging nicht ins Dorf. Er sah seine Mutter nicht.
b. Er hat nicht lange gesucht. Er hat das Buch nicht gefunden.
c. Wir waren nicht lange da. Wir haben nicht viel getanzt.
d. Sie war kein Vöglein. Sie ist nicht zu ihm geflogen.
e. Sie waren nicht froh. Sie haben sich nicht viel erlaubt.
f. Der Jäger hatte nicht auf mich geschossen. Ich fiel nicht um.
g. Ihr habt sie nicht angerufen. Sie haben das nicht gewußt.
h. Siegfrieds Freund badete nicht in dem Fett. Er war nicht unverwundbar.
i. Du bist nicht vorsichtig gewesen. Du hast die Flasche nicht nach Hause gebracht.
j. Die Lorelei sang keine wundersame Melodei. Der Schiffer fuhr nicht gegen den Felsen.

ANTWORTEN:
a. Wenn er ins Dorf gegangen wäre, hätte er seine Mutter gesehen.
b. Wenn er lange gesucht hätte, hätte er das Buch gefunden.
c. Wenn wir lange da gewesen wären, hätten wir viel getanzt.
d. Wenn sie ein Vöglein gewesen wäre, wäre sie zu ihm geflogen.
e. Wenn sie froh gewesen wären, hätten sie sich viel erlaubt.
f. Wenn der Jäger auf mich geschossen hätte, wäre ich umgefallen.
g. Wenn ihr sie angerufen hättet, hätten sie das gewußt.
h. Wenn Siegfrieds Freund in dem Fett gebadet hätte, wäre er unverwundbar gewesen.
i. Wenn du vorsichtig gewesen wärest, hättest du die Flasche nach Hause gebracht.
j. Wenn die Lorelei eine wundersame Melodei gesungen hätte, wäre der Schiffer gegen den Felsen gefahren.

F. Evaluation: Refer to Section A.

"Wenn ich das gewußt hätte, . . ."

LESSONS 66 and 67

A. **Your objectives:** To demonstrate your ability to express conditional sentences in several of the possible variations, by being able to do the exercises in Section E fluently without error.

B. **How to get there:** Study carefully the explanations in Section D. When they are clear to you, practice the exercises in Section E. You can afford to spend twice the usual amount of time on this material, since it constitutes two lessons.

C. **What to learn:** Refer to Section D.

D. **Analysis or explanations:** We have been practicing conditional-type sentences which follow one fairly standard pattern. There are, however, numerous variations possible. The "would do something" idea can be expressed in two ways:

  Wenn ich Geld hätte, **würde** ich auch **gehen.**
  Wenn ich Geld hätte, **ginge** ich auch.

In other words, in German we can get the "would do" feeling by using **würde** . . . **gehen** *or* by using the subjunctive form

ginge. This has no parallel in English in the conclusion. We rely on the auxiliary "would" to give us the conditional feeling. A German can experience this feeling either through **würde** . . . *or* the subjunctive form of the verb.

In German the "if" clause can also be expressed in two ways:

Wenn ich Geld hätte, . . .
Hätte ich Geld, . . .

This is sometimes possible in English:

If I had been there . . .
Had I been there . . .

But this is possible only with a few words in English, and even then it is beginning to sound archaic to our ears. In German we *can* always leave out the **wenn** and start with a subjunctive form of the verb:

Wenn ich spät nach Hause käme, . . .
Käme ich spät nach Hause, . . .

As in English, we can also *reverse* the position of the clauses in German. Therefore, with two possibilities for the "if" clause in German, and two possibilities for the conclusion clause, and with all four of these combinations reversed, we have a total of eight possible combinations:

Wenn ich Geld hätte, würde ich auch gehen.
Wenn ich Geld hätte, ginge ich auch.
Hätte ich Geld, würde ich auch gehen.
Hätte ich Geld, ginge ich auch.

Ich würde auch gehen, wenn ich Geld hätte.
Ich ginge auch, wenn ich Geld hätte.
Ich würde auch gehen, hätte ich Geld.
Ich ginge auch, hätte ich Geld.

This is not as complex as it might appear. It reduces to the fact that you can express each clause in two ways, and that the clauses can be reversed. (In the *past* where we do not use **würde,** the number of possibilities is reduced to half.)

Lessons 66 and 67

E. **Practice:** Express the following English sentences in German

> a. using the common "**Wenn . . . , würde . . .**" (except with **sein, haben,** the modals, or in past time);
> b. omitting the use of **würde** in any conclusion clause;
> c. using neither **wenn** nor **würde** (this results in the somewhat literary-sounding construction used in the song "Ach, wie ist's möglich dann"); and
> d. reversing the clauses in the sentence obtained in "a" above.

1. If I were Gisela, I would go home.
2. If we were eating now, I would be happy.
3. If you should happen to be reading now, you wouldn't be thinking so much.
4. If they were driving to Berlin, I'd be very nervous.
5. If Gisela would be (were) sitting here, you'd believe me (**mir**).
6. If you-all had seen the dragon, you'd have been afraid too.
7. If she'd have spoken with me, I would have given her the money.
8. If I'd have found the hawk, I'd have shot it (**ihn**).
9. Had I known that, I would have come immediately (**gleich**).
10. She would have danced all night, if he had stayed with her.

ANTWORTEN:
1. a. Wenn ich Gisela wäre, würde ich nach Hause gehen.
   b. Wenn ich Gisela wäre, ginge ich nach Hause.
   c. Wäre ich Gisela, ginge ich nach Hause.
   d. Ich würde nach Hause gehen, wenn ich Gisela wäre.

2. a. Wenn wir jetzt äßen, wäre ich froh.
   b. (same as a.)
   c. Äßen wir jetzt, wäre ich froh.
   d. Ich wäre froh, wenn wir jetzt äßen.

3. a. Wenn du jetzt läsest, würdest du nicht so viel nachdenken.
   b. Wenn du jetzt läsest, dächtest du nicht so viel nach.
   c. Läsest du jetzt, dächtest du nicht so viel nach.
   d. Du würdest nicht so viel nachdenken, wenn du jetzt läsest.

4. a. Wenn sie nach Berlin führen, wäre ich sehr nervös.
   b. (same as a.)
   c. Führen sie nach Berlin, wäre ich sehr nervös.
   d. Ich wäre sehr nervös, wenn sie nach Berlin führen.

"Wäre er mit ihr geblieben, hätte sie die ganze Nacht getanzt."

5. a. Wenn Gisela hier säße, würdest du mir glauben.
   b. Wenn Gisela hier säße, glaubtest du mir.
   c. Säße Gisela hier, glaubtest du mir.
   d. Du würdest mir glauben, wenn Gisela hier säße.

6. a. Wenn ihr den Drachen gesehen hättet, hättet ihr auch Angst gehabt.
   b. (same as a.)
   c. Hättet ihr den Drachen gesehen, hättet ihr auch Angst gehabt.
   d. Ihr hättet auch Angst gehabt, wenn ihr den Drachen gesehen hättet.

7. a. Wenn sie mit mir gesprochen hätte, hätte ich ihr das Geld gegeben.
   b. (same as a.)
   c. Hätte sie mit mir gesprochen, hätte ich ihr das Geld gegeben.
   d. Ich hätte ihr das Geld gegeben, wenn sie mit mir gesprochen hätte.

8. a. Wenn ich den Habicht gefunden hätte, hätte ich ihn geschossen.
   b. (same as a.)
   c. Hätte ich den Habicht gefunden, hätte ich ihn geschossen.
   d. Ich hätte den Habicht geschossen, wenn ich ihn gefunden hätte.

9. a. Wenn ich das gewußt hätte, wäre ich gleich gekommen.
   b. (same as a.)

c. Hätte ich das gewußt, wäre ich gleich gekommen.
d. Ich wäre gleich gekommen, wenn ich das gewußt hätte.

10. a. Wenn er mit ihr geblieben wäre, hätte sie die ganze Nacht getanzt.
b. (same as a.)
c. Wäre er mit ihr geblieben, hätte sie die ganze Nacht getanzt.
d. Sie hätte die ganze Nacht getanzt, wenn er mit ihr geblieben wäre.

F. **Evaluation:** Refer to Section A.

LESSON 68

A. **Your objectives:** To be able to do the exercises in Section E (involving conditional sentences with modal auxiliaries) fluently and without error.

B. **How to get there:** Study Section D thoroughly; then practice the exercises in Section E until you are able to do them fluently.

C. **What to learn:** Refer to Section D.

D. **Analysis or explanations:**

CONDITIONAL SENTENCES WITH MODALS

The modals can, of course, be part of conditional sentences. We have already been concerned with the modals in the present tense subjunctive. With the past tense we use the proper form of **hätte** (never **wäre**, since no modals have **sein** as the auxiliary in the perfect tenses):

Wenn er das Auto **kaufen wollte, könnte** er es **kaufen.**
Wenn er das Auto **hätte kaufen wollen, hätte** er es **kaufen können.**
Wenn er nach Hause **hätte gehen wollen, hätte** er **gehen dürfen.**

Can you give English equivalents of the above sentences?

E. **Practice:** Express each of the pairs of ideas below first as a conditional sentence in the present, and then as a conditional sentence in the past. Don't use **würde**, even if possible. (The "X" indicates where the auxiliary should go when the conditional sentence is stated in the past, in case it wouldn't be found just before the verb forms.)

EXAMPLE: (sie) (^Xzu Hause bleiben müssen)   (ich) (davon wissen)
Wenn sie zu Hause bleiben müßten, wüßte ich davon.
Wenn sie zu Hause hätten bleiben müssen, hätte ich davon gewußt.

a. (ich) (zu dir fliegen können)   (glücklich sein)
b. (Hans) (^Xbesser schwimmen können)   (mit uns gehen dürfen)
c. (du) (die Hausarbeit machen können)   (Fußball spielen dürfen)
d. (wir) (dieses Blümlein nicht pflücken sollen)   (nicht im Garten sein)
e. (ihr) (^Xzusammen sein wollen)   (tanzen gehen können)
f. (Sie) (in der Schmiede arbeiten sollen)   (sie) (Ihnen einen Hammer geben)
g. (ich) (in dem Fett baden können)   (unverwundbar werden)

ANTWORTEN:
a. Wenn ich zu dir fliegen könnte, wäre ich glücklich.
   Wenn ich zu dir hätte fliegen können, wäre ich glücklich gewesen.
b. Wenn Hans besser schwimmen könnte, dürfte er mit uns gehen.
   Wenn Hans hätte besser schwimmen können, hätte er mit uns gehen können. *dürfen*

"Wenn Hans hätte besser schwimmen können, ..."

Lesson 69

    c. Wenn du die Hausarbeit machen könntest, dürftest du Fußball spielen.
       Wenn du die Hausarbeit hättest machen können, hättest du Fußball spielen können. *dürfen*
    d. Wenn wir dieses Blümlein nicht pflücken sollten, wären wir nicht im Garten.
       Wenn wir dieses Blümlein nicht hätten pflücken sollen, wären wir nicht im Garten gewesen.
    e. Wenn ihr zusammen sein wolltet, könntet ihr tanzen gehen.
       Wenn ihr zusammen hättet sein wollen, hättet ihr tanzen gehen können.
    f. Wenn Sie in der Schmiede arbeiten sollten, gäben sie Ihnen einen Hammer.
       Wenn Sie in der Schmiede hätten arbeiten sollen, hätten sie Ihnen einen Hammer gegeben.
    g. Wenn ich in dem Fett baden könnte, würde ich unverwundbar.
       Wenn ich in dem Fett hätte baden können, wäre ich unverwundbar geworden.

F. Evaluation: Refer to Section A.

LESSON 69
Self-Test on Lessons 63-68

A. Your objectives: To be able to do the Self-Test in Section E with at least 90% accuracy.

B. How to get there: Look over the Self-Test. If there is any section you feel unsure about, review and practice that type of exercise in the appropriate E section of Lessons 63-68.

                                      When you believe you can do the test with no difficulty, do so.

C. What to learn: Review, if necessary.

D. Analysis or explanations: Review, if necessary.

E. Practice: SELF-TEST

1. Form conditional sentences by using the following ideas and subjects. The first idea should be the **wenn** clause.

        a. (ich) (Geld haben)   (seinen VW kaufen)
        b. (er) (nach Hause gehen)   (schneller laufen)
        c. (du) (hier sein)   (ein Steak kochen)

d. (Gisela) (nicht so viel sprechen)   (Hans) (mehr arbeiten können)
e. (wir) (das wissen)   (es dir nicht sagen)
f. (ihr) (in Berlin wohnen dürfen)   (oft ins Theater gehen wollen)
g. (Sie) (immer zu Hause bleiben)   (mehr Arbeit tun)
h. (sie) *they* (Bier trinken)   (ich) (nicht mitfahren dürfen)
i. (du) (neben Gisela sitzen)   (sie) (den Film nicht ansehen)
j. (ich) (sterben)   (nicht in dem Himmel fliegen)

2. Express each of the sentences in 1 above to refer to *past* conditions.

3. Express in German:

a. If I understood that, I wouldn't ask.
b. If we stayed home, they would find us.
c. If you came along, she would stay home.
d. If she had picked the flower, we would have been angry.
e. If you-all had fallen into the lake, we would have laughed.
f. If I had played football, would we have won?
g. If I wanted to go, would I have to buy the ticket?
h. If they were permitted to play, they could stay here.
i. If he had wanted to become (a) soldier, he would have had to be healthy (**gesund**)
j. If you (**du**) had been able to go home, would you have gone?

4. a. Write 3b with **würde** in the second clause.
   b. Write the same sentence without **würde** in the second clause.
   c. Write b (in this section) without a **wenn** in the first clause.
   d. Write a (in this section) with the clauses reversed.

F. Evaluation: If you did well (90% or better), go on to Lesson 70. If you did not do well on this test, review where necessary; then try the test (or an alternate version, if your teacher has one) again.

LESSON 70
A Review Self-Test

A. Your objectives: To demonstrate your ability to use verbs in all the forms and tenses we have practiced in German up to this point,

Lesson 70   177

"Wenn ich ein Vöglein wär',
flög' ich zu dir!"

including present tense, past tense, present perfect tense, past perfect tense, and the subjunctive forms—and including the modal auxiliaries—by being able to express sentences of the type called for in Section E below in German with at least 90% accuracy.

B. **How to get there**   Do the Self-Test with no review.

C. **What to learn:**   Review, if necessary, after attempting the test once.

D. **Analysis or explanations:**   Refer to Section C.

E. **Practice:** REVIEW SELF-TEST

1. Using the idea **in Deutschland wohnen,** tell your friends that they

   a. can do this;
   b. could do this (simple past tense);
   c. have been able to do this;
   d. had been able to do this;
   e. know they aren't allowed to do this;
   f. know they weren't allowed to do this;
   g. know they haven't been allowed to do this;
   h. know they hadn't been allowed to do this;
   i. Tell your friends that if they had money they would want to do this.
   j. Tell your friends that if they had had money they would have wanted to do this.

2. Using the idea **nach Berlin fahren,** how would you express the fact that

   a. you are doing this?
   b. you were doing this?
   c. you have done this?
   d. you had done this?
   e. you would do this?
   f. you would have done this?
   g. you must do this?
   h. you had to do this (simple past)?
   i. you have had to do this?
   j. you would have to do this?
   k. you would have had to do this?
   l. you know that Hans has done this?
   m. Hans knows that you would have had to do this?
   n. you know that Hans has had to do this?

F. **Evaluation:** Check (or have checked) your answers. If you had no difficulty, you are ready for the test covering Lessons 63-68. If you do have difficulty, have your teacher analyze the type of mistakes you are making and prescribe review exercises for you. Re-take the test as often as necessary.

Lesson 70 179

VIERTER TEIL

Das Thema: FANTASIEWELT "Sonne, Mond und Sterne"

"Als es nun gar nichts mehr hatte, fielen auf einmal die Sterne vom Himmel, und es waren lauter harte, blanke Taler, und obwohl es sein Hemdlein eben weggegeben hatte, trug es doch ein neues, das von allerfeinstem Linnen war. Das Mädchen sammelte die Taler ein und war reich für sein ganzes Leben."

Lessons 71-73	184
Ein Lied: "La, la, la, la"	
Ein Märchen: "Die Sterntaler"	
Lesson 74	192
Die deutsche Sprache: Wiederholung (Adjektivendungen)	
Lessons 75-79, 81-84	192
Die deutsche Sprache: Etwas Neues (Relativpronomen, Pronomen, Pronominaladverbien)	
Lessons 86-90	216
Zum Lesen: "Hänsel und Gretel" (Ein Märchen) (original Grimm version)	
Lessons 91-95	230
A comprehensive review	

Test Lessons

Lesson 80	206
Lesson 85	216
Lesson 96	237

"Laterne, Laterne, Sonne, Mond und Sterne!"

LESSON 71
Ein Lied: "La, la, la, la"

A. Your objectives: To be able to read the words of the song in Section C out loud with pronunciation and intonation as close to that of your model as possible (and acceptable to your teacher); to be able to explain (English or German, whichever your teacher directs) the meaning of any words or passages; and to be able to do the exercises in Section E without error.

B. How to get there: Listen to the song (recorded) a few times while looking at the text. You should understand most of it readily.

Then go over the text carefully to work out any sentences you don't understand. Check Section D for explanatory notes. Then practice pronouncing and reading the sentences aloud.

Finally, practice the exercises in Section E.

C. What to learn:

*LA, LA, LA, LA

Die Sonne,[1] die am Morgen durch unsre Fenster[2] scheint,
Hat alles Leben in sich[3] vereint.[4]
Sie läßt[5] die Blumen blüh'n
Und wärmt jeden Stein;
Sie läßt die Herzen schlagen,
Und mich läßt sie glücklich sein.
La, la, la, la, la, la, la, la, la, la
la, la, la, la, la, la, la, la,
La, la, la, la, la, la, la, la, la,
La, la, la, la, la, la, la.

Die Sonne, die am Abend die Welt für uns dunkel macht,
Schenkt[6] mir die Träume für eine Nacht.
Und wenn du von mir gehst,
Und ich bin allein,
Dann weiß ich, du kommst wieder
Genau[7] wie der Sonnenschein.
La, la, la, la, ... u.s.w.[8]

*COPYRIGHT © 1968 by ZAFIRO S.A. Ed. Musicales; Southern Music Espanola
German Recordings: Heidi Brühl, Philips, 384529 PF; Geschwister Jacob, CBS 3422; Massiel, Vogue, DV 14736; The Tattoos, Telefunken, U 56012.

Lesson 71

1	sun	5	causes (see Section D)
2	window	6	to give; to present
3	itself	7	just; exactly
4	united	8	= **und so weiter** (which means *et cetera*)

D. Analysis or explanations:

This unit concentrates on relative clauses. Two typical clauses of this type appear in the song:

(line 1) Die Sonne, **die am Morgen durch unsere Fenster scheint,** ...

(line 11) Die Sonne, **die am Abend die Welt für uns dunkel macht,** ...

Die Sonne, die ... would be equivalent to English "The sun, which (or that) ..." The verb is, of course, at the end of the clause, since this is a dependent, or subordinate, clause. Thus the first passage above would read as follows:

"The sun, which shines through our window in the morning, ..."

Although **lassen** basically means *to let,* when it appears with the infinitive of another verb its meaning is closer to *to cause*:

Sie läßt die Blumen blüh'n ...

As has been stated previously, relative pronouns (which are pronouns which *relate* to some previously mentioned noun) are commonly repetitions of some form of the articles of the nouns referred to:

Der Mann, **der** da drüben ist, ist mein Vater.
(*The man who is over there is my father.*)

Das Buch, **das** ich gelesen habe, heißt *Faust*.
(*The book which I read is called* Faust.)

Die Lampe, **die** über dem Tisch hängt, sollst du reparieren.
(*You should repair the lamp which hangs over the table.*)

The verb is at the end of the relative clause, as is usual in dependent clauses (i.e., clauses which depend on the rest of the statement to complete or make clear their meaning).

Also, a relative clause is set off from the main clause by commas. This is *always* the case in German (even though it is not always the case in English).

E. **Practice:** Express the following English sentences in German:

1. The man who is drinking beer is my teacher. Der Mann, der Bier trinkt, ist mein Lehrer.
2. The lady who is coming through the door wants to see Hans. Die Frau, die durch die Tür kommt, will Hans sehen.
3. The girl who was playing the guitar has gone home. Das Mädchen, das Gitarre spielte, ist nach Hause gegangen.
4. Where is the Volkswagen which was over there? Wo ist der Volkswagen, der da drüben war?
5. I like the house which is (stands) next to the tree over there. Mir gefällt das Haus, das neben dem Baum da drüben steht.

F. **Evaluation:** Refer to Section A.

"Und mich läßt sie glücklich sein!"

Lesson 72

Fantasiewelt

LESSON 72
Ein Märchen: Die Sterntaler

A. Your objectives: To be able to read the fairy tale in Section C out loud with acceptable (to your teacher) pronunciation and intonation; and to be able to explain (German or English, whichever your teacher expects) the meaning of any words, phrases, or sentences.

B. How to get there: Follow the usual procedures (see Section B of Lesson 71, for instance).

C. What to learn:

DIE STERNTALER[1]

Es war einmal ein kleines Mädchen, dessen[2] Vater und Mutter gestorben waren. Es war so arm,[3] daß es kein Kämmerchen[4] mehr hatte, um darin zu wohnen, und kein Bettchen mehr besaß,[5] in dem es schlafen konnte. Es hatte auch nur die Kleider, die es auf dem Leib[6] trug, und zu essen besaß es nur ein Stückchen Brot, das ihm
5   ein mit leidiger[7] Mensch geschenkt hatte. Doch es war gut und fromm.[8] Weil es von allen[9] verlassen war, zog[10] es im Vertrauen[11] auf den lieben Gott hinaus auf das Feld. Da begegnete[12] ihm ein armer Mann und sprach: "Ach, gib mir etwas zu

essen, ich bin so hungrig!" Das Mädchen reichte[13] ihm das ganze Brot und sagte: "Gott segne[14] dir's,"[15] und ging danach[16] gleich weiter. Dann kam ein Kind, das jammerte:[17] "Es friert mich so an meinem Kopf, schenke mir etwas, damit[18] ich ihn bedecken[19] kann!" Da nahm das Mädchen seine Mütze[20] ab und gab sie ihm. Nach einer Weile kam wieder ein Kind, das hatte kein Leibchen[21] an und fror. Da gab es ihm seins. Als es weitergegangen war, bat[22] ein anderes Kind um ein Röcklein.[23] Auch das gab es hin.[24] Endlich gelangte[25] es in einen Wald. Es war inzwischen schon dunkel geworden, da begegnete ihm noch ein Kind und bat um ein Hemdlein.[26] Das fromme Mädchen dachte: Es ist so dunkel in der Nacht, da erkennt dich niemand, und du kannst dein Hemd getrost[27] weggeben. Es zog[28] das Hemd aus und verschenkte es auch noch. Als es nun gar nichts mehr hatte, fielen auf einmal die Sterne vom Himmel, und es waren lauter[29] harte, blanke[30] Taler, und obwohl[31] es sein Hemdlein eben weggegeben hatte, trug es doch ein neues, das von allerfeinstem[32] Linnen war. Das Mädchen sammelte[33] die Taler ein und war reich für sein ganzes Leben.

1	**der Taler** was an old German coin ("dollar"); **der Stern** means *star*	15	= **dir es**
2	whose (a relative pronoun)	16	after that
3	poor	17	to cry
4	small room, chamber	18	so that
5	**besitzen** = to possess (the past is **besaß**)	19	to cover
		20	cap, hat
6	body	21	vest
7	compassionate, sympathetic	22	**bitten um** = to ask for, request
8	pious; devout; religious	23	little dress
9	everyone	24	**hingeben** = to give away
10	**hinausziehen** = to go or move out	25	to reach, arrive
11	**im Vertrauen auf** = relying on; having confidence in	26	undershirt
		27	confidently
12	to meet (note that these and most other verbs are in the simple, or narrative, *past* form)	28	**ausziehen** = to take off
		29	nothing but
		30	shiny
		31	although
13	to hand	32	finest of all
14	to bless	33	**einsammeln** = to gather in, collect

D. Analysis or explanations:

NOTES on the text (The text is in the original form. You may not find it quite as easy as previous edited texts.):

line 1   **dessen** is a relative pronoun meaning *whose*

Lesson 72

line 2   **es**, rather than **sie**, is used as the pronoun here (*she* in English) as it was in **Rotkäppchen** because it refers to a **das** word: **das Mädchen**.

line 2   **um darin zu wohnen** is best translated as "in which to live"

line 3   **in dem** is a relative pronoun: "in which"

line 4   notice the relative pronouns

line 5   **doch** = however; nevertheless

line 7   **Feld** = field

line 7   **ihm** is the dative form of **es** (*her* in English here) ("There a poor man met her . . .")

line 8   **ihm** is *him* here

line 9   **gleich weiter** (*immediately away*) meaning she left immediately afterwards

line 10   **Es friert mich so an meinem Kopf**: If translating, it would, of course, be better to say "My head is freezing so" than to give the awkward literal translation "It's freezing me so on my head."

line 11   **ihn** (*it*) refers to her head

line 12   **fror** is the past of **frieren** (*to freeze*)

line 13   **seins** = hers

line 15   **inzwischen** = meanwhile

line 17   **erkennen** = to recognize

line 18   **gar nichts** = nothing at all

line 18   **fielen** = past of **fallen**

line 19   **es waren** = they were

line 20   **trug** is the past of **tragen** (*to wear*)

E. **Practice:** See Section C. There are no exercises in this lesson.

F. **Evaluation:** Refer to Section A and make certain you can perform these objectives well. You are then ready for evaluation.

LESSON 73

A. **Your objectives:** To be able to give oral and written German equivalents for the vocabulary in Section C when given the English as cues; and to be able to answer the German questions in German concerning the story in Lesson 72—all without error.

B. **How to get there:** Memorize the vocabulary in the usual manner. These are some common words from the song and the story in the previous two lessons (some of which you have had earlier).

   Then practice answering the questions in Section E. You should be able to answer them briefly without referring to the answers. If you can't, you should re-read the story in Lesson 72 until you can.

   Then refer to the answers to the questions and practice giving accurate answers in complete sentences.

C. **What to learn:**

sun	die Sonne, -n
window	das Fenster, -
God	(der) Gott, ̈er
sky; heaven	der Himmel, -
cap	die Mütze, -n
exactly	genau
poor	arm
rich	reich
devout, religious	fromm
meanwhile; in between	inzwischen
to give; present	schenken (regular verb)
to hand; reach	reichen (regular verb)
to cover	bedecken (regular verb)
to request	bitten um (bat, gebeten)
to take off; undress	ausziehen (zog, gezogen)

Lesson 73

Heidelberg. Schoßbeleuchtung.

D. **Analysis or explanations:** Refer to Lesson 73.

E. **Practice:** Answer the following questions in German in complete sentences:

1. Wo waren der Vater und die Mutter des kleinen Mädchens?
   Der Vater und die Mutter waren gestorben.
2. Warum hatte das Mädchen kein Kämmerchen mehr?
   Das Mädchen war zu arm.
3. Wieviel Kleidung hatte das Mädchen?
   Es hatte nur die Kleidung, die es auf dem Leib trug.
4. Wer hat dem Mädchen etwas zu essen gegeben?
   Ein mitleidiger Mensch hat dem Mädchen etwas zu essen gegeben.
5. Warum ging das Mädchen auf das Feld?
   Es ging auf das Feld, weil es von allen verlassen war.

6.	Was gab das Mädchen dem hungrigen Mann?	Es gab ihm das ganze Brot.
7.	Wo fror es das erste Kind?	Es fror das erste Kind an seinem Kopf.
8.	Wohin ging das Mädchen, nachdem es das Röcklein weggegeben hatte?	Es ging in einen Wald.
9.	Wie war es im Wald?	Es war dunkel im Wald.
10.	Wer konnte das Mädchen im dunklen Wald erkennen?	Niemand konnte es erkennen.
11.	Was geschah, als das Mädchen das Hemd weggab?	Die Sterne fielen vom Himmel.
12.	Was waren die Sterne, die vom Himmel fielen?	Sie waren Taler.
13.	Nachdem die Sterne gefallen waren, was trug das Mädchen?	Es trug ein neues Hemdlein von Linnen.
14.	Was machte das Mädchen mit den "Sternen?"	Es sammelte sie ein.
15.	Warum wurde das Mädchen reich?	Es wurde reich, weil es so gut und fromm war.

F. Evaluation: Refer to Section A for the objectives you should have reached before you are ready for evaluation.

LESSON 74
Wiederholung: Adjektivendungen

In preparation for extensive work with relative pronouns, which depends on your facility and feeling for case (nominative, accusative, dative, etc.), you will repeat Lesson 26. Be certain to study Section D of that lesson thoroughly again too!

LESSON 75
Etwas Neues: Relativpronomen
(Relative Pronouns)

A. Your objectives: To be able to do the drills in Section E fluently and without error, both orally and written.

Lesson 75

B. How to get there: Make certain you know the forms of **der, die,** and **das** as relative pronouns in the four cases listed in Section C. Study Section D very carefully. Then practice Section E with the recordings. Intonation is important for proper oral expression involving relative clauses.

C. What to learn: Go over the following forms until you can give the accusative, dative, and genitive forms of each article when referring only to the nominative form (and covering up the rest).

NOMINATIVE	ACCUSATIVE	DATIVE	GENITIVE
(subject)	(object)	(other)	(possessive)
der	den	dem	dessen (*whose*)
das	(das)	(dem)	(dessen) (*whose*)
die	(die)	der	deren (*whose*)

D. Analysis or explanations:
"Die Sonne, **die** am Morgen durch unsre Fenster scheint, ..."
"Es war einmal ein kleines Kind, **dessen** Vater und Mutter ..."
"... und kein Bettchen besaß, in **dem** es schlafen konnte ..."
"... ein neues, **das** von allerfeinstem Linnen war."

"Es war einmal ..."

As you should be able to recognize by now, the words in boldface above are relative pronouns. In German relative pronouns are essentially repetitions of the **der, die, das** of the word to which they refer.

But the *form* in which they appear depends on the function of the pronoun *in the clause in which it appears*. The relative pronoun may refer to a **der** word, yet have four different forms because it is used in four different ways in the relative clause. For example:

Der Mann, **der** hier war, ist mein Vater.	(subject)
Der Mann, **den** ich gestern sah, ging in den Park.	(object)
Der Mann, **dem** wir das Geld gaben, ist sehr arm.	("to whom")
Der Mann, **dessen** Frau ich kenne, arbeitet nicht.	("whose")

The English equivalents would be

The man *who* . . .
The man *whom* . . .
The man *to whom* . . .
The man *whose* . . .

In English, if the thing referred to is not a person, the relative pronoun is usually *which* (or *that*), no matter what the function. In German we still use a form of **der, das,** or **die**:

Der Wagen, mit **dem** er fährt, . . .
Die Tasse, **die** er zerbrochen hatte, . . .
Das Buch, **das** auf dem Tisch liegt, . . .

E. Practice:

Substitute the given nouns in the sentences. Don't forget to change the relative pronouns correspondingly.

1. NOMINATIVE (the relative pronouns being the *subjects* in the clauses in which they appear):

Der Mann, der da drüben ist, ist sehr alt.

a.	das Buch	Das Buch, das da drüben ist, ist sehr alt.
b.	die Lampe	Die Lampe, die da drüben ist, ist sehr alt.
c.	der Drachen	Der Drachen, der da drüben ist, ist sehr alt.
d.	die Katze	Die Katze, die da drüben ist, ist sehr alt.
e.	das Haus	Das Haus, das da drüben ist, ist sehr alt.

Lesson 75   195

"Das Fenster,
vor dem wir stehen, ..."

2. ACCUSATIVE (the relative pronouns being the objects or "targets" of the verbs in the clauses):

Das Rad, das ich gestern kaufte, war nicht teuer.

a. der Wagen   Der Wagen, den ich gestern kaufte, war nicht teuer.
b. die Mütze   Die Mütze, die ich gestern kaufte, war nicht teuer.
c. das Glas   Das Glas, das ich gestern kaufte, war nicht teuer.
e. Die Hütte   Die Hütte, die ich gestern kaufte, war nicht teuer.

3. DATIVE (the relative pronouns showing "where at" or "to whom"):

Der Baum, vor dem wir stehen, ist sehr alt.

a. das Haus   Das Haus, vor dem wir stehen, ist sehr alt.
b. die Stube   Die Stube, vor der wir stehen, ist sehr alt.
c. der Bahnhof   Der Bahnhof, vor dem wir stehen, ist sehr alt.
d. die Kirche   Die Kirche, vor der wir stehen, ist sehr alt.
e. das Fenster   Das Fenster, vor dem wir stehen, ist sehr alt.

4. GENITIVE (the relative pronoun indicates a relationship of "possession," of "belonging to"):

Die Frau, deren Freund weg ist, wartet auf ihn.

    a. der Mann   Der Mann, dessen Freund weg ist, wartet auf ihn.
    b. das Mädchen   Das Mädchen, dessen Freund weg ist, wartet auf ihn.
    c. die Tochter   Die Tochter, deren Freund weg ist, wartet auf ihn.
    d. der Sohn   Der Sohn, dessen Freund weg ist, wartet auf ihn.
    e. die Lehrerin   Die Lehrerin, deren Freund weg ist, wartet auf ihn.

F. Evaluation: Refer to Section A.

LESSON 76

A. Your objectives: To be able to do the exercises in Section E in German without error.

B. How to get there: Study Section D carefully before attempting the exercises in Section E.

C. What to learn: No new material.

D. Analysis or explanations: It is important to note that the relative pronoun is not a mere repetition of the article as it appears in the antecedent. This should have become clear to you in the last lesson. A **der** word might appear in any of *four* forms (**der, dem, den, dessen**), depending on its function in the relative clause.

It is also important to realize that the antecedent might be in a form other than the nominative:

    Ich sehe **den** Mann, **der** das gemacht hat.
    Ich spreche mit **dem** Mann, **den** du gesehen hast.

Therefore, the problem in a relative clause is not only the one of giving the proper form of a prior **der, die,** or **das** word, but also of recognizing whether this antecedent is, in its basic (or nominative) form, a **der, die,** or **das** word.

In doing the following exercises you will need to know the plural forms of the relative pronouns too, since they are

Lesson 76

required in a few of the exercises. You may refer to the following chart while doing the exercises, although by the end of your practice you should know them.

Nominative:	die
Accusative:	die
Dative:	denen
Genitive:	deren

E. Practice: Which forms of the relative pronouns would correctly complete each of the following sentences in German? (The answers appear *after* this practice section.)

1. Where is the man who was driving my car?
   Wo ist der Mann, _____ meinen Wagen fuhr?
2. The child whom we found was deep in the forest.
   Das Kind, _____ wir gefunden haben, war tief im Wald.
3. Here is the room in which I saw the sick old lady.
   Hier ist die Stube, in _____ ich die kranke alte Frau sah.
4. The people whose homes are here are rich.
   Die Leute, _____ Häuser hier stehen, sind reich.
5. He knows the man who came through this door.
   Er kennt den Mann, _____ durch diese Tür gekommen ist.
6. The floor onto which he fell was especially hard.
   Der Boden, auf _____ er gefallen ist, war besonders hart.
7. I love the last picture which Picasso painted.
   Ich liebe das letzte Bild, _____ Picasso gemalt hat.
8. The picture in which you see the green horse is not by him.
   Das Bild, in _____ du das grüne Pferd siehst, ist nicht von ihm.
9. I hate the streetcar whose bell keeps going "ding-a-ling."
   Ich hasse die Straßenbahn, _____ Klingel immer "tingel-tangel" macht.
10. Did she write the letters that are in his pocket?
    Hat sie die Briefe geschrieben, _____ in seiner Tasche sind?
11. There is the dog I gave a bone to (to whom I gave a bone).
    Da ist der Hund, _____ ich einen Knochen gegeben habe.
12. We sang the song whose melody goes like this: . . .
    Wir haben das Lied gesungen, _____ Melodie so geht: . . .
13. You ought to hang it on the tree that is over there.
    Sie sollen es an den Baum hängen, _____ da drüben ist.
14. The wolves which the hunter killed were very wild.
    Die Wölfe, _____ der Jäger getötet hat, waren sehr wild.

15. The mountain on whose peak the girl was sitting is called the Lorelei.
    Der Berg, auf _____ Gipfel das Mädchen saß, heißt die Lorelei.
16. That is the movie house that shows the best films.
    Das ist das Kino, _____ die besten Filme zeigt.
17. In this book I have the flower which I was wearing at the dance.
    In diesem Buch habe ich die Blume, _____ ich auf den Tanz trug.
18.-20. The dragon which he saw and whose head he cut off, and before which he is now standing, was about to kill him.
    Der Drachen, _____ er gesehen hat und _____ Kopf er abgeschnitten hat und vor _____ er jetzt steht, wollte ihn töten.

1.	der	6.	den	11.	dem	16.	das
2.	das	7.	das	12.	dessen	17.	die
3.	der	8.	dem	13.	der	18.	den
4.	deren	9.	deren	14.	die	19.	dessen
5.	der	10.	die	15.	dessen	20.	dem

F. Evaluation: You will be asked to read the German sentences in Section E aloud, filling in the proper relative pronouns as you read along. You may be asked to write them also.

LESSON 77

A. Your objectives: To be able to do the drills in Section E fluently and without error.

B. How to get there: Follow the normal procedure for lessons of this type.

C. What to learn: No new material.

D. Analysis or explanations: See Lesson 76, Section D.

E. Practice: Read the following German sentences out loud, filling in the blanks with the proper relative pronouns in German. When you can do this orally, make certain you can spell the relative pronouns also. (The answers follow exercise 18.)

1. Der Mann, _____ hier wohnt, arbeitet mit meinem Vater.
2. Hier ist das Buch, _____ ich gelesen habe.
3. Die alte Frau, hinter _____ er steht, ist seine Mutter.
4. Der Jäger, _____ wir jetzt sehen können, hat den Wolf.
5. Wo ist die Tasse, _____ er zerbrochen hat?
6. Das Mädchen, _____ Vater Autos verkauft, heißt Gisela.
7. Siehst du den Hund, _____ wir etwas zu essen gegeben haben?
8. Die Männer, _____ Musik spielen, sind Brüder.
9. Sind diese die Frauen, _____ du gehört hast?
10. Er hat einen Sohn, _____ Haus neben meinem Haus steht.
11. Die kleine Katze, _____ Haare schwarz sind, ist am schönsten.
12. Die Mutter, _____ eben in die Schule kommt, ist sehr böse.
13. Ich liebe das Kind, _____ so schön singt.
14. Siehst du das Sofa, unter _____ die Katze schläft?
15. Da sind die Soldaten, _____ wir Brot geben sollen.
16. Wir wollen die Tische reparieren, _____ Beine kaputt sind.
17. Hier ist das Fenster, in _____ die Katze immer schläft.
18. Hier ist das Fenster, durch _____ die Katze immer springt.

ANTWORTEN:
1. der   7. dem   13. das
2. das   8. die   14. dem
3. der   9. die   15. denen
4. den   10. dessen   16. deren
5. die   11. deren   17. dem
6. dessen   12. die   18. das

F. **Evaluation:** Refer to Sections A and E.

LESSON 78

A. **Your objectives:** To be able to do the exercises in Section E fluently and without error according to the directions given there.

B. **How to get there:** Study Section D first. Use the recordings!

C. **What to learn:** No new material.

D. **Analysis or explanations:**

Although the position of a relative clause may vary under certain conditions, we shall, at this point, standardize its position: *place the relative clause immediately after its antecedent* unless the only sentence element in the main clause following the antecedent is the verb or part of it.

EXAMPLES:

1. Der Mann geht jetzt nach Hause. **Er stand lange an der Ecke.**
   Der Mann, **der lange an der Ecke stand,** geht jetzt nach Hause.

(Don't forget that the verb comes at the end of the relative clause!)

2. Sie hat den Mann gesehen. **Er steht an der Ecke.**
   Sie hat den Mann gesehen, **der an der Ecke steht.**

(It would be highly unusual to delay **gesehen** until the end of the entire sentence.)

"Der Mann, der an der Ecke steht, ..."

Lesson 78

E. **Practice:** Combine the following sentences, making the second sentence a relative clause. Refer to the examples in Section D. (Intonation is important, so practice with the recordings.)

1. Die Blume blüht auch im Winter. Die Blume wächst (*grows*) auf dem Grab.
2. Der Krieg beginnt schon. Die Männer sollen in dem Krieg kämpfen.
3. Das Blatt sieht krank aus. Es fällt vom Baum.
4. Der Soldat war in der Infantrie. Er kommt jetzt nach Hause.
5. Der Friseur hat meine Haare geschnitten. Du siehst ihn da drüben.
6. Die Suppe schmeckt gut. Du hast sie gekocht.
7. Das Bild gefällt mir. Mutter hat es gekauft.
8. Die Straßenbahn war gelb. Fischer fuhr mit der Straßenbahn.
9. Der Arbeiter läuft davon. Sie gab ihm das Geld.
10. Das Bett ist weich. Wir schlafen in dem Bett.
11. Der Schaffner nimmt unser Geld. Sein Gesicht hat zehn-tausend Falten.
12. Wohin fährt die gelbe Straßenbahn? Ihre Klingel macht "tingel-tangel."

ANTWORTEN:

1. Die Blume, die auf dem Grab wächst, blüht auch im Winter.
2. Der Krieg, in dem die Männer kämpfen sollen, beginnt schon.
3. Das Blatt, das vom Baum fällt, sieht krank aus.
4. Der Soldat, der in der Infantrie war, kommt jetzt nach Hause.
5. Der Friseur, den du da drüben siehst, hat meine Haare geschnitten.
6. Die Suppe, die du gekocht hast, schmeckt gut.
7. Das Bild, das Mutter gekauft hat, gefällt mir.
8. Die Straßenbahn, mit der Fischer fuhr, war gelb.
9. Der Arbeiter, dem sie das Geld gab, läuft davon.
10. Das Bett, in dem wir schlafen, ist weich.
11. Der Schaffner, dessen Gesicht zehntausend Falten hat, nimmt unser Geld.
12. Wohin fährt die gelbe Straßenbahn, deren Klingel "tingel-tangel" macht?

F. **Evaluation:** When you can combine these sentences accurately and fluently, and with the intonation you hear on the recordings, you are ready for evaluation.

"..., deren Klingel 'tingel-tangel' macht."

LESSON 79

A. Your objectives: To be able to do the exercises in Section E (based on the forms in Section C) in German fluently and without error—using only the English sentences as cues.

B. How to get there: First, read Section D carefully. Then make certain you know the *forms* in Section C.
Finally, practice the exercises in Section E.

C. What to learn:

	FORMS OF **wer** (*who*)	PLURALS OF RELATIVES
Nominative:	wer	die
Accusative:	wen	die
Dative:	wem	denen
Genitive:	wessen	deren

D. Analysis or explanations:

Some relative clauses have no *stated antecedent*, or if there is one, it is not in a form from which we can determine its gender. When a situation exists where we can't point to a **der**, **die**, or **das** antecedent, we use a form of **wer** (see Section C), or we use **was**. We use **wer** if we are referring to a *person*, and **was** if referring to a *thing*.

In learning the forms of **wer**, note that they parallel the **der** forms exactly:

der	wer
den	wen
dem	wem
dessen	wessen

In learning the plural forms, note that they parallel the plural forms we have already learned, but with the addition of endings in two cases. (The plural forms were introduced in Lesson 76. Memorize them now if you haven't done so yet.)

Nominative:	die	die
Accusative:	die	die
Dative:	den	denen
Genitive:	(der)	deren

EXAMPLES:

1. Relative pronouns with no definite antecedent:

   a. Ich gebe ihm, **was** er haben will.
      (*I'll give him what he wants to have.*)
   b. Weißt du, **was** das ist?
      (*Do you know what that is?*)
   c. Es gibt fast nichts, **was** er essen kann.
      (*There is almost nothing that he can eat.*)
   d. Ich sehe, **wer** jetzt kommt.
      (*I see who is coming now.*)
   e. Er will wissen, **wen** wir besuchen wollen.
      (*He wants to know whom we want to visit.*)
   f. Er sagt nicht, **wem** er den Ring kauft.
      (*He's not saying for whom he's buying the ring.*)
   g. Hat er vergessen, **wessen** Auto er fährt?
      (*Has he forgotten whose car he's driving?*)

2. The plural forms of the relative pronouns:

   a. Die Mädchen, **die** hier waren, sind jetzt weg.
      (*The girls who were here are now gone.*)
   b. Wo sind die Soldaten, **deren** Mädels auf sie warten?
      (*Where are the soldiers whose girl friends are waiting for them?*)
   c. Die Autos, mit **denen** sie hierher gefahren sind, stehen jetzt auf dem Parkplatz.
      (*The cars in which they drove here are in the parking lot now.*)

E. Practice: Express the following English sentences in German. (Use the recordings to assure proper intonation.)

1. Have you seen what Gisela has?
2. We can eat what's on the table.
3. He couldn't see who was coming into the room.
4. Who knows who took the money?
5. Do they know whom you found in the woods?
6. It isn't very clear (**klar**) to whom he gave the gun.
7. Have you-all forgotten whose car that is?
8. I don't know what he's doing.
9. I can't hear with whom she's speaking.
10. We don't understand whose child they want to take.
11. Who are the men who are coming around the corner?
12. Here are the trees in which the birds live.

Lesson 79

"Ich weiß nicht, was er macht."

13. The girls whose books I found have not come back (**zurückkommen**).
14. The flowers which you picked are very beautiful.

ANTWORTEN:
1. Hast du gesehen, was Gisela hat?
2. Wir können essen, was auf dem Tisch steht.
3. Er konnte nicht sehen, wer ins Zimmer kam.
4. Wer weiß, wer das Geld genommen hat?
5. Wissen sie, wen du im Wald gefunden hast?
6. Es ist nicht sehr klar, wem er das Gewehr gegeben hat.
7. Habt ihr vergessen, wessen Auto das ist?
8. Ich weiß nicht, was er macht.
9. Ich kann nicht hören, mit wem sie spricht.
10. Wir verstehen nicht, wessen Kind sie nehmen wollen.
11. Wer sind die Männer, die um die Ecke kommen?
12. Hier sind die Bäume, in denen die Vögel wohnen.
13. Die Mädchen, dessen Bücher ich gefunden habe, sind nicht zurückgekommen.
14. Die Blumen, die du gepflückt hast, sind sehr schön.

F. Evaluation: Refer to Section A.

LESSON 80
Review Self-Test (Lessons 75-79)

A. Your objectives: To be able to do the Self-Test in Section E without error; and to pass the test referred to in Section F with at least 90% accuracy.

B. How to get there: Review any exercises or explanations in Lessons 75-79 you find necessary. If you feel you need to spend time to study or practice any of them, do so.

Then practice Section E. If you make no more than 3 or 4 errors, analyze why you are having difficulty and do the sentences correctly. (Several times!) Then you are ready to do the test which accompanies this lesson (see Section F).

If you make more than 4 errors in Section E, you need to review Lessons 75-79 more thoroughly before attempting the test.

C. What to learn: Review.

D. Analysis or explanations: Review.

E. Practice:

REVIEW SELF-TEST

Say or/and write the following sentences in German, filling in the missing relative pronouns as you go:

1. Sie liebt den Mann, _____ in München wohnt.
2. Die Blumen, _____ die Mädchen pflückten, waren alle rot.
3. Wir sehen eine Frau, _____ schnell über die Straße läuft.
4. Wo ist der Soldat, _____ Freund gestorben ist?
5. Das ist ein schönes Auto, _____ du gekauft hast.
6. Niemand hat mir gesagt, _____ heute abend zur Party kommt.
7. Wir stehen in dem Garten, in _____ die schönsten Rosen blühen.
8. Da kommt die gelbe Straßenbahn, mit _____ Fischer fahren soll.
9. Das Bein, _____ er gebrochen hat, ist jetzt ganz gesund.
10. Die Hunde, _____ Herr weg war, wollten uns beißen.
11. Du kannst alles haben, _____ du hier findest.
12. Wo wohnen die Kinder, _____ ihr die Geschenke geben wollt?
13. Das Bett, über _____ die Lampe hängt, ist besonders schön.
14. Er schmiedete ein Schwert, _____ Klinge (*blade*) sehr scharf war.

Lesson 80

15. Ich hatte Angst vor dem Drachen, _____ Siegfried tötete.
16. Warum will Gisela wissen, _____ Hans das Hemd gab?
17. Sehen Sie nicht, _____ Körper (*body*) vor uns liegt?
18. Die Kohle, _____ er bringt, brennt besonders langsam.
19. Sie sammelte die Taler ein, _____ vom Himmel fielen.
20. Die Geschichte, _____ Mutter uns erzählte, war interessant.
21. Mein Gott! Habt ihr gehört, _____ sie jetzt liebt?!
22. Gib mir die Rose, _____ Blätter so frisch und grün sind!
23. Das Blatt, _____ vom Baum fiel, fiel auf Siegfrieds Schulter.
24. Sie haben so viel, _____ wir lesen könnten.
25. Du hättest sehen können, hinter _____ er stand.
26. Das ist ein dunkler Wald, durch _____ er geht.
27. & 28. Wir müssen das Haus finden, in _____ er gegangen ist und in _____ er jetzt bleibt.
29. & 30. Wie soll ich wissen, _____ sie da getroffen hat und mit _____ sie so lange gesprochen hat?

F. Evaluation: Read the evaluation instructions in Section B again.
   Check your performance in Section E by comparing your answers with those in the key, or by having your teacher check you (whichever your teacher directs).
   When you can do Section E without error, you are ready to be tested.

LESSON 81

A. Your objectives: To be able to use the proper pronouns for German words as demonstrated by your ability to do the exercises in Section E fluently and with no errors.

B. How to get there: Study Section D carefully; then do the exercises in Section E until you can do them readily and accurately.

C. What to learn: No new forms or vocabulary.

D. Analysis or explanations: We learned the German pronoun forms in *Deutsch: Kernstufe* and reviewed them earlier in this text. Let us focus now on the third person pronouns **er, sie,** and **es** for the singular forms and **sie** for the plural. These third person pronouns present a problem to English-speaking people. We are not used to having to assign "gender" to *things*. In English the pronoun "it" is usually sufficient when we refer to *things,* rather than to people. In German our "it" may be **er, sie,** or **es** or other forms of these pronouns. Which pronoun and which form to use depends on whether the noun referred to was a **der, die,** or **das** noun, and on how it functions in the sentence.

Therefore we shall have to get out of our "English-conditioned" habit of thinking of **er, sie, es,** etc., as biologically determined pronouns such as "he," "she," "it," etc. For example:

> **Das Haus** ist nicht weiß; **es** ist gelb.
> Wo ist **der Spiegel**? **Er** ist hinter der Tür.
> **Der Zug** soll schon hier sein, aber ich sehe **ihn** nicht.
> **Die Musik** ist laut, aber **sie** ist auch schön.

The plural forms don't present any difficulty. Even in English we represent plural nouns with "they" or "them," whether they are persons or not. It is only in English in the singular that we have a different pattern from the German. Since things don't normally have gender in English, we are used to applying only one pronoun, "it," to all *things.* With persons we use "he" or "she." So we shall need to practice the German patterns until we have a feeling for referring to

Lesson 81

nouns with different pronouns, whether they are persons or not.

Following is a summary of the third person pronoun forms in German. (The dative forms are not used very often. Instead we use the compounds described in Lesson 82 whenever possible.)

	NOMINATIVE	ACCUSATIVE *Target*	DATIVE *Other*
der words:	er	ihn	ihm
das words:	es	es	ihm
die words:	sie	sie	ihr
plurals:	sie	sie	ihnen

E. **Practice:** Give German equivalents of the following English sentences:

1. The sun (**die Sonne**) is shining and it is very hot.
2. The moon (**der Mond**) is shining too, but it isn't hot.
3. I have hit (**treffen**) the window and broken it.
4. The dress is beautiful, but it is expensive.
5. I had the comb (**der Kamm**), but I can't find it now.
6. I have read the story, and it is really beautiful.
7. If I had a car (**der Wagen**) I would drive it.
8. He's buying the shirt (**das Hemd**) because he needs it.
9. They don't live in the room (**die Stube**) because it is too small.
10. The mirror which I want is never here when I want it.

ANTWORTEN:
1. Die Sonne scheint, und sie ist sehr heiß.
2. Der Mond scheint auch, aber er ist nicht heiß.
3. Ich habe das Fenster getroffen und es zerschlagen.
4. Das Kleid ist schön, aber es ist teuer.
5. Ich habe den Kamm gehabt, aber ich kann ihn jetzt nicht finden.
6. Ich habe die Geschichte gelesen, und sie ist wirklich schön.
7. Wenn ich einen Wagen hätte, würde ich ihn fahren.
8. Er kauft das Hemd, weil er es braucht.
9. Sie wohnen nicht in der Stube, weil sie zu klein ist.
10. Der Spiegel, den ich haben will, ist nie hier, wenn ich ihn haben will.

F. **Evaluation:** Refer to Section A.

LESSON 82

A. Your objectives: To be able to say and write the German prepositions when given the English equivalents as cues (Section C); to be able to give the "**da**-compound" form, in German, of each preposition which can form one; and to be able to do the exercises in Section E as directed—all without error.

B. How to get there: First, study Section D carefully. Then memorize any prepositions in Section C which you don't already know.

Then practice giving the **da**-compounds for each preposition while looking at only the English cues.

Finally, practice expressing the italicized English passages in Section E in German until you can do them readily without error.

C. What to learn: Be certain you know all the following prepositions. You have had most of them before. (Mark lightly any which you don't know; then concentrate on learning these.)

GROUP A		GROUP B	
to, at, on	an+	through	durch+
upon, on, onto	auf+	for	für+
behind	hinter+	against, toward	gegen+
in, into	in+	without	ohne
near, next to	neben+	around	um+
over, above	über+		
below, under	unter+		
in front of, before	vor+		
between	zwischen+		

GROUP C	
out of	aus+
except for, besides	außer
at (see a dictionary)	bei+
with	mit+
after; to (a city, country, etc.)	nach+
since	seit
from	von+
to	zu+
opposite, across from	gegenüber

+These prepositions can form compounds with **da** and **wo**.

Lesson 82

D. Analysis or explanations:

PREPOSITIONS

Up to now we have determined the case (dative or accusative) of nouns or pronouns after prepositions by whether or not they were the "target" in the sentence. We can still do this—with very few exceptions—but it might be more convenient for you to use another approach with some of the pronouns.

The group C prepositions above *all* "govern" the dative case—always!

The group B prepositions govern the accusative—*always*!

(There is a group of prepositions requiring the genitive forms. We shall deal with them and the genitive later.)

Objects of the group A prepositions can go either way, dative or accusative. We still have to determine or feel whether the question **wo** (*where at*) or **wohin** (*where to*, "target") is being answered.

It might be well to review the meanings of these "doubtful" (as to case governed) prepositions:

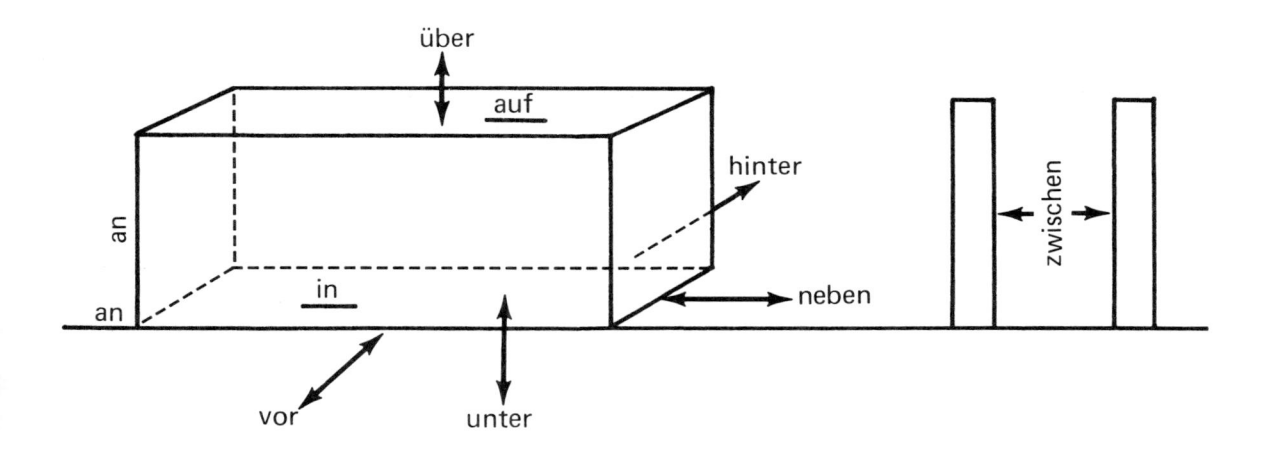

COMPOUNDS WITH da AND wo

Compounds formed with the adverb "there" in English do not occur very frequently any more. Instead of "thereunder" we now prefer "under it," "under that," "under them," or "under there," etc. We sometimes still find such compounds as "therefrom," "therein," "thereinto," "thereof," "thereon," etc., in written texts or in dictionaries; but except for a few words, such as "therefore," "thereabouts," etc., we use or come across them infrequently, except, perhaps, in certain formal or legal documents.

In German these compounds are still common, because it is simpler to use them than not. We could have the forms **ihn, es, sie, ihm, ihr,** and **ihnen** after such a preposition as **unter,** and we commonly do use all these forms if we are referring to a person, but when we are referring to a *thing* we can avoid such choices of the proper pronoun and its case. We simply use **darunter,** no matter what the gender or function of the pronoun after the preposition is.

All the prepositions in Section C with a + mark *can* combine with **da.** *If the preposition begins with a vowel,* an "**r**" is used between the **da** and the preposition. Some examples of these compounds are as follows:

dabei	danach	daran
dafür	davon	darauf
dagegen	davor	darin
dahinter	dazu	darüber
damit	dazwischen	darunter

Notice the connecting "**r**" in the last column of words. (These **da**-compounds with the connecting "**r**" are often contracted: **dran, drauf, drin, drum,** etc.)

If such a compound exists in a question, it occurs as a **wo**-compound. (A **wo**-compound can occur under other circumstances too. We shall practice them later, since they are far down on the priority list of what you need to function adequately in German.)

Here are some examples of **da** and **wo** compounded with prepositions in sentences:

Wo ist das Messer? Ich schneide **damit** (*with it*).
Ich sehe den Tisch schon, aber ich sehe nichts **darauf.**
Die Tür ist zu; was kann **dahinter** (*behind it*) sein?

Womit (*with what*) schneidet er? Mit dem neuen Messer.
Worauf (*on what*) schläft das Kind? **Darauf!** (*On that!*)
Wovon hat er gesprochen? (*What was he talking about?*)

Lesson 82   213

E. Practice: Express the italicized parts in German:

I can't find my little car anywhere. *Are you playing with it?*[1] No? *What are you playing with?*[2] I looked in my closet, *but it is not in there.*[3] The toy shelf is empty. *It can't be on that.*[4] *What did you find your car in?*[5] No, I didn't look under the stove. *It can't be under that!*[6] *But maybe it is behind it.*[7] No, not there either. *What was I playing in front of?*[8] The TV and the hi-fi. *Maybe it's* (stecken) *in between them.*[9] Oh, you have found it? *Under what?!*[10]

ANTWORTEN:
1. Spielst du damit?
2. Womit spielst du?
3. aber es ist nicht darin (drin).
4. Es kann nicht darauf (drauf) sein.
5. Worin hast du dein Auto gefunden?
6. Es kann nicht darunter sein!
7. Aber vielleicht ist es dahinter.
8. Wovor spielte ich?
9. Vielleicht steckt es dazwischen.
10. Worunter?!

F. Evaluation: See Section A.

Worüber sprechen sie?

LESSONS 83 and 84
Review Self-Test (Lessons 71-82)

A. Your objectives: To be able to do the Self-Test in Section E as directed in each part—with at least 90% accuracy.

B. How to get there: Look over Lessons 71-82. Stop to practice any exercises you feel you may have forgotten to some degree. When you feel confident that you will be able to score 90% or better, do the test in Section E.

C. What to learn: Review.

D. Analysis or explanations: Review.

E. Practice:

SELF-TEST

1. Give English equivalents of the following German words:

   a. die Sonne
   b. das Fenster
   c. schenken
   d. genau
   e. u.s.w.
   f. arm
   g. fromm
   h. begegnen
   i. reichen
   j. der Stern
   k. sammeln
   l. blank
   m. gelangen
   n. frieren
   o. besitzen
   p. jammern
   q. der Kopf
   r. bedecken
   s. die Mütze
   t. das Hemd

2. Read the following sentences aloud, filling in the blanks with the proper relative pronouns (or write them, if so requested). Do this in German, of course. You will be using the proper forms of **der, die, das** or **wer** or **was**:

   a. Wo kann ich das Buch finden, _____ du gelesen hast?
   b. Der Wagen, _____ ich fahre, fährt sehr schnell.
   c. Ist das nicht die Ecke, _____ er meint?
   d. Wir waren in der Stube, _____ neben der Küche ist.
   e. Warum sitzt er in dem Zimmer, _____ Fenster alle kaputt sind?
   f. Der See, in _____ sie schwimmen, ist besonders kalt.
   g. Ich verstehe nicht, _____ das Auto hätte nehmen können.
   h. Hat er nicht gesagt, _____ Gitarre er gespielt hätte?
   i. Wer soll den Fußball bringen, mit _____ wir spielen werden?
   j. Was machen die Leute, _____ Häuser gebrannt sind?
   k. Der Polizist hatte mit der Frau gesprochen, _____ Mann jetzt tot ist.

Lessons 83 and 84

l. Der Spiegel war teuer, _____ Glas du zerbrochen hast.
m. Sagst du mir bald, _____ du zu Weihnachten haben willst?
n. Ich habe den Sport gern, _____ "baseball" heißt.
o. Sag mir, wo die Blumen sind, _____ auf den Gräbern waren.
p. Das Haus, in _____ Großmutter wohnt, steht im Wald.
q. Hier wohnt die arme Familie, _____ wir Geschenke geben.
r. Sie erzählt gerade, von _____ sie geträumt hat.
s. Die Gammler, _____ er die Gitarre geliehen hat, sind weg!
t. Siegfried konnte nicht wissen, _____ er in der Dunkelheit getötet hatte.
u. Wir dürfen in das Boot steigen, _____ hier liegt.
v. Die Eltern kommen, _____ uns gesehen haben.
w. Der Baum, auf _____ er gestiegen ist
x. und _____ Früchte er gegessen hat
y. und aus _____ er dann gefallen ist, steht in Frau Schmidts Garten!

3. Express in German:

a. The streetcar is over there. It is yellow.
b. I ate the green salad. It was very good.
c. I bought the book and I have read it.
d. Books are expensive when you buy them.
e. The hunter sees the wolf and shoots it.

4. Express the following in German, using compounds of **da** or **wo** where possible:

a. There is the house. A Volkswagen is standing in front of it.
b. He found the ball and he's playing with it.
c. If you want it, you must pay for it.
d. What are you sitting on?
e. What are you writing with? (With what...?)
f. The train is arriving (**ankommen**). Three people are getting (**steigen**) out of it.
g. I know (**kennen**) the house. One tree stands next to it and two trees stand behind it.

F. **Evaluation:** See Section A. If you scored below 90%, review; then repeat the test.

LESSON 85
Test

A.	Your objectives:	To pass the final test on Lessons 71-82 with a score of at least 90%.
B.	How to get there:	Use your performance on the Self-Test in Lessons 83 and 84 as a guide to reviewing and practicing whatever is necessary.
C.	What to learn:	Review.
D.	Analysis or explanations:	Review.
E.	Practice:	See Section B.
F.	Evaluation:	If you did 90% or better on the previous Self-Test, or you have reviewed and practiced carefully any types of exercises you missed, you should be ready to take the test.

LESSON 86
Ein Märchen: Hänsel und Gretel

A.	Your objectives:	To be able to read and understand the first installment of *Hänsel und Gretel* in German, as demonstrated by your ability (1) to read it out loud with acceptable (to your teacher) pronunciation and intonation; (2) to explain any word, phrase, or sentence in English (or German, if your teacher so directs); and (3) to answer German questions in German about the story (Section E).
B.	How to get there:	Listen to the recorded version while reading the text. You should be able to follow the main story line, at least, while doing this—especially since you are undoubtedly familiar with the story already. Then study the text more carefully, referring to notes in Section D or vocabulary (following the text) as necessary.

Lesson 86

When you can read the story, understanding it completely without referring to any notes, you should be ready to answer the questions in Section E.

Finally, using the recordings, practice reading the story out loud.

"Vor einem großen Walde wohnte . . ."

C. **What to learn:**

HÄNSEL UND GRETEL

Vor einem großen Walde wohnte ein armer Holzhacker,[1] der hatte nichts zu beißen und zu brechen und verdiente[2] kaum[3] das tägliche Brot für seine Frau und seine beiden Kinder Hänsel und Gretel. Einmal konnte er auch das nicht mehr schaffen[4] und wußte sich in seiner Not[5] nicht zu helfen. Wenn er abends sich vor Sorge[6] in
5 seinem Bett herumwälzte,[7] sagte seine Frau zu ihm: "Höre, Mann, morgen früh nimmst du die beiden Kinder, gibst jedem noch ein Stückchen Brot und führst[8] sie

in den Wald hinaus. In der Mitte, wo er am dichtesten[9] ist, mach ihnen ein Feuer[10] an und geh dann weg und laß sie dort; wir können sie nicht mehr ernähren!"[11]

10 "Nein, Frau," sagte der Mann, "das kann ich nicht über mein Herz[12] bringen, meine eigenen[13] Kinder zu den wilden Tieren zu führen, die sie bald im Wald zerreißen[14] würden!"

"Wenn du das nicht tust," sprach die Frau wieder, "müssen wir alle miteinander Hungers sterben!" Sie ließ ihm keine Ruhe,[15] bis er einwilligte.[16]

15 Die beiden Kinder waren vor Hunger auch noch wach[17] und hatten alles gehört, was die Mutter zum Vater gesagt hatte. Gretel dachte, nun sei es um sie geschehen,[18] und fing an, erbärmlich[19] zu weinen; doch Hänsel sprach: "Sei still, Gretel, und gräm[20] dich nicht, ich will uns helfen." Damit stand er auf, zog sein Röcklein an, öffnete die Tür und schlich[21] hinaus. Der Mond schien hell, und die weißen Kieselsteine[22] glänzten[23] wie lauter Silbermünzen.[24] Hänsel bückte[25] sich

20 und füllte sich sein ganzes Rocktäschlein[26] damit, soviel nur hineingingen, dann sprang er zurück ins Haus: "Tröste[27] dich, Gretel, und schlaf nur ruhig!"[28] sagte er zu seinem Schwesterchen, legte sich wieder ins Bett und schlief ein.

Morgens früh, ehe[29] die Sonne aufgegangen war, kam die Mutter und weckte[30] sie beide: "Steht auf, Kinder, wir wollen in den Wald gehen; da habt ihr

25 jedes ein Stücklein Brot. Teilt es euch gut ein[31] und hebt[32] euch etwas für den Mittag auf!" Gretel nahm das Brot unter die Schürze, weil Hänsel die Steine in der Tasche hatte, dann machten sie sich auf den Weg in den Wald hinein. Als sie ein Weilchen gegangen waren, stand Hänsel still und guckte nach dem Haus zurück, bald darauf wieder und immer wieder. Der Vater sprach: "Hänsel, was guckst du zurück

30 und hältst dich auf,[33] gib acht[34] und marschier[35] tüchtig[36] zu!"

1	woodchopper	19	pitifully
2	earned	20	fret; grieve
3	hardly	21	sneaked
4	do; provide	22	pebbles
5	trouble, distress	23	shone; gleamed
6	worry, concern	24	silver coins
7	toss and turn	25	bent down
8	lead, guide	26	coat pocket
9	thickest, most dense	27	take comfort
10	fire	28	peacefully
11	feed; support	29	before
12	heart	30	awakened
13	own	31	**einteilen** = to divide up
14	tear apart	32	**aufheben** = to save
15	peace; rest	33	**aufhalten** = to delay
16	agreed	34	pay attention (**achtgeben**)
17	awake	35	march
18	**es sei um sie geschehen** = they're done for, finished	36	energetically

Lesson 87

D. **Analysis or explanations:**

line 1   **nichts zu beißen und zu brechen** = nothing to eat (literally, nothing to bite and to break)

line 4   **wußte sich in seiner Not nicht zu helfen** = didn't know how to get himself out of this distressing situation

line 9   **nicht über mein Herz bringen** = can't find it in my heart to do it

line 13   **miteinander Hungers sterben** = die together of hunger; starve

line 30   **marschier tüchtig zu!** = "get going!"

E. **Practice:** Answer the following questions in German with complete sentences. *Possible* answers follow the questions.

1. Warum mußte der Vater die Kinder im Wald verlassen?
2. Was könnte den Kindern im Wald geschehen?
3. Warum waren die Kinder noch wach, als die Eltern sprachen?
4. Warum schlich Hänsel aus dem Haus hinaus?
5. Wie wissen wir, daß es sehr früh war, als die Kinder geweckt wurden?

MÖGLICHE ANTWORTEN:
1. Die Eltern hatten nichts mehr zu essen im Haus.
2. Die wilden Tiere könnten sie im Wald zerreißen.
3. Sie waren noch wach vor Hunger.
4. Er wollte weiße Kieselsteine holen.
5. Sie mußten aufstehen, ehe die Sonne aufgegangen war.

F. **Evaluation:** Refer to Section A.

LESSON 87
Hänsel und Gretel (Continued)

A. **Your objectives:** See Lesson 86.

B. **How to get there:** See Lesson 86.

C. What to learn:

"Ach, Vater, ich sehe nach meinem weißen Kätzchen, das sitzt oben auf dem Dach[1] und will mir ade[2] sagen."

Die Mutter sprach: "Ei, du Narr,[3] das ist nicht dein Kätzchen, das ist die Morgensonne, die auf den Schornstein[4] scheint!" Doch Hänsel hatte nicht nach
5 dem Kätzchen gesehen, sondern immer einen von den blanken Kieseln aus seiner Tasche auf den Weg geworfen.

Als sie mitten in den Wald gekommen waren, sprach der Vater: "Nun sammelt Holz, ihr Kinder, ich will ein Feuer anmachen, damit wir nicht frieren!" Hänsel und Gretel trugen Reisig[5] zusammen, einen kleinen Berg hoch. Dann
10 steckten sie es an,[6] und als die Flamme recht groß brannte, sagte die Mutter: "Nun legt euch ans Feuer und schlaft, wir wollen in den Wald und das Holz fällen,[7] wartet, bis wir wiederkommen und euch abholen!"

Hänsel und Gretel saßen an dem Feuer und warteten bis zum Mittag. Dann aß jedes sein Stücklein Brot. Sie warteten auch noch den Abend ab,[8] doch Vater und
15 Mutter kamen nicht, um sie abzuholen. Als es nun finstere[9] Nacht wurde, fing Gretel an zu weinen, Hänsel aber sprach: "Wart nur noch ein Weilchen, bis der Mond aufgegangen ist!" Und als er aufgegangen war, faßte Hänsel Gretel bei der Hand. Da lagen die Kieselsteine wie neugeschlagenes[10] Silber und schimmerten und zeigten[11] den Kindern den Weg. Die ganze Nacht gingen sie, und beim
20 Morgengrauen kamen sie bei dem Haus ihrer Eltern an. Der Vater freute sich[12] von Herzen, als er seine Kinder wiedersah; denn er war traurig, daß er sie allein gelassen hatte. Die Mutter tat auch so,[13] als freute sie sich, doch heimlich[14] war sie böse.

Nicht lange danach war wieder kein Brot im Hause, und Hänsel und Gretel hörten, wie die Mutter abends zum Vater sagte: "Einmal haben die Kinder den Weg
25 zurückgefunden, und ich habe es so hingenommen.[15] Jetzt ist wieder nichts als nur ein halber Laib[16] Brot im Hause! Du mußt sie morgen tiefer in den Wald führen, damit sie nicht wieder heimkommen können, es gibt sonst keine Hilfe mehr für uns!"

Dem Mann fiel es schwer aufs Herz, und er dachte, es wäre doch besser, wenn
30 er auch den letzten Bissen mit den Kindern teilte.[17] Weil er es aber einmal getan und die Kinder fortgeführt hatte, durfte er jetzt nicht nein sagen. Hänsel und Gretel hörten das Gespräch[18] der Eltern; Hänsel stand auf und wollte wieder Kieselsteine auflesen,[19] als er aber an die Tür kam, da hatte sie die Mutter zugeschlossen.[20] Doch er tröstete Gretel und sagte: "Schlaf nur, liebe Gretel, der Liebe Gott wird
35 uns schon helfen!"

1	roof	6	**anstecken** = to light, ignite
2	goodbye	7	to fell (chop or saw down)
3	fool	8	**abwarten** = await, wait for
4	chimney	9	dark
5	twigs; brush	10	newly minted

Lesson 87

11	showed	16	loaf
12	**sich freuen** = rejoice	17	shared, divided
13	**tat auch so, als . . .** = also acted as if . . .	18	conversation
14	secretly	19	pick up
15	**so hinnehmen** = to put up with	20	locked

D. Analysis or explanations:

line 8   **damit** = so that

line 27   **damit** = so that

line 27   **es gibt sonst . . .** = otherwise there won't be any help for us any longer

line 29   it weighed heavily on the husband's heart

E. Practice:

1. Warum sah Hänsel immer wieder nach dem Haus um?
2. Wie wissen wir, daß es kein warmer Sommertag ist?
3. Warum gehen Hänsel und Gretel nicht nach Hause, sobald es dunkel ist?
4. Wie fühlen sich die Eltern, als die Kinder nach Hause kommen?
5. Warum holte Hänsel keine Kieselsteine das zweite Mal?

MÖGLICHE ANTWORTEN:
1. Er wollte Kieselsteine auf den Weg werfen.
2. Sie wollen ein Feuer anmachen, damit sie nicht frieren.
3. Sie müssen warten, bis der Mond aufgegangen ist.
4. Der Vater freut sich, aber die Mutter ist böse.
5. Die Tür war zugeschlossen, und er konnte nicht hinausschleichen.

F. Evaluation: See Lesson 86.

LESSON 88
Hänsel und Gretel (Continued)

A. Your objectives: See Lesson 86.

B. How to get there: See Lesson 86.

C. What to learn:

Morgens früh erhielten[1] sie ihr Stücklein Brot, es war noch kleiner als das vorige[2] Mal. Auf dem Wege zerbröckelte[3] es Hänsel in der Tasche, stand oft still und warf ein Bröcklein auf die Erde.

"Was bleibst du immer stehen, Hänsel, und guckst dich um," sagte der Vater,
5 "geh deiner Wege!"

"Ach, ich seh' nach meinem Täubchen,[4] das sitzt auf dem Dach und will mir ade sagen!"

"Du Narr," sagte die Mutter, "das ist nicht dein Täubchen, das ist die Morgensonne, die auf den Schornstein oben scheint."

10 Hänsel zerbröckelte all sein Brot und warf die Bröcklein auf den Weg. Die Mutter führte sie noch tiefer in den Wald hinein, wo sie ihr Lebtag nicht gewesen waren. Da sollten sie wieder einschlafen, und abends wollten die Eltern kommen und sie abholen. Zu Mittag teilte Gretel ihr Brot mit Hänsel, weil der seins auf den Weg gestreut[5] hatte. Der Mittag verging[6] und der Abend verging, doch niemand
15 kam zu den armen Kindern. Hänsel tröstete Gretel und sagte: "Wart, wenn der Mond aufgeht, dann seh' ich die Brotbröcklein, die ich ausgestreut habe, die zeigen uns den Weg nach Hause."

Der Mond ging auf, doch als Hänsel nach den Bröcklein sah, waren sie alle weg. Die vielen tausend Vöglein im Wald hatten sie gefunden und aufgepickt.
20 Hänsel meinte,[7] dennoch[8] den Weg nach Hause zu finden, und zog Gretel mit sich; sie verirrten[9] sich aber bald in der großen Wildnis[10] und gingen die Nacht und den ganzen Tag, dann schliefen sie vor Müdigkeit ein. Noch einen Tag gingen sie, doch sie kamen nicht aus dem Wald heraus und waren so hungrig. Sie hatten nichts zu essen als ein paar Beerlein,[11] die auf der Erde standen.

25 Am dritten Tage gingen sie wieder bis zum Mittag. Da kamen sie an ein Häuslein, das war ganz aus Brot gebaut[12] und war mit Kuchen gedeckt.[13] Die Fenster waren aus hellem Zucker.[14]

"Hier wollen wir uns niedersetzen und uns satt[15] essen!" sagte Hänsel. "Ich will vom Dach essen, iß du vom Fenster, Gretel, das ist schön süß für dich!" Hänsel
30 hatte schon ein großes Stück vom Dach und Gretel schon ein paar runde[16] Fensterscheiben[17] gegessen und brach sich eben eine neue aus, da hörten die Kinder eine feine Stimme,[18] die von innen herausrief:

Lesson 88   223

"Knusper, knusper, Kneuschen![19]
Wer knuspert an meinem Häuschen?"

35   Hänsel und Gretel erschraken[20] so gewaltig,[21] daß sie fallenließen, was sie in der Hand hielten, und gleich darauf sahen sie aus der Tür eine kleine, steinalte Frau schleichen. Sie wackelte[22] mit dem Kopf und sagte: "Ei, ihr lieben Kinder, wo seid ihr denn hergelaufen, kommt herein zu mir, ihr sollt es gut haben!" Dabei faßte sie die Kinder an der Hand und führte sie in ihr Häuschen. Gutes Essen, Pfannkuchen
40   mit Zucker, Äpfel und Nüsse[23] trug sie auf, und als sich die Kinder satt gegessen hatten, bereitete[24] ihnen die Alte zwei schöne Bettlein; in die legten sich Hänsel und Gretel hinein und meinten, es sei wie im Himmel.

1	received	15	full, "satiated"
2	former, last	16	round
3	crumbled	17	window panes
4	pigeon	18	voice
5	scattered	19	**knuspern** = nibble (**Kneuschen** is probably a "made up" word, as often occur in nursery rhymes, such as "Hickory, dickory, dock..."
6	went by, passed		
7	was of the opinion, thought, believed		
8	nevertheless		
9	got lost, went astray	20	were startled, frightened
10	wilderness	21	strongly, violently
11	little beeries	22	shook
12	built	23	nuts
13	covered	24	prepared
14	sugar		

D. **Analysis or explanations:**

line 4   **was** = why

line 22   **vor müdigkeit** = from fatigue

line 32   **von innen herausrief** = called out from inside

line 35   **fallenließen** = let fall or drop

line 38   **hergelaufen** = come (to here) from

line 40   **trug sie auf** = she brought out; served

E. **Practice:**

1. Warum bröckelte Hänsel sein Brot? Wollte er Brotpudding machen?
2. Warum konnten sie diesmal den Weg nach Hause nicht finden?
3. Wie viele Tage wanderten sie durch den Wald?
4. Was fanden sie zu essen am dritten Tag?
5. Warum glaubten Hänsel und Gretel, es wäre im Haus der alten Frau wie im Himmel?

MÖGLICHE ANTWORTEN:
1. Er wollte die Bröcklein auf den Weg werfen, damit sie den Weg nach Hause finden konnten.
2. Die Vögel haben die Bröcklein aufgepickt.
3. Sie wanderten drei Tage lang. (Wenigstens waren sie drei Tage im Wald.)
4. Sie fanden ein Haus aus Brot, Kuchen und Zucker gebaut.
5. Sie hatten sehr viel zu essen und sie hatten schöne Bettlein.

F. **Evaluation:**   See Section A, Lesson 86.

LESSON 89
Hänsel und Gretel (Conclusion)

A. **Your objectives:**   See Lesson 86.

B. **How to get there:**   See Lesson 86.

C. **What to learn:**

Die alte Frau aber war eine böse Hexe,[1] die lauerte[2] den Kindern auf und hatte, um sie zu locken,[3] ihr Brothäuslein gebaut. Wenn ein Kind in ihre Gewalt[4] kam, dann machte sie es tot, kochte es und aß es, und das war ihr Festtag. Da war sie nun recht froh, daß Hänsel und Gretel ihr zugelaufen waren. Früh, ehe sie erwachten, stand
5   die Hexe schon auf, ging an ihre Bettlein, und als sie die beiden so friedlich[5] ruhen sah, freute sie sich und dachte, das würde ein guter Bissen für sie sein. Sie packte Hänsel und steckte ihn in einen kleinen Stall. Als er dort aufwachte, war er von einem Gitter umschlossen[6] und konnte nur ein paar Schritte[7] gehen. Gretel aber wurde von der Hexe geschüttelt,[8] und sie rief: "Steh auf, du Faulenzerin,[9] hol

"..., war er von einem Gitter umschlossen..."

10 Wasser und geh in die Küche und koch ein gutes Essen. Dort steckt dein Bruder in einem Stall, den will ich erst fett machen. Und wenn er fett ist, dann will ich ihn essen; jetzt sollst du ihn füttern!"[10] Gretel erschrak und weinte, mußte aber tun, was die Hexe von ihr verlangte.[11] Hänsel bekam[12] nun alle Tage das beste Essen, damit er fett werde. Doch Gretel bekam nichts als die mageren Abfälle.[13] Alle Tage
15 kam die Alte und sagte: "Hänsel, streck deine Finger heraus, damit ich fühlen kann, ob du fett genug bist!" Hänsel streckte ihr aber immer ein Knöchlein[14] heraus, und die böse Hexe wunderte sich, daß er gar nicht zunehmen[15] wollte.

    Nach vier Wochen sagte sie eines Abends zu Gretel: "Sei flink,[16] geh und trag Wasser herbei, dein Brüderchen mag[17] nun fett genug sein oder nicht, morgen will
20 ich es schlachten[18] und kochen. Ich werde inzwischen den Teig[19] anrühren,[20] damit wir auch dazu backen können." Da ging Gretel mit traurigem Herzen und holte das Wasser, in dem Hänsel gekocht werden sollte. Frühmorgens mußte Gretel aufstehen, Feuer anmachen und den Kessel[21] mit Wasser aufhängen. "Gib nun acht,[22] bis es kocht," sagte die Hexe, "ich will Feuer in dem Backofen[23] machen
25 und das Brot hineinschieben!"[24]

    Gretel stand in der Küche, weinte bittere Tränen[25] und dachte: "Hätten uns lieber die wilden Tiere im Walde gefressen, dann wären wir zusammen gestorben und müßten nun nicht das Herzeleid[26] tragen, und ich müßte nicht selber das

Wasser zu dem Tod meines lieben Bruders kochen; lieber Gott, hilf uns armen Kindern aus der Not!"

Da rief die Alte: "Gretel, komm gleich einmal hierher zu dem Backofen!" Und als Gretel kam, sagte sie: "Guck hinein, ob das Brot schon hübsch braun ist, meine Augen sind schwach, ich kann nicht so weit sehen, und wenn du es auch nicht kannst, setz dich auf das Brett, dann will ich dich hineinschieben, damit du darin umhergehen und nachsehen[27] kannst!"

Wenn aber Gretel drinnen wäre, wollte sie die Ofentür zuschlagen,[28] und Gretel sollte in der Glut[29] backen, und dann wollte es die Hexe auch aufessen. Nur deshalb hatte die böse Alte Gretel gerufen. Doch der liebe Gott gab Gretel ein,[30] der Hexe zu antworten: "Ich weiß nicht, wie ich das anfangen soll, zeig's mir erst, setz dich drauf, ich will dich hineinschieben." Die Hexe setzte sich auf das Brett, und weil sie leicht[31] war, schob sie Gretel hinein, so weit sie konnte, and dann machte sie geschwind die Tür zu und steckte den eisernen Riegel[32] vor. Da fing die Alte an, in dem heißen Backofen zu schreien und zu jammern; Gretel aber lief fort und ließ die Hexe elendig[33] verbrennen.

Schnell befreite[34] Gretel ihren Bruder, und Hänsel sprang froh aus seinem Ställchen heraus und küßte sein Schwesterchen, und sie tanzten fröhlich herum. Das ganze Häuschen war voll von Edelsteinen[35] und Perlen. Davon füllten die Kinder ihre Taschen, eilten fort[36] und fanden jetzt den Weg nach Hause.

Der Vater freute sich, als er sie wiedersah; er hatte keinen vergnügten[37] Tag gehabt, seit seine Kinder im Walde geblieben waren. Nun wurde er ein reicher Mann, als er von den Kindern die Schätze bekam. Die Mutter aber war gestorben.

1	witch	20	mix
2	**auflauern** = to lie in wait for	21	kettle
3	lure, entice	22	watch out
4	power	23	oven
5	peacefully	24	shove in
6	enclosed by a grate (**Gitter**)	25	tears
7	steps	26	great sorrow
8	shaken	27	inspect; check out
9	"lazy bones"	28	slam shut
10	feed	29	heat
11	demanded	30	**eingeben** = to inspire
12	received	31	light (not heavy)
13	**mageren Abfälle** = meager scraps	32	iron bolt
14	little bone	33	miserably
15	gain weight	34	to free
16	quick, nimble	35	precious stones; jewels
17	may	36	**forteilen** = to hurry away
18	slaughter	37	happy
19	dough; pastry		

D. **Analysis or explanations:**

    line 13   **alle Tage** = every day

    line 21   **dazu** = in addition

    line 26   **Hätten uns lieber** ... = It would have been better if the wild animals in the forest had eaten us

    line 28   **müßten ... nicht ... tragen** = wouldn't have to bear

    line 37   **deshalb** = for that reason

    line 41   **schob sie Gretel** = *Gretel* shoved *her*

E. **Practice:**

1. Was machte die Hexe mit Kindern?
2. Warum glaubte die Hexe, daß Hänsel nicht zunähme?
3. Warum wäre Gretel lieber im Wald gestorben?
4. Warum setzte sich die Hexe auf das Brett, das in den Backofen geschoben werden konnte?
5. Was nahmen die Kinder mit nach Hause?

MÖGLICHE ANTWORTEN:
1. Sie machte sie tot, kochte sie und aß sie.
2. Er streckte immer ein Knöchlein heraus.
3. Dann müßte sie den Tod ihres Bruders nicht ansehen.
4. Sie wollte Gretel zeigen, wie man das macht.
5. Sie nahmen Edelsteine und Perlen mit nach Hause.

F. **Evaluation:**   See Section A, Lesson 86.

LESSON 90
Self-Test/Review (Lessons 86-89)

A. **Your objectives:**   To be able to answer the questions about content and vocabulary in *Hänsel und Gretel* as directed in the test in Section E, with at least 90% accuracy.

228 Deutsch: ZWEITE STUFE

B. How to get there: Review each of the lessons (86-89) containing the story of *Hänsel und Gretel*. If you can still answer all the questions and explain or give English equivalents for all new vocabulary, you should be ready to do the test in Section E.
If you can't do all of the tasks well, practice until you can.

C. What to learn: Review.

D. Analysis or explanations: Review.

E. Practice: SELF-TEST

1. Match the German words in column **A** with equivalent English words in column **B**:

	A		B
_____	a. Holzhacker	a.	pebbles
_____	b. führen	b.	pitifully
_____	c. zerreißen	c.	secretly
_____	d. erbärmlich	d.	fool
_____	e. schleichen (schlich)	e.	to crumble
_____	f. Kieselsteine	f.	to scatter
_____	g. das Dach	g.	to lose one's way
_____	h. der Narr	h.	woodchopper
_____	i. finster	i.	dark
_____	j. sich freuen	j.	to feed
_____	k. heimlich	k.	to tear apart
_____	l. zugeschlossen	l.	to free
_____	m. zerbröckeln	m.	to shove into
_____	n. der Schornstein	n.	kettle
_____	o. streuen	o.	roof
_____	p. meinen	p.	step
_____	q. sich verirren	q.	witch
_____	r. Zucker	r.	to mean; be of the opinion
_____	s. die Stimme	s.	to lead
_____	t. die Hexe	t.	voice
_____	u. der Schritt	u.	locked
_____	v. füttern	v.	rejoice
_____	w. der Kessel	w.	sugar
_____	x. hineinschieben	x.	chimney
_____	y. befreien	y.	to sneak

Lesson 90

Kein armer Holzhacker wohnt hier.

2. Answer the following questions in German (one word answers are sufficient):

a. Was war der Vater von Hänsel und Gretel?
b. Was sollte der Vater den Kindern geben, wenn er sie in den Wald führte?
c. Was glänzte im Mondschein wie Silbermünzen?
d. Wo hatte Hänsel die Steine?
e. Hänsel sagte, er wollte jemandem "ade" sagen. Wer (was) war das?
f. Warum mußten die Kinder im Wald Holz und Reisig sammeln?
g. Wie fühlte sich der Vater, als die Kinder zurückkamen?
h. Wer hatte die Tür zugeschlossen, als Hänsel das zweite Mal hinausschleichen wollte?
i. Was zerbröckelte Hänsel in seiner Tasche?
j. Was fanden sie im Wald zu essen (ehe sie das Haus der Hexe fanden)?
k. Woraus waren die Fenster im Hexenhaus gemacht?

l. Wohin steckte die Hexe Hänsel?
m. Was wollte die Hexe mit Hänsel und Gretel machen?
n. Was sollte in dem Kessel mit heißem Wasser kochen?
o. Wo ist die Hexe gestorben?

F. **Evaluation:** Check your answers against the key, or have them checked. If you did well (90% or better), go on to Lesson 91.

If you did not do so well, review and try the test again.

LESSONS 91-95
Comprehensive Review

The next 5 lessons consist of a total of 100 sentences in English for you to express in German. These 100 sentences contain almost all the structural problems (grammar) which you have encountered in *Deutsch: Kernstufe* and *Deutsch: Zweite Stufe,* including
1. all verb forms practiced,
2. noun phrases in every gender and case practiced,
3. all pronouns in every case practiced,
4. relative pronouns in every gender and case, and
5. **da**-compounds

We shall give the objectives for all 100 sentences only once.

Each group of 20 sentences constitutes one lesson. (Thus, sentences 1-20 = Lesson 91; 21-40 = Lesson 91; 41-60 = Lesson 93; 61-80 = Lesson 94; 81-100 = Lesson 95.)

A. **Your objectives:** (For all of Lessons 91-95) To be able to give a correct German equivalent, oral and/or written, for each English sentence, 20 sentences at each evaluation, with at least 90% accuracy.

B. **How to get there:** The main verb used in each sentence is given. Express the sentence as best you can; then refer to the correct answer (all

Lessons 91 — 95

answers follow sentence number 100) and correct your version as necessary.

Repeat the correct version several times.

When you have done all 20 sentences, try doing them again. Keep going through them until you make no (or *very few*) errors.

C. What to learn: No new material.

D. Analysis or explanations: You will need to make an individual analysis (with the help of your teacher, if necessary) of any errors you make. Do not merely memorize the correct version of each sentence, without understanding why it is correct and why your version was wrong. You may wish to do the analysis independently.

E. Practice: Give German equivalents of the following English sentences. Use the German verb in parentheses.

Lesson 91

1. (*angeln*) The little boy is fishing in the lake.
2. (*anfangen*) Yes, the book is here. Do you want to begin it?
3. (*aufmachen*) We are opening the door which is behind you-all.
4. (*bleiben*) Does she know who would have stayed?
5. (*aufwachen*) The friendly cat woke up under the bed. *past tense*
6. (*beginnen*) The story was good, and you wanted to begin it.
7. (*bestellen*) We were ordering the newspaper which I wanted to read.
8. (*bringen*) We'd like to know whom you are bringing.
9. (*brauchen*) We don't have to do that.
10. (*denken*) The nice girl (has) always thought that.
11. (*fragen*) You would want to ask him if he were here.
12. (*entscheiden*) Gisela has to decide who she wants to sit next to (next to whom she wants . . .).
13. (*fühlen*) But sometimes I feel (myself) all alone.
14. (*essen*) I know who could have eaten it.
15. (*füllen*) They had filled the garden with beautiful flowers.
16. (*fahren*) Did you want to drive it (*der VW*)?
17. (*glauben*) We believed what he told us.
18. (*fallen*) Did you know that she fell into the lake?
19. (*herumgucken*) Red Riding Hood, don't nose around in all the corners! *all en Ecken*
20. (*finden*) I must find the next man.

21. (*holen*) You had wanted to get me.
22. (*gehen*) The lieutenant killed the farmers, whose workers had gone.
23. (*hören*) Can you hear with that?
24. (*gewinnen*) We should have won.
25. (*kaufen*) I had to buy the expensive watch (*die Uhr*).
26. (*haben*) Would you have wanted to have them?
27. (*klopfen*) They knocked on the doors that the soldiers were sleeping behind (behind which the soldiers . . .).
28. (*heißen*) His name is Rudolf.
29. (*kosten*) It would have cost too much.
30. (*kennen*) I would know the old house.
31. (*lachen*) Did you laugh with her?
32. (*kommen*) If he came home, I'd be happy.
33. (*legen*) Put the gun on the table!
34. (*laufen*) Run home, children!
35. (*machen*) I too have had to make the fast movements.
36. (*lesen*) Were you (*Sie*) reading with them?
37. (*merken*) You would notice it if they were playing here.
38. (*liegen*) The gun is lying on the table.
39. (*packen*) Put (pack) the umbrella in the suitcase, Miss Braun.
40. (*nehmen*) I had had to take it in the big basket.
41. (*reden*) Were you (*du*) talking to (with) him?
42. (*nennen*) We had named the lady to whom he had given the jewels.
43. (*retten*) If I had been there I would have saved her.
44. (*rufen*) My mother should have called.
45. (*schauen*) I would have looked into the mirror from (*aus*) the dark corner.
46. (*scheinen*) You had seemed stupid to me.
47. (*schenken*) We can give you the lamp whose light is especially bright.
48. (*schießen*) If he had a gun he'd shoot us.
49. (*schmecken*) I wouldn't taste that!
50. (*schlafen*) I would have to sleep in the cold room.
51. (*schnarchen*) You-all were snoring behind us.
52. (*schneiden*) The paper, which we were able to cut, is on the table.
53. (*setzen*) If you had set it on the table, I would have found it.
54. (*sein*) They would have been there if they had had a car.
55. (*spielen*) I would have had to play in the bad jazz clubs.
56. (*sehen*) Do you-all see me?
57. (*starren*) We had all been able to stare at (*auf*) the girl who was there.
58. (*singen*) If she had been able to sing, he would not have fired (*entlassen*) her.
59. (*stecken*) Put the money in your pocket.
60. (*sinken*) A German ship is sinking into the lake.

Lessons 91 – 95   233

61. (*suchen*) Did you-all look for me at his place?
62. (*sitzen*) The chair on which we could have sat (would have been able to sit) was gone.
63. (*tanzen*) We could have danced all night.
64. (*sprechen*) Don't talk about (*über*) it.
65. (*träumen*) A poor woman was dreaming about (*von*) money.
66. (*steigen*) Had you-all climbed into the car with it (a thing)?
67. (*verkaufen*) Here is the ham which we can sell.
68. (*tragen*) If you wore it would he be happy?
69. (*verschlucken*) A wolf couldn't swallow the grandmother!
70. (*trinken*) A green dragon has drunk from (*aus*) the lake.
71. (*warten*) You-all ought to wait in front of me.
72. (*tun*) I had a VW that could do that.
73. (*weinen*) Gisela, don't cry so loudly!
74. (*vergessen*) Has she forgotten everything that I've given her?
75. (*winken*) Who had waved with the white cap (*die Mütze*)?
76. (*verlassen*) Were you-all supposed to leave the house?
77. (*wohnen*) We may live in the house whose owner (*Besitzer*) is in America.
78. (*verstehen*) Please understand me (you-all)!
79. (*wundern*) We wonder (ourselves) about (*über*) it.
80. (*werden*) Can I become a good child?
81. (*zahlen*) Had you-all been obligated to pay us?
82. (*wissen*) We were permitted to know who would come.
83. (*zuhören*) Listen, Mrs. Schmidt!
84. (*zerbrechen*) I believe that they had wanted to break it.
85. (*anzünden*) Would I be able to light a nice fire?
86. (*geschehen*) We were permitted to say what happened.
87. (*schenken*) Give me something, please!
88. (*aufstehen*) Mr. Müller, get up now!
89. (*reichen*) Now I have to hand her the bread!
90. (*einschlafen*) Fritz, go to sleep!
91. (*einsammeln*) Would you-all be obligated to collect them?
92. (*sterben*) Here are the flowers which would have had to die.
93. (*kämpfen*) I shouldn't have fought with her.
94. (*bitten um*) We could have asked for more.
95. (*schicken*) Hans and Fritz, send the pious girl a new slip (*der Unterrock*).
96. (*anziehen*) Would you-all have been permitted to put them on?
97. (*lieben*) These are the stories that we love.
98. (*besitzen*) Do you know what you own now?
99. (*atmen*) Can one breathe under there?
100. (*scheinen*) The sun could not have shone onto the treasure.

E3
Hamburg
-Stadtmitte
-Georgswerder
E3 E4
Kiel
500 m
E3 Hamburg E3
-Stadtmitte
-Georgswerder
E4 Lübeck E4
Kiel
Hamburg
Moorfleet
70-90
km
800 m
HAMBURGER SPEDITION

E3
Hamburg
-Stadtmitte
-Georgswerder
E3 E4
Kiel
500 m
E3 Hamburg E3
-Stadtmitte
-Georgswerder
E4 Lübeck E4
Kiel
Hamburg
Moorfleet
70-90
km
800 m

Lessons 91 — 95

ANTWORTEN:
1. Der kleine Junge angelt in dem (im) See.
2. Ja, das Buch ist hier. Willst du es anfangen?
3. Wir machen die Tür auf, die hinter euch ist.
4. Weiß sie, wer geblieben wäre?
5. Die freundliche Katze wachte unter dem (unterm) Bett auf.
6. Die Geschichte war gut, und du wolltest sie beginnen.
7. Wir bestellten die Zeitung, die ich lesen wollte.
8. Wir möchten wissen, wen du bringst.
9. Wir brauchen das nicht zu machen.
10. Das nette Mädchen hat das (schon) immer gedacht.
11. Du wolltest ihn fragen, wenn er hier wäre.
12. Gisela muß sich entscheiden, neben wem sie sitzen will.
13. Aber manchmal fühle ich mich ganz allein.
14. Ich weiß, wer es hätte essen können.
15. Sie hatten den Garten mit schönen Blumen gefüllt.
16. Hast du ihn fahren wollen?
17. Wir glaubten (das), was er uns gesagt hat.
18. Hast du gewußt, daß sie in den See gefallen ist (in den See fiel)?
19. Rotkäppchen, guck nicht in allen Ecken herum!
20. Ich muß den nächsten Mann finden.

21. Du hattest mich holen wollen.
22. Der Leutnant hat die Bauern getötet, deren Arbeiter (weg)gegangen waren.
23. Kannst du damit hören?
24. Wir hätten gewinnen sollen.
25. Ich habe die teure Uhr kaufen müssen (mußte die teure Uhr kaufen).
26. Hättest du sie haben wollen?
27. Sie klopften an die Türen, hinter denen die Soldaten schliefen.
28. Er heißt Rudolf.
29. Es hätte zuviel gekostet.
30. Ich kennte das alte Haus.
31. Hast du mit ihr gelacht?
32. Wenn er nach Hause käme, wäre ich glücklich.
33. Leg das Gewehr auf den Tisch!
34. Lauft nach Hause, Kinder!
35. Ich habe auch die schnellen Bewegungen machen müssen.
36. Lasen Sie mit ihnen?
37. Du würdest es merken, wenn sie hier spielten.
38. Das Gewehr liegt auf dem Tisch.
39. Packen Sie den Regenschirm in den Koffer, Fräulein Braun!
40. Ich hatte es in dem großen Korb nehmen müssen.

41. Redetest du mit ihm?
42. Wir hatten die Frau genannt, der er die Juwelen gegeben hatte.
43. Wenn ich da gewesen wäre, hätte ich sie gerettet.
44. Meine Mutter hätte rufen sollen.
45. Ich hätte aus der dunklen Ecke in den Spiegel geschaut.
46. Du hattest mir dumm geschienen.
47. Wir können dir die Lampe schenken, deren Licht besonders hell ist.
48. Wenn er ein Gewehr hätte, würde er auf uns schießen.
49. Ich würde das nicht schmecken.
50. Ich müßte in dem kalten Zimmer schlafen.
51. Ihr schnarchtet hinter uns.
52. Das Papier, das wir haben schneiden können, ist (liegt) auf dem Tisch.
53. Wenn du es auf den Tisch gesetzt hättest, hätte ich es gefunden.
54. Sie wären da gewesen, wenn sie einen Wagen gehabt hätten.
55. Ich hätte in den schlechten Jazzkellern spielen müssen.
56. Seht ihr mich?
57. Wir hatten alle auf das Mädchen starren können, das da war.
58. Wenn sie hätte singen können, hätte er sie nicht entlassen.
59. Steck das Geld in die (deine) Tasche!
60. Ein deutsches Schiff sinkt in den See.

61. Habt ihr mich bei ihm gesucht?
62. Der Stuhl, auf dem wir hätten sitzen können, war weg.
63. Wir hätten die ganze Nacht tanzen können.
64. Sprich nicht darüber!
65. Eine arme Frau träumte von Geld.
66. Wart ihr damit in den Wagen gestiegen?
67. Hier ist der Schinken, den wir verkaufen können (dürfen).
68. Wenn du es trügest, wäre er glücklich?
69. Ein Wolf könnte die Großmutter nicht verschlucken!
70. Ein grüner Drachen hat aus dem See getrunken.
71. Ihr sollt vor mir warten.
72. Ich hatte einen VW, der das tun konnte.
73. Gisela, wein nicht so laut!
74. Hat sie alles vergessen, was ich ihr gegeben habe?
75. Wer hatte mit der weißen Mütze gewinkt?
76. Habt ihr das Haus verlassen sollen?
77. Wir dürfen in dem Hause wohnen, dessen Besitzer in Amerika ist.
78. Bitte versteht mich!
79. Wir wundern uns darüber.
80. Kann ich ein gutes Kind werden?

Lesson 96

       81. Hattet ihr uns (be)zahlen sollen?
       82. Wir durften wissen, wer käme (kommen würde).
       83. Hören Sie zu, Frau Schmidt!
       84. Ich glaube, daß sie es hatten zerbrechen wollen.
       85. Könnte ich ein nettes Feuer anzünden?
       86. Wir haben sagen dürfen, was geschehen ist.
       87. Schenk mir etwas bitte!
       88. Herr Müller, stehen Sie jetzt auf!
       89. Jetzt muß ich ihr das Brot reichen!
       90. Fritz, schlaf ein!
       91. Solltet (müßtet) ihr sie einsammeln?
       92. Hier sind die Blumen, die hätten sterben müssen.
       93. Ich hätte mit ihr nicht kämpfen sollen.
       94. Wir hätten um mehr bitten können.
       95. Hans und Fritz, schickt dem frommen Mädchen einen neuen Unterrock!
       96. Hättet ihr sie anziehen dürfen?
       97. Diese sind die Geschichten, die wir lieben.
       98. Weißt du, was du jetzt besitzt (besitzest)?
       99. Kann man darunter atmen?
     100. Die Sonne hat nicht auf den Schatz scheinen können.

F. Evaluation: Refer to Sections A and B and to the introduction to Lessons 91-95.

LESSON 96
Final Unit Test (Lessons 71-95)

A. Your objectives: To be able to pass the final test accompanying this lesson with a score of 90% or better. (The test will consist of 25 sentences chosen at random from the 100 sentences in Lessons 91-95 and a multiple choice test designed to determine your understanding of the content and vocabulary of *Hänsel und Gretel*.)

B. How to get there: Reviewing Lessons 86-95 will be sufficient, since any grammar learned is reviewed and contained in the 100 sentences practiced in Lessons 91-95.

C. What to learn: See Section B.

D.	Analysis or explanations:	Review.
E.	Practice:	See Section B.
F.	Evaluation:	When you have reviewed enough so that you feel confident you can score 90% or better on any of the material in Lessons 86-95, you are ready to take the test. You will have to repeat the test if you score less than 90%.

"Hallooo, Baby!"

Deutsch: ZWEITE STUFE
Complement

TABLE OF CONTENTS Complement

Language Problem	Lesson(s)	Page
Passive Voice	C-1 to C-8	244
Comparison of Adjectives	C-9 to C-12	253
Ordinal Numbers and Fractions	C-13 to C-14	259
Present Participles	C-15, C-16	262
Genitive Case	C-17, C-18	265
Reflexive Verbs	C-19, C-20	268
Time Phrasess	C-21, C-22	270
Indirect Discourse	C-23 to C-25	274
Wishes	C-26	277
Negation	C-27, C-28	277
Words Often Confused	C-29	281
Common Idioms	C-30 to C-32	282

COMPLEMENT

Following are 32 lessons dealing with German grammar and structure. The problems presented here have not been practiced before in either *Deutsch: Kernstufe* or *Deutsch: Zweite Stufe.* The author considers them as having less priority for basic communication skills than the structures already practiced. This does not mean, however, that they are not common and eventually necessary.

These lessons may be made an integral part of the second year course, or they may be done in the initial phases of a third year course. The teacher and/or the student will need to decide whether these lessons are added to the 96 lessons of the core, or whether other activities such as more reading, conversation, listening comprehension, etc., are of more value.

You will notice that the format of the lessons has been changed somewhat. There is no special section entitled "How to get there" nor one for "Evaluation." It is assumed that these procedures should be obvious by now and do not have to be stated for each lesson.

Complement

LESSON C-1
The Passive Voice

Objectives: To demonstrate your understanding of the passive as shown by your ability to do the exercises in the practice section in oral and written German with no difficulty.

What to learn: Be certain you still know the forms of the verb **werden**. This verb, as you will see, is essential for operating in the passive.

werden (to become, get)

Principal parts: **werden, wird, wurde, ist geworden**

ich **werde**	ich **wurde**	ich **bin geworden**
du **wirst**	du **wurdest**	du **bist geworden**
er **wird**	er **wurde**	er **ist geworden**
wir **werden**	wir **wurden**	wir **sind geworden**
ihr **werdet**	ihr **wurdet**	ihr **seid geworden**
sie **werden**	sie **wurden**	sie **sind geworden**

Explanation: We have been familiar with the use of the verb **werden** in its meaning "to become" or "to get" since early in beginning German:

Es **wird** dunkel.	It's getting (becoming) dark.
Hans **wurde** böse.	Hans was getting (becoming) angry.
Sie **ist** müde **geworden**.	She got (became) tired.
Wir **waren** sehr freundlich **geworden**.	We had gotten (become) very friendly.

In both English and German we can use past participles instead of adjectives in this basic structure:

Ich **werde** geschlagen.	I'm *getting beaten.*
Hans **wurde** geküßt.	Hans *was (getting) kissed.*
Sie **ist** überfahren **worden**.	She *got (was) run over.*

This construction is called the *passive*. Look over the previous four sentences again. Are the subjects *doing* anything? No, something is *being done* to them.

COMPARE:

> Er **schrieb** den Brief.
> Der Brief **wurde** von ihm **geschrieben**.

The first sentence is in what is termed grammatically the *active voice.* The subject is the actor, is active. The second sentence is in the *passive voice.* Here the subject is inactive, passive, acted on. (If the actor is stated in such a sentence, it is called the *agent.*)

In English we express the passive either by using a form of "get" or a form of "to be": *We're getting beaten; we were beaten; we got beaten* . . . The feeling to focus on, however, is the feeling that the subject is receiving the action.

Practice: 1. How would you express the following in German?

geschlagen

a.	this is happening to you:	**Ich werde geschlagen.**
b.	this was happening to you:	**Ich wurde geschlagen.**
c.	this did happen to you:	**Ich bin geschlagen worden.**
d.	this had happened to you:	**Ich war geschlagen worden.**

schnell gegessen

a.	this is happening to the cake:	**Der Kuchen wird schnell gegessen.**
b.	this had happened to the cake:	**Der Kuchen war schnell gegessen worden.**
c.	this was happening to the cake:	**Der Kuchen wurde schnell gegessen.**
d.	this happened to the cake:	**Der Kuchen ist schnell gegessen worden.**

2. Study the following possible forms of the passive and give English equivalents:

a.	**Mein Auto wird repariert.**	My car is being repaired.
b.	**Mein Auto wurde repariert.**	My car was being repaired.
c.	**Mein Auto ist repariert worden.**	My car has been repaired.
d.	**Mein Auto war repariert worden.**	My car had been repaired.
e.	**Mein Auto muß repariert werden.**	My car must be repaired.
f.	**Mein Auto mußte repariert werden.**	My car had to be repaired.
g.	**Mein Auto hat repariert werden müssen.**	My car had to be repaired.
h.	**Mein Auto hatte repariert werden müssen.**	My car had had to be repaired.
i.	**Mein Auto würde repariert.**	My car would be repaired.

"Die Zeitung wird gelesen werden müssen."

j.	**Mein Auto wäre repariert worden.**	My car would have been repaired.
k.	**Mein Auto müßte repariert werden.**	My car would have to be repaired.
l.	**Mein Auto hätte repariert werden müssen.**	My car would have had to be repaired.

3. Using **bringen**,

a.	ask *what* this was done to:	**Was ist gebracht worden? (Was wurde gebracht?)**
b.	ask what this had been done to:	**Was war gebracht worden?**
c.	ask what this is being done to:	**Was wird gebracht?**
d.	ask what this has been done to:	**Was ist gebracht worden?**

LESSON C-2
The Passive

Objectives: To be able to do the exercises in the practice section in oral and written German with no errors.

Lesson C-2

What to learn: Make sure you can give the equivalent passive statement (on the right) for each active statement (on the left):

	(die Zeitung lesen)	die Zeitung (gelesen werden)
1.	Er **liest** die Zeitung.	Die Zeitung **wird gelesen**.
2.	Er **las** die Zeitung.	Die Zeitung **wurde gelesen**.
3.	Er **hat** die Zeitung **gelesen**.	Die Zeitung **ist gelesen worden**.
4.	Er **hatte** die Zeitung **gelesen**.	Die Zeitung **war gelesen worden**.
5.	Er **wird** (die Zeitung lesen).	Die Zeitung **wird** (gelesen werden).
6.	Er **muß** (die Zeitung lesen).	Die Zeitung **muß** (gelesen werden).
7.	Er **mußte** (die Zeitung lesen).	Die Zeitung **mußte** (gelesen werden).
8.	Er **hat** (die Zeiting lesen) **müssen**.	Die Zeitung **hat** (gelesen werden) **müssen**.
9.	Er **hatte** (die Zeitung lesen) **müssen**.	Die Zeitung **hatte** (gelesen werden) **müssen**.
10.	Er **wird** (die Zeitung lesen) **müssen**.	Die Zeitung **wird** (gelesen werden) **müssen**.
11.	Er **würde** (die Zeitung lesen).	Die Zeitung **würde** (gelesen).
12.	Er **hätte** die Zeitung **gelesen**.	Die Zeitung **wäre gelesen** worden.
13.	Er **müßte** die Zeitung lesen.	Die Zeitung **müßte** gelesen werden.
14.	Er **hätte** die Zeitung lesen **müssen**.	Die Zeitung **hätte** gelesen werden müssen.

Explanations: Look carefully at sentences 5-11. Notice that the auxiliaries have exactly the same form whether we are expressing an idea in the passive or the active. The only difference is the infinitive phrase:

(die Zeitung **lesen**) vs. **gelesen werden**
to read vs. *to be read.*

The subjects are, of course, also different.

Practice: Using the phrase **das Radio reparieren**, state in German that

1.	he is doing this	this is being done
2.	he was doing this	this was being done
3.	he has done this	this has been done
4.	he had done this	this had been done
5.	he will do this	this will be done
6.	he must do this	this must be done
7.	he had to do this	this had to be done
8.	he has had to do this	this has had to be done
9.	he had had to do this	this had had to be done
10.	he will have to do this	this will have to be done

11.	he would do this	this would be done
12.	he would have done this	this would have been done
13.	he would have to do this	this would have to be done
14.	he would have had to do this	this would have had to be done

To check your answers, refer to the "What to learn" section above. Instead of **die Zeitung lesen** and **gelesen werden** you will have **das Radio reparieren** and **repariert werden**.

LESSON C-3
The Passive

Objectives: To be able to say and write in German the sentences called for in the practice section—without error.

Practice:

1. Using the phrase **drei Autos verkaufen**, how would you say that Udo

a.	had done this?	Udo hatte drei Autos verkauft.
b.	was doing this?	Udo verkaufte drei Autos.
c.	has done this?	Udo hat drei Autos verkauft.
d.	is doing this?	Udo verkauft drei Autos.
e.	would have done this?	Udo hätte drei Autos verkauft.

2. Using the phrase **drei Autos verkaufen**, how would you say that

a.	this had been done?	Drei Autos waren verkauft worden.
b.	this was being done?	Drei Autos wurden verkauft.
c.	this has been done?	Drei Autos sind verkauft worden.
d.	this is being done?	Drei Autos werden verkauft.
e.	this would have been done?	Drei Autos wären verkauft worden.

3. How would you say that

a.	we must read the book?	Wir müssen das Buch lesen.
b.	the book must be read?	Das Buch muß gelesen werden.
c.	Hans will read the book?	Hans wird das Buch lesen.

d.	the book will be read?	Das Buch wird gelesen werden.
e.	he would have read the book?	Er hätte das Buch gelesen.
f.	the book would have been read?	Das Buch wäre gelesen worden.

4. Express in German:

a.	The bread had been eaten.	Das Brot war gegessen worden.
b.	The car was being driven.	Das Auto wurde gefahren.
c.	The book has never been read.	Das Buch ist nie gelesen worden.
d.	The paper is being cut.	Das Papier wird geschnitten.
e.	What has been played?	Was ist gespielt worden?
f.	Who is being asked?	Wer wird gefragt?
g.	They had been shot.	Sie waren geschossen worden.
h.	You're being called.	Du wirst gerufen.
i.	We have been seen.	Wir sind gesehen worden.
j.	I wasn't forgotten.	Ich bin nicht vergessen worden.

LESSON C-4
The Passive

Objectives: To be able to say and write in German the sentences called for in the practice section—without error.

Practice: 1. Using the phrases **der Film** and **gezeigt werden**, how would you say that

a.	this is being done?	Der Film wird gezeigt.
b.	this was being done?	Der Film wurde gezeigt.
c.	this has been done?	Der Film ist gezeigt worden.
d.	this had been done?	Der Film war gezeigt worden.
e.	this will be done?	Der Film wird gezeigt werden.
f.	this may not be (is not allowed to be) done?	Der Film darf nicht gezeigt werden.
g.	this had to be done?	Der Film mußte gezeigt werden.
h.	this would be done?	Der Film würde gezeigt (werden).
i.	this would have been done?	Der Film wäre gezeigt worden.
j.	this would not have been permitted?	Der Film hätte nicht gezeigt werden dürfen.

2. Using the phrases **der Brief** and **von uns geschrieben werden**, how would you say in German that

a.	this has been done?	Der Brief ist von uns geschrieben worden.
b.	this ought to be done?	Der Brief soll von uns geschrieben werden.
c.	this could be done?	Der Brief könnte von uns geschrieben werden.
d.	this is being done?	Der Brief wird von uns geschrieben.
e.	this will be done?	Der Brief wird von uns geschrieben werden.
f.	this could have been done?	Der Brief hätte von uns geschrieben werden können.
g.	this had been done?	Der Brief war von uns geschrieben worden.
h.	this was supposed to have been done?	Der Brief hätte von uns geschrieben werden sollen.
i.	this should be done?	Der Brief soll von uns geschrieben werden.

LESSON C-5
The Passive

Objectives: To be able to give German equivalents for the English sentences in the practice section with no errors.

Practice: SELF-TEST

Using the phrases **die Zeitung** and either **lesen** or **gelesen werden**, how would you say or write in German that

1.	Hans is reading the paper?	Hans liest die Zeitung.
2.	the paper is being read now?	Die Zeitung wird jetzt gelesen.
3.	I have wanted to read the paper?	Sie haben die Zeitung lesen wollen.
4.	the paper has had to be read?	Die Zeitung hat gelesen werden sollen (or müssen).
5.	we were reading the paper?	Wir lasen die Zeitung.
6.	we will be permitted to read the paper?	Wir werden die Zeitung lesen dürfen.
7.	you read (past) the paper?	Ich habe die Zeitung gelesen.
8.	the newspaper would have been read?	Die Zeitung wäre gelesen worden.
9.	the paper would have had to be read?	Die Zeitung hätte gelesen werden müssen.
10.	she would be able to read the paper?	Sie könnte die Zeitung lesen.
11.	the paper had been read?	Die Zeitung war gelesen worden.
12.	the paper had to be read?	Die Zeitung mußte gelesen werden.
13.	they will read the paper?	Sie werden die Zeitung lesen.

14. the paper must be read?	Die Zeitung muß gelesen werden.
15. you-all had had to read the paper?	Wir hatten die Zeitung lesen müssen.
16. the paper would be read?	Die Zeitung würde gelesen werden.

LESSON C-6
The Passive

Objectives: To be able to do the exercises in the practice section as requested there—without error.

Explanations: The passive is often used in German to emphasize an activity as such—where nothing is stated about who is carrying on the activity.

EXAMPLES:

Was ist denn da drinnen los?	**Es wird gesungen.** (Indicating that singing is the activity going on.)
What's going on in there?	**Es wird getanzt.**
	Gestern wurde hier gearbeitet.
	Es wird geflüstert. (Somebody's whispering.)

"Hier wird gearbeitet."

The passive is not used as commonly by German speakers as it is by English speakers. If the subject is unknown or is meant "generally," the German speaker will often use an active sentence with the general term **man** as the subject.

Man braucht einen Paß instead of **Ein Paß wird gebraucht.**
Man muß das Geld umwechseln instead of **Das Geld muß umgewechselt werden.**

As in most languages, one usually uses the simpler forms, if one has a choice.

Practice: 1. If you were asked what is or what was happening somewhere, how might you express in German that the following activities were going on by using the passive?

a. people are singing	**Es wird gesungen.**
b. there was a lot of dancing	**Es wurde viel getanzt.**
c. people are playing	**Es wird gespielt.**
d. there was talking here	**Hier wurde gesprochen.**
e. here there's always musicmaking	**Hier wird immer musiziert.**

2. How would you express the following passive sentences in the active voice using **man**?

a. Wir wurden in Berlin gesehen.	**Man sah uns in Berlin.**
b. Das Auto wird jetzt repariert.	**Man repariert jetzt das Auto.**
c. Das darf nicht gemacht werden.	**Man darf das nicht machen.**
d. Das Geld ist nicht gefunden worden.	**Man hat das Geld nicht gefunden.**
e. Der VW war schon verkauft worden.	**Man hatte den VW schon verkauft.**
f. Hier wird alles gemacht.	**Man macht hier alles.**
g. Der Brief hätte schon längst geschrieben werden sollen.	**Man hätte den Brief schon längst schreiben sollen.**

LESSONS C-7, C-8
The Passive

Objectives: To choose any one of the German phrases listed in the practice section and to be able to express it in German in all of the 14 active forms and also the 14 passive forms listed in the "What to learn" section of Lesson C-2.

Lesson C-9

Explanation: You should be able to express any given verb phrase in all 14 forms, active and passive, listed in Lesson C-2. Review Lesson C-2.

Practice: Pick one or two of the following phrases and express them in the forms listed in English below. Check your responses against the forms in Lesson C-2, or have your teacher check your responses:

ACTIVE	PASSIVE
(Max) (das Buch finden)	(das Buch) (gefunden werden)
(der Kaiser) (den Brief schreiben)	(der Brief) (geschrieben werden)
(die Soldaten) (die Stadt zerstören)	(die Stadt) (zerstört werden)

State that the subject
1. is doing this
2. was doing this
3. has done this
4. had done this
5. will do this
6. must do this
7. had to do this
8. has had to do this
9. had had to do this
10. will have to do this
11. would do this
12. would have done this
13. would have to do this
14. would have had to do this

State that this
1. is being done
2. was being done
3. has been done
4. had been done
5. will be done
6. must be done
7. had to be done
8. has had to be done
9. had had to be done
10. will have to be done
11. would be done
12. would have been done
13. would have to be done
14. would have had to be done

LESSON C-9
Comparison of Adjectives

Objectives: To be able to do the exercises in the practice section below in German with no errors.

Explanation: The comparison of adjectives in German is similar to the comparison of adjectives in English. The main difference is that we must be concerned often with case endings in German.

ENGLISH:
fresh, fresher, freshest

GERMAN:
frisch-, frischer-, frischest-
Haben Sie einen frischeren Salat?
Hier ist der frischeste Salat, den wir haben.

ein frisches Ei
ein frischeres Ei
das frischeste Ei

ein frischer Salat
ein frischerer Salat
der frischeste Salat

Practice: (All the adjectives called for form the comparative and superlative as described above.)

1. Change the adjective in each of the following sentences to the comparative *and* to the superlative:

a. Das ist der kleine Wagen. — Das ist der kleinere Wagen.
Das ist der kleinste Wagen.

b. Wir sind in dem schönen Park. — Wir sind in dem schöneren Park.
Wir sind in dem schönsten Park.

c. Dieser Mann kauft den schnellen Wagen. — Dieser Mann kauft den schnelleren Wagen.
Dieser Mann kauft den schnellsten Wagen.

d. Wo ist das neue Haus? — Wo ist das neuere Haus?
Wo ist das neu(e)ste Haus?

e. Er fährt mir der langsamen Straßenbahn. — Er fährt mit der langsameren Straßenbahn.
Er fährt mit der langsamsten Straßenbahn.

2. How would you express the following English sentences in German?

a. He is a nice man. — **Er ist ein netter Mann.**
b. Hans is a nicer man. — **Hans ist ein netterer Mann.**
c. But Fritz is the nicest man. — **Aber Fritz ist der netteste Mann.**
d. Is that an expensive house? — **Ist das ein teures Haus?**

Lesson C-10

e. Yes, but that is a more expensive house.	Ja, aber das ist ein teureres Haus.
f. Here is a more expensive car.	Hier ist ein teurerer Wagen.
g. He lives in the most expensive house.	Er wohnt in dem teuersten Haus.
h. Who has the happiest child?	Wer hat das glücklichste Kind?
i. My most interesting teacher is Mr. Braun.	Mein interessantester Lehrer ist Herr Braun.
j. Our more interesting books are over there.	Unsre interessanteren Bücher sind da drüben.

LESSON C-10
Comparison of Adjectives

Objectives: (1) To be able to give the comparative and superlative forms in German of the adjectives listed in the explanation section below; and (2) to be able to do the exercises in the practice section—without error.

Explanations: 1. No German adjectives form the comparative with the help of "more" or "most." All adjectives, no matter how many syllables they contain, add an **-er** or an **-(e)st** ending to the basic form.

2. Many adjectives have an umlaut in the comparative and superlative forms. Look up any adjective in a dictionary if you are not sure. Memorize the following common ones, however:

    alt, älter, ältest-
    jung, jünger, jüngst-
    lang, länger, längst-
    oft, öfter, öftest-
    groß, größer, größt-
    kalt, kälter, kältest-
    warm, wärmer, wärmst-
    schwach, schwächer, schwächst-
    stark, stärker, stärkst-
    arm, ärmer, ärmst-

(If you aren't sure of any adjective, it pays to be "suspicious" of any which have vowels which could have an umlaut!)

In German, as in English, some adjectives are irregular in their forms. Memorize the following common ones:

gut, besser, best-
viel, mehr, meist-
gern, lieber, liebst-
nah, näher, nächst-
hoch (hoh-), höher, höchst-

(You will have noticed by now that most adjectives whose basic forms end in **-e, -el, -en,** or **-er** drop the "e" before adding comparative or superlative endings.)

"hoch, höher, am höchsten"

Lesson C-11

Practice: Give the comparative and superlative forms of the following phrases:

1. ein junger Mann — ein jüngerer Mann / der jüngste Mann
2. der kalte Winter — der kältere Winter / der kälteste Winter
3. bei der schwachen Großmutter — bei der schwächeren Großmutter / bei der schwächsten Großmutter
4. sein großer Baum — sein größerer Baum / sein größter Baum
5. die hohen Berge — die höheren Berge / die höchsten Berge
6. Ihr gutes Kleid — Ihr besseres Kleid / Ihr bestes Kleid
7. Wer hat viel Geld? — Wer hat mehr Geld? / Wer hat das meiste Geld?

LESSON C-11
Comparison of Adjectives and Adverbs

Objectives: To be able to do the exercises in the practice section with no errors.

Explanations: Study the following examples:

Das Auto fährt schnell (*fast*).
Das Auto fährt schneller (*faster*).
Das Auto fährt **am schnellsten** (*the fastest*).

Ich spreche viel.
Ich spreche mehr.
Er spricht **am meisten**.

When adjectives do not precede or modify a noun directly (or if we are comparing adverbs), the superlative form always has the **am** —**sten** form illustrated above.

Practice: Change the following sentences to the comparative and superlative forms:

1. Spielt er gut?
   Spielt er besser?
   Spielt er am besten?

2. Wessen Mutter ist alt?
   Wessen Mutter ist älter?
   Wessen Mutter ist am ältesten?

3. Sie wohnen nah.
   Sie wohnen näher.
   Sie wohnen am nächsten.

4. Habt ihr das gern?
   Habt ihr das lieber?
   Habt ihr das am liebsten?
   (Can you give English equivalents of these two sentences?)

5. Hier sind die Leute arm.
   Hier sind die Leute ärmer.
   Hier sind die Leute am ärmsten.

6. Wir hätten hoch springen sollen.
   Wir hätten höher springen sollen.
   Wir hätten am höchsten springen sollen.

7. Du hast sicher viel getrunken.
   Du hast sicher mehr getrunken.
   Du hast sicher am meisten getrunken.

LESSON C-12
Comparison

Objectives: To be able to do the exercises in the practice section without error.

Explanations: Comparisons often are on an "equal level" or they express an obvious difference. Compare German and English:

Ich bin **so** intelligent **wie** er. — I'm *as* intelligent *as* he.
Ist dein Wagen **so** teuer **wie** mein Wagen? — Is your car *as* expensive *as* mine?
Mein Wagen ist teu**rer als** dein Wagen. — My car is *more* expensive *than* your car.
Das ist viel **besser, als** ich erwartet habe. — That is much *better than* I expected.

Practice: Express in German:

1. Does he have more than I? — **Hat er mehr als ich?**
2. She plays as well as Hans. — **Sie spielt so gut wie Hans.**

Lesson C-13

3. He is as old as my father.
4. The steak tastes better than the chicken.
5. But the chicken is not as expensive as the steak.
6. My old car goes faster than my new one.
7. An older man is not as strong as a younger one.
8. I like beer, but I prefer wine to beer. I like white wine best.

Er ist so alt wie mein Vater!
Das Steak schmeckt besser als das Hähnchen.
Aber das Hähnchen ist nicht so teuer wie das Steak.
Mein alter Wagen fährt schneller als mein neuer.
Ein älterer Mann ist nicht so stark wie ein jüngerer.
Ich trinke Bier gern, aber ich trinke Wein lieber als Bier. Ich trinke Weißwein am liebsten.

LESSON C-13
Ordinal Numbers; Fractions

Objectives: To be able to do the exercises in the practice section without error.

Explanations: Ordinal numbers (*first, fourth, twenty-fifth,* etc.) are used as adjectives and must have endings depending upon gender, case, number, etc.

    der (or **die**, or **das**)   **erste**
    zwei**te**
    dritte
    vier**te**, fünf**te**, . . .
    neunzehn**te**
    zwanzig**ste**
    neunundzwanzig**ste**
    dreißig**ste**
    neunundneunzig**ste**
    hundert**ste**

Practice: Express in German:

1. My first wife is dead.
2. Our fourth child is a boy.
3. Today is the twelfth day.
4. That is (**steht**) on the twenty-fifth page.

Meine erste Frau ist tot.
Unser viertes Kind ist ein Junge.
Heute ist der zwölfte Tag.
Das steht auf der fünfundzwanzigsten Seite.

5. They were in the second or third car.
6. His fifth book was the best.
7. I won't sit in the thirteenth row!
8. Her eighth husband is as young as her first.
9. The thirtieth student was more intelligent than the twenty-third.
10. Your last week here will not be as interesting as your first.

Sie waren im zweiten oder (im) dritten Wagen.
Sein fünftes Buch war das beste (am besten).
Ich sitze nicht in der dreizehnten Reihe!
Ihr achter Mann ist so jung wie ihr erster.

Der dreißigste Student war intelligenter als der dreiundzwanzigste.
Ihre letzte Woche hier wird nicht so interessant sein wie die erste.

"Ich sitze nicht in der dreizehnten Reihe!"

LESSON C-14
Numbers and Fractions

Objectives: To be able to do the exercises in the practice section with no errors.

Explanations: 1. Reading German numbers can often be confusing to English-speaking natives because the German uses commas and periods ("decimal points") in a manner opposite to that to which we are accustomed.

ENGLISH	GERMAN
1,000 (one thousand)	1.000 (tausend)
25.33 (twenty-five *point* thirty-three)	25,33 (fünfundzwanzig **komma** dreiunddreißig)

2. Fractions in German follow a pattern similar to the English pattern.

ein halb (1/2)
ein drittel (1/3)
ein viertel (1/4)
ein fünftel (1/5)
ein sechstel (1/6)

ein fünfzehntel (1/15)
ein zwanzigstel (1/20)
ein dreiunddreißigstel (1/33)
fünf achtel (5/8)
neun zehntel (9/10)
neunundneunzig hundertstel (99/100)

Practice

Read the following numbers *in German* (the numbers are written in the German manner):

a.	65	fünfundsechzig
b.	999	neunhundertneunundneunzig
c.	1.588	(ein)tausendfünfhundertachtundachtzig
d.	16.439	sechzehntausendvierhundertneununddreißig
e.	3.678.123	drei Millionen sechshundertachtundsiebzigtausendeinhundertdreiundzwanzig
f.	3,414	drei komma vier eins vier
g.	0,055	null komma null fünf fünf
h.	1.101,606	tausendeinhunderteins komma sechs null sechs
i.	1/7	ein siebtel
j.	9/10	neun zehntel
k.	19/45	neunzehn fünfundvierzigstel
l.	5 3/4	fünf drei viertel (read with a slight pause after the whole number, and with the fraction sounding like one word)
m.	25 2/3	fünfundzwanzig zwei drittel

LESSON C-15
Present Participles

Objectives: To be able to do the exercises in the practice section with no errors.

Explanations: There *is* such a thing as a present participle in German—that is, a form equivalent to an *-ing* ending in English: *running, sleeping, crying,* etc. In German these participles are not used as they are in such English sentences as "He is running." "He is running" must be expressed in German as **Er läuft**.

But we can use the present participle in German as an adjective. The ending in German equivalent to *-ing* in English is **-end**: **laufend, schlafend, weinend,** etc. In essence, one forms such a participle by adding a **-d** to the infinitive of a verb.

When using such a participle as an adjective, the proper ending must be added:

ein weinendes Kind	*a crying child*
das schlafende Mädchen	*the sleeping girl*
in dem abfahrenden Zug	*in the departing train*

If an adverb is added to modify the adjective, no ending is required on the adverb, of course.

ein laut weinendes Kind
das langsam sinkende Schiff

Practice: Give German equivalents of the following sentences:

1. Do you see the sleeping dog? — Siehst du den schlafenden Hund?
2. A blooming apple tree is beautiful. — Ein blühender Apfelbaum ist schön.
3. He heard the snoring grandmother. — Er hat die schnarchende Großmutter gehört.
4. She was standing behind the waving people. — Sie stand hinter den winkenden Leuten.
5. A flying bird is faster than a swimming fish. — Ein fliegender Vogel ist schneller als ein schwimmender Fisch.
6. The arriving train is not as long as the departing train. — Der ankommende Zug ist nicht so lang wie der abfahrende Zug.

LESSON C-16

Objectives: To be able to do the exercises in the practice section with no errors.

Explanations: Sometimes in German an "adjective phrase" containing a participle can be quite long compared to what one finds in English. In English such long modifying phrases are usually expressed as relative clauses. We *could* say in English, for example:

> The unusually popular and very long-running musical, *Hair*, has finally ended its engagement in New York.

But we are more likely to say something like the following:

> The musical, *Hair,* which was unusually popular and ran for a very long time, has finally ended its engagement in New York.

In German it would not be unusual to read a sentence such as:

> Der alte **auf zwei Rädern so schnell um die Ecke und gerade auf die kleinen Kinder fahrende** Wagen wurde von einer alten Frau gefahren.

An English-speaking native would find the sentence more familiar if the long boldfaced phrase were expressed as a relative clause:

> Der alte Wagen, **der auf zwei Rädern so schnell um die Ecke und gerade auf die kleinen Kinder fuhr,** wurde von einer alten Frau gefahren.

Practice: Express each of the following English sentences in two ways in German:
a. with a relative clause, as in the English sentence;
b. with the content in the relative clause expressed as an adjective phrase.

EXAMPLE:
The train which is just arriving at the station will soon continue on to Stuttgart.

a. Der Zug, der eben im Bahnhof ankommt, wird bald nach Stuttgart weiterfahren.
b. Der eben im Bahnhof ankommende Zug wird bald nach Stuttgart weiterfahren.

BEGIN:
1. The man who was standing at the corner over there didn't see the car.

a. Der Mann, der da drüben an der Ecke stand, hat das Auto nicht gesehen.
b. Der da drüben an der Ecke stehende Mann hat das Auto nicht gesehen.

2. I want to talk to the man who is just now running into the building.

a. Ich will mit dem Mann sprechen, der eben in das Gebäude läuft.
b. Ich will mit dem eben in das Gebäude laufenden Mann sprechen.

3. The people who are dancing in the streets have drunk too much.

a. Die Leute, die auf den Straßen tanzen, haben zu viel getrunken.
b. Die auf den Straßen tanzenden Leute haben zu viel getrunken.

"Die auf den Straßen tanzenden Leute haben zuviel getrunken."

4. My teacher, who at that time was still living in Dortmund, lives in America now.

   a. **Mein Lehrer, der damals noch in Dortmund wohnte, wohnt jetzt in Amerika.**
   b. **Mein damals noch in Dortmund wohnender Lehrer wohnt jetzt in Amerika.**

5. Who are the soldiers who are shooting at us out of the forest?

   a. **Wer sind die Soldaten, die aus dem Wald auf uns schießen?**
   b. **Wer sind die aus dem Wald auf uns schießenden Soldaten?**

LESSON C-17
The Genitive Case

Objectives: To be able to do the exercises in the practice section with no errors.

Explanations: We have encountered the genitive (possessive) case before (Lesson 75). However, we have delayed extensive practice, since the genitive form, except in relative clauses, can be avoided to a great degree.

However, it *is* used in German, and it will be frequently encountered, even though there seems to be a modern trend toward replacing it with the dative.

Some examples of the genitive:

ENGLISH	GERMAN
my father's friend	der Freund **meines** Vater**s**
	(or: der Freund **von meinem Vater**)
the lady's purse	die Handtasche **der** Frau
the windows of the old house	die Fenster **des** alt**en** Hause**s**
the men's cars	die Autos **der** Männer
whose?	wessen?

Summary of German genitive forms:

MASCULINE	NEUTER	FEMININE	PLURAL
des –n –(e)s	des –n –(e)s	der –n –	der –n –
eines –n –(e)s	eines –n –(e)s	einer –n –	keiner –n –

Some notes:

1. There are basically only *two* forms to learn for the genitive: **-es -n -(e)s** (for masculine and neuter nouns) and **-er -n -** (for feminine and plural).
2. The **-es** ending is generally added to masculine and neuter nouns of one syllable. An **-s** only is added to nouns of two or more syllables.
3. There *are* nouns with an irregular genitive ending (**Herz/ Herzens**), but they are infrequent. Consult a dictionary for certainty.
4. Neither the genitive nor **von** are used with measurements:

> **ein Glas Wasser**
> **eine Tasse Tee**
> **ein Pfund Fleisch**
> **eine Flasche Milch**

5. With names the genitive is similar to that in English:

> **Erikas Mutter**
> **Schmidts Familie**

6. Apostrophes are *not* used with these possessive forms in German.

Practice: Give German equivalents, using the genitive where possible, of the following expressions:

1.	the wolf's fur	der Pelz des Wolf(e)s
2.	the girl's face	das Gesicht des Mädchens
3.	the lady's umbrella	der Regenschirm der Frau
4.	the children's friend	der Freund der Kinder
5.	my old friend's wife	die Frau meines alten Freundes
6.	her sick mother's house	das Haus ihrer kranken Mutter
7.	the color of our new house	die Farbe unsres neuen Hauses
8.	the leaves of his little trees	die Blätter seiner kleinen Bäume
9.	a glass of wine	ein Glas Wein
10.	the color of the wine	die Farbe des Weines
11.	the story of the good old days	die Geschichte der guten alten Tage
12.	Erika's mother	Erikas Mutter

LESSON C-18
Genitive

Objectives: To be able to do the exercises in the practice section with no errors.

Explanations: A few common prepositions are generally followed by genitive forms:

während des Tages	during the day
trotz des Wetters	in spite of the weather
wegen der Zeit	on account of the time
statt seiner Freunde	instead of his friends

(Do not be surprised if you should see the dative used in some phrases similar to those above, especially after **trotz**.)

Practice: Express in German:

1. The children's mother is coming in spite of the war.
   Die Mutter der Kinder kommt trotz des Krieges.
2. My father's grandmother stays with (**bei**) us during the summer.
   Die Großmutter meines Vaters bleibt während des Sommers bei uns.
3. We have to stay in the old hunter's cabin on account of the weather.
   Wir müssen wegen des Wetters in der Hütte des alten Jägers bleiben.
4. They brought a bottle of wine instead of a bouquet.
   Sie haben statt eines Blumenstraußes eine Flasche Wein gebracht.
5. Gisela's mother likes the colors of the new rooms.
   Giselas Mutter hat die Farben der neuen Zimmer gern.
6. Siegfried smeared the fat of the dead dragon on his skin.
   Siegfried schmierte das Fett des toten Drachens auf seine Haut.
7. Hänsel and Gretel ate the sugar windows of the little house in spite of the witch.
   Hänsel und Gretel aßen die Zuckerfenster des kleinen Hauses trotz der Hexe.
8. On account of the short (amount of) time we can't read the end of this beautiful story.
   Wegen der kurzen Zeit können wir das Ende dieser schönen Geschichte nicht lesen.

LESSON C-19
Reflexive Verbs

Objectives: To be able to give the German equivalents, orally and written, of the vocabulary in the explanation section below; and to be able to do the exercises in the practice section—all without error.

Explanations: There are a great number of reflexive verbs in German. They are recognizable in dictionaries by the third person reflexive pronoun **sich**, or by the abbreviation **r.** Some of them require the accusative, some the dative. We shall practice accusative forms in this lesson.

Study the forms of the reflexive below. It should not be difficult to learn them. Note that the third person reflexive forms (equivalent to English *himself, herself, itself, themselves*) are all expressed by one form in German, **sich**. The formal *you* (**Sie**) also has the reflexive form **sich**. The reflexive forms of the other second persons and the first persons are exactly the same as the accusative forms of these pronouns (**mich, dich, uns, euch**), which you have learned previously.

sich erkälten	to catch (a) cold
Ich erkälte **mich.**	I'm catching cold.
Du erkältest **dich.**	You are catching cold.
Er erkältet **sich.**	He's catching cold.
Sie erkältet **sich.**	She's catching cold.
Wir erkälten **uns.**	We're catching cold.
Ihr erkältet **euch.**	You're catching cold.
Sie erkälten **sich.**	They're catching cold.
	You are catching cold.

Memorize the following common reflexive verbs:

to wash oneself	**sich waschen/er wäscht sich/wusch/gewaschen**
to shave	**sich rasieren** (regular verb)
to catch cold	**sich erkälten** (reg.)
to get married	**sich verheiraten** (reg.)
to rest	**sich ausruhen** (reg.)
to fall in love with	**sich verlieben in** (reg.)
to sit down	**sich (hin)setzen** (reg.)

to put on (clothes)	sich anziehen/zog an/angezogen
to take off (clothes)	sich ausziehen/zog aus/ausgezogen
to change (clothes)	sich umziehen/zog um/umgezogen

Practice: Express in German:

1. She's washing herself. — Sie wäscht sich.
2. He's shaving. — Er rasiert sich.
3. We have to change clothes. — Wir müssen uns umziehen.
4. You've caught cold. — Du hast dich erkältet.
5. I want to sit down and rest. — Ich will mich setzen und mich ausruhen.
6. Gisela has fallen in love with Hans. — Gisela hat sich in Hans verliebt.
7. Will they get married? — Werden sie sich verheiraten?
8. Undress, please! — Ziehen Sie sich bitte aus!
9. You-all are not getting dressed as fast as we. — Ihr zieht euch nicht so schnell an wie wir.
10. Do you see the man shaving over there? — Siehst du den sich rasierenden Mann da drüben?
    Or: Siehst du den Mann da drüben, der sich rasiert?

LESSON C-20
Reflexives

Objectives: To be able to do the drills in the practice section; and to memorize the vocabulary in the explanation section—all without error.

Explanations: The reflexive pronoun is in the *dative* form if a direct object is named for the reflexive verb. Since the dative pronouns for the third person, for **wir**, and for **uns** are the same as the accusative (at least in the reflexive forms), we need be concerned only about the pronouns **mir** and **dir**.

EXAMPLES:
Ich wasche **mir** das Gesicht.
Du sollst **dir** das Kinn rasieren.

Note the contrast:
>Ich wasche **mich** jeden Morgen.
>Ich wasche **mir** das Gesicht jeden Morgen.

In the first sentence **mich** is the object. In the second sentence **das Gesicht** is the object, and it belongs *to me*. *Me* is an indirect object in the sense of *me* in the colloquial sentence "I bought me a new car."

Memorize the following dative reflexive phrases:

to brush one's teeth	sich die Zähne putzen
to comb one's hair	sich die Haare kämmen
to buy oneself something	sich etwas kaufen
to look at something (for oneself)	sich etwas ansehen
to build something (for oneself)	sich etwas bauen

Practice: Express in German:

1. When are you going to brush your teeth? — Wann putzt du dir die Zähne?
2. I would have built myself a house if I had had the time. — Ich hätte mir ein Haus gebaut, hätte ich die Zeit gehabt.
3. The smaller children can't brush their teeth. — Die kleineren Kinder können sich die Zähne nicht (selber) putzen.
4. I didn't want to watch the movie. — Ich habe mir den Film nicht ansehen wollen.
5. Buy yourselves a newer car. — Kauft euch ein neueres Auto!

LESSON C-21
Time Phrases

Objectives: To be able to do the drills in the practice section with no errors.

Explanations: Time phrases in German can often be a problem to speakers of English, since the two languages sometimes have basically different forms for expressing the same elements of time.

Lesson C-21

Notice the differences:

1. I've worked here for two years.   Ich arbeite hier seit zwei Jahren.
  (or: schon zwei Jahre)
2. I worked there for five years.   Ich habe da fünf Jahre (lang) gearbeitet.
3. I worked there seven years ago.   Ich habe vor sieben Jahren da gearbeitet.
4. for a long time   lange
5. for two years   zwei Jahre (lang) (except in a sentence like number 1 above) (See note below.)

Note especially that in number 1 above there are two differences. The action of beginning to work *began in the past and is still going on.* The English uses the *verb* in the present perfect tense to get this idea across.

The German, however, does not use the verb to show that the action began in the past (the verb is in the present tense). Instead, it is the time phrase itself which takes us back two years: **seit zwei Jahren** (or **schon zwei Jahre**).

The English phrase *for two years* indicates nothing about when these two years occurred. We have to rely on the verb for that.

Practice: Express in German:

1. We have been living in Duisburg for seven months.   Wir wohnen (schon) seit sieben Monaten in Duisburg.
2. They want to stay in Italy for three weeks.   Sie wollen drei Wochen (lang) in Italien bleiben.
3. Six years ago I was much heavier than I am now.   Vor sechs Jahren war ich viel schwerer, als ich jetzt bin.
4. At seven o'clock he was seen in Motzenhofen.   Um sieben Uhr wurde er in Motzenhofen gesehen.
5. A year ago nothing could be seen there.   Vor einem Jahr konnte da nichts gesehen werden.
6. Have you been living here long?   Wohnen Sie schon lange (seit langem) hier?
7. Yes, I've lived here for eight years.   Ja, ich wohne schon acht Jahre (seit acht Jahren) (schon seit acht Jahren) hier.

"Vor einem Jahr konnte da nichts gesehen werden."

LESSON C-22
More About Time

Objectives: To be able to do the exercises in the practice section with no errors.

Practice: Study the following expressions. If they are new to you, memorize them.

the twenty-fifth of June	den 25. (fünfundzwanzigsten) Juni
on the fifteenth of May	am fünfzehnten Mai
every Monday	jeden Montag
every year	jedes Jahr
every five years	alle fünf Jahre
on Wednesday	(am) Mittwoch
in August	im August
half past nine	halb zehn
quarter to six	viertel vor sechs
	dreiviertel sechs
in one year	nach einem Jahr

Practice: Express in German:

1.	the 7th of July	den siebten Juli
2.	every Friday	jeden Freitag
3.	3 days ago	vor drei Tagen
4.	every 3 days	alle drei Tage
5.	in 3 days	nach drei Tagen
6.	for 3 days	drei Tage lang
7.	the third day	der dritte Tag
8.	in August	im August
9.	on the 10th of August	am zehnten August
10.	on Tuesday	am Dienstag
11.	11:45	dreiviertel zwölf (elf Uhr 45)
12.	since last year	seit letztem Jahr

LESSON C-23
Indirect Discourse

Objectives: To be able to do the exercises in the practice section without error.

Explanations: The subjunctive forms are used in German in indirect discourse and in expressing wishes, as well as in the conditional sentences practiced in Lessons 59-70.

In indirect discourse we are reporting what someone else has said:

DIRECT QUOTE	INDIRECT DISCOURSE
"I'm going home."	He said he was going home.
"I ate too much."	She said she ate too much.
	She said she had eaten too much.

In German the indirect statement would be in the subjunctive form:

"Ich gehe nach Hause."	Er sagte, er **ginge** nach Hause.
"Ich habe zuviel gegessen."	Er sagte, er **hätte zuviel gegessen**.

If the direct quote is in the present tense, the indirect quote will be in the present subjunctive form. But remember that the present subjunctive form is based on the simple past stem—umlauted if possible.

If the direct quote is in *any* past tense, the indirect quote will be in the past subjunctive, a form with **wäre** or **hätte** plus a past participle.

Practice: Change each of the following direct quotations into indirect discourse, beginning with **Er sagte,** ...

1. "Hans hat einen neuen VW." — Er sagte, Hans hätte einen neuen VW.
2. "Die Leute singen zu laut." — Er sagte, die Leute sängen zu laut.
3. "Ich schlafe bald ein." — Er sagte, er schliefe bald ein.
4. "Ihr müßt Hans finden." — Er sagte, wir müßten Hans finden.
5. "Gisela darf nicht gehen." — Er sagte, Gisela dürfte nicht gehen.
6. "Ich war nicht da." — Er sagte, er wäre nicht da gewesen.
7. "Udo wollte mitkommen." — Er sagte, Udo hätte mitkommen wollen.

8.	"Ihr habt das gesehen."	Er sagte, wir hätten das gesehen.
9.	"Ich bin nicht gefallen."	Er sagte, er wäre nicht gefallen.
10.	"Die Mutter wohnt in Nürnberg."	Er sagte, die Mutter wohnte in Nürnberg.

LESSON C-24
Indirect Discourse

Objectives: To be able to do the exercises in the practice section with no errors.

Practice: Express in German:

1.	My mother said that she was riding with us.	Meine Mutter sagte, daß sie mit uns führe.
2.	Who said that Mr. Braun had written the letter?	Wer sagte, daß Herr Braun den Brief geschrieben hätte?
3.	They said that the 10th day was the longest.	Sie sagten, daß der zehnte Tag am längsten wäre.
4.	She said that the car had not been repaired.	Sie sagte, daß das Auto nicht repariert worden wäre.
5.	He said he was combing his hair.	Er sagte, daß er sich die Haare kämmte.
6.	She said I ought to wash my hands and face.	Sie sagte, daß ich mir die Hände und das Gesicht waschen sollte.

LESSON C-25
Indirect Discourse

Objectives: To be able to do the exercises in the practice section with no errors.

Explanations: Indirect discourse sentences can begin with **Er fragte, ob**...

"Er fragte, ob ich mir den Film noch nicht angesehen hätte."

Practice: Change to indirect questions beginning with **Er fragte,** ...

1. "Hat Gisela nicht einmal Gitarre gespielt?" — Er fragte, ob Gisela nicht einmal Gitarre gespielt hätte.
2. "Warum schießt er den Wolf?" — Er fragte, warum er den Wolf schösse.
3. "Hast du dir den Film noch nicht angesehen?" — Er fragte, ob ich mir den Film noch nicht angesehen hätte.
4. "Ist er oft mit dem Motorrad gefahren?" — Er fragte, ob er oft mit dem Motorrad gefahren wäre.
5. "Wann ist der Zug angekommen?" — Er fragte, wann der Zug angekommen wäre.
6. "Wie lange bleibt Tante Emma hier in Bayreuth?" — Er fragte, wie lange Tante Emma hier in Bayreuth bliebe.
7. "Mit wem wollten sie Fußball spielen?" — Er fragte, mit wem sie hätten Fußball spielen wollen.
8. "Ist das verlorene Geld schon gefunden worden?" — Er fragte, ob das verlorene Geld schon gefunden worden wäre.

LESSON C-26
Expressing Wishes

Objectives: To be able to do the drills in the practice section with no errors.

Explanations: One can express wishes in various ways. Here are a few. Note the subjunctive:

Ich wollte, ich wäre reich!	I wish I were rich.
Ich wünschte, ich wäre reich!	I wish I were rich.
Wenn ich nur reich wäre!	If only I were rich!
Es wäre schön, wenn ich reich wäre.	It would be wonderful if I were rich.
Wäre ich nur reich!	Would that I were rich!
Ich wäre gern reich!	I would like to be rich.

Practice: Express in German (coming as close to the English structure as possible):

1. I wish you were here. — Ich wollte (wünschte), du wärest hier.
2. If only I had seen that! — Wenn ich das nur gesehen hätte!
3. It would be nice if they had not gone home. — Es wäre nett, wenn sie nicht nach Hause gegangen wären.
4. I wish I hadn't forgotten my umbrella. — Ich wollte, ich hätte meinen Regenschirm nicht vergessen.
5. Had he only not fallen into the lake! — Wäre er nur nicht in den See gefallen!
6. I would have liked to win that. — Ich hätte das gern gewonnen!
7. If only she had not been seen there! — Wenn sie nur nicht da gesehen worden wäre.
8. I wish she had as much money as you. — Ich wollte, sie hätte so viel Geld wie du.

LESSON C-27
Negation

Objectives: To be able to do the exercises in the practice section without error.

Explanations: Negation in German involves two problems: form and position. In this lesson we shall concentrate on several forms.

1. If we are negating a *noun* directly, we use **kein**.

a. Ich habe ein Buch.
   Ich habe **kein** Buch.   (*I have no book. I haven't any book.*)
b. Hast du Geld?
   Hast du **kein** Geld?   (*Don't you have any money?*)

2. Otherwise (negating a sentence, a verb, an adverb, an adjective, a predicate noun), we use **nicht**.

a. Wir gehen.
   Wir gehen **nicht**.
b. Es ist da drüben.
   Es ist **nicht** da drüben.
c. Das Mädchen ist schön.
   Das Mädchen ist **nicht** schön.
d. Das Auto fährt schnell.
   Das Auto fährt **nicht** schnell.
e. Sie geht heute nach Hause.
   Sie geht heute **nicht** nach Hause.
f. Das ist mein Buch.
   Das ist **nicht** mein Buch.

3. Some words have special negative forms. Learn them as pairs of "opposites."

a. **schon** (*already*):   **noch kein** (*referring to noun*)
                               noch nicht (*otherwise*)
                               (meanings: *not yet; still don't*)
b. **noch** (*still*):   **kein . . . mehr** (*if a noun*)
                               nicht mehr (*otherwise*)
                               (meanings: *no more; no longer*)
c. **müssen**:   **brauchen nicht** zu

EXAMPLES:
a. Sie haben **schon** ein Auto.   Er geht **schon** nach Hause.
   Sie haben **noch kein** Auto.   Er geht **noch nicht** nach Hause.

   Hans ist **schon** hier.
   Hans ist **noch nicht** hier.

Lesson C-27

    b. Ich habe Papier. Ich habe **noch** Papier   Es ist **noch** voll.
        Ich habe **kein** Papier **mehr**.   Es ist **nicht mehr** voll.

        Er ist **noch** in der Schule.   Sie spielt **noch**.
        Er ist **nicht mehr** in der Schule.   Sie spielt **nicht mehr**.

Practice: Give the negative or "opposite" of the following phrases. (Be certain you can give English equivalents.):

1.	ein Buch	kein Buch
2.	mein Auto	nicht mein Auto
3.	singen	nicht singen
4.	in der Straßenbahn	nicht in der Straßenbahn
5.	Wasser	kein Wasser
6.	schöner	nicht schöner
7.	schon eine Frau (*wife*)	noch keine Frau
8.	noch Bier	kein Bier mehr
9.	. . . müssen abfahren	. . . brauchen . . . nicht abzufahren
10.	. . . essen schon	. . . essen noch nicht
11.	. . . schreiben noch	. . . schreiben nicht mehr
12.	Wienerschnitzel	kein Wienerschnitzel
13.	schwer	nicht schwer
14.	. . . brauchen nicht zu bleiben	müssen bleiben
15.	keine Sahne mehr	noch Sahne
16.	noch keinen Regen	schon Regen
17.	. . . regnet noch nicht	. . . regnet schon
18.	. . . regnet nicht mehr	regnet noch

LESSON C-28
Negation

Objectives: To be able to do the drills in the practice section without error.

Explanations: The negating word or phrase *usually* precedes the word or phrase being negated, including verb forms like participles and infinitives at the end of sentences or clauses. If there is part of the predicate which is closely tied to the verb, the negation precedes this too.

If we are negating a verb which is not at the end of a sentence, the negation is then usually at the end of the sentence.

EXAMPLES:
- Es ist **nicht** rot.
- Er ist **nicht** da.
- Wir haben **keinen** Wein.
- Wir dürfen **nicht** trinken.
- Ich habe **kein** Auto **mehr**.
- Erika ist **noch nicht** nach Hause gegangen.

BUT:
- Wir singen heute **nicht**.
- Ich sehe den Zug **noch nicht**.
- Ich habe das **nicht mehr**.

(We are negating the verb or the whole idea, rather than one specific element.)

Practice: Express in German:

1. I don't have a glass. — Ich habe kein Glas.
2. We're *not* playing today. — Wir spielen heute nicht.
3. We're not playing *today*. — Wir spielen nicht heute.
   (Or: Wir spielen *heute* nicht.)
4. He's not working yet. — Er arbeitet noch nicht.
5. They're not at home yet. — Sie sind noch nicht zu Hause.
6. You don't know me any more. — Du kennst mich nicht mehr.
7. Have you already seen the house? — Hast du das Haus schon gesehen?
8. We don't have to go home. — Wir brauchen nicht nach Hause zu gehen.

9. She doesn't want any more ice cream.   **Sie will kein Eis mehr.**
10. The little child can't read the book yet.   **Das kleine Kind kann das Buch noch nicht lesen.**

LESSON C-29
Words Often Confused

Objectives: To memorize the German pairs of words in the explanation section; and to be able to use them as requested in the practice section, with no errors.

Explanations: Certain pairs (or even triplets) of words are often confused by new speakers of German, especially if their mother tongue is English. We should learn to distinguish between them readily. A few common ones:

sitzen	to sit (to be in position)
setzen	to set (to put into position)
liegen	to lie (to be in position)
legen	to lay (to put into a lying position)
stehen	to stand (to be in this position)
stellen	to place (put into an upright position)
begegnen (dat.)	to meet (without planning to)
treffen	to meet (intentionally) *or* to hit
kennen	to know (be acquainted with)
wissen	to know (a fact; have knowledge)
können	to know (a language)
werden	to get (become)
bekommen	to get (receive)
wohnen	to live (reside)
leben	to live (be alive; spend one's life)
stehenbleiben	to stop (oneself)
anhalten	to stop (a vehicle)

Students should get used to consulting a dictionary to distinguish between various shades of meaning. Most words have many. For instance, the word *stop* in English can have more than ten German equivalents, depending on exactly in which sense we mean it. (Of course, it has just about as many synonyms in English!)

Practice: Express in German:

1.	Lay that on the table.	Leg das auf den Tisch!
2.	Do you know whom we met in Berlin?	Weißt du, wem wir in Berlin begegneten?
3.	I get too tired.	Ich werde zu müde.
4.	He lived well at that time.	Er lebte damals gut.
5.	They know German.	Sie können Deutsch.
6.	Put (stand) the bicycle there.	Stellen Sie das Rad da!
7.	He always sits here.	Er sitzt immer hier.
8.	It's lying behind me.	Es liegt hinter mir.
9.	I'll meet you at ten.	Ich treffe dich um Zehn (Uhr).
10.	The bicycle is still standing there.	Das Rad steht noch da.
11.	You know that she knows me.	Du weißt, daß sie mich kennt.
12.	I get enough money.	Ich bekomme genug Geld.
13.	He lived in Hamburg at that time.	Er wohnte damals in Hamburg.
14.	I stopped the car.	Ich habe das Auto angehalten.
15.	I stopped walking.	Ich bin stehengeblieben. (Ich blieb stehen.)

LESSON C-30
Common Idioms

Objectives: To learn the common idioms in the practice section so that you can give them in German with any subject and in any tense (if a verb is involved) when given only the English equivalents as cues.

Practice:

1.	What's the matter with you?	Was fehlt Ihnen?
2.	to get used to	sich gewöhnen an (accus.)
	(I'll get used to him.)	(Ich gewöhne mich an ihn.)

Lesson C-31

3. to be interested in (I'm interested in the car.) — sich interessieren für (acc.) (Ich interessiere mich für den Wagen.)
4. in any case — auf jeden Fall
5. to be proud of (He's proud of his dog.) — stolz sein auf (acc.) (Er ist stolz auf seinen Hund.)
6. to rely on (One can't rely on them.) — sich verlassen auf (acc.) (Man kann sich nicht auf sie verlassen.)
7. to wait for — warten auf (acc.)
8. It occurs to me. — Es fällt mir ein.
9. to consider (something as. . .) (I consider him stupid.) (I think he's dumb.) — halten für Ich halte ihn für dumm.
10. to ask a question (She asked three questions.) — eine Frage stellen (Sie hat drei Fragen gestellt.)

LESSON C-31
Idioms

Objectives: See Lesson C-30.

Practice:

1. That's right. — Das stimmt!
2. gradually; by and by — nach und nach
3. to be right (You're right.) — recht haben (Du hast recht.)
4. to get angry about (He got mad at her.) — sich ärgern über (acc.) (Er hat sich über sie geärgert.)
5. neither . . . nor — weder . . . noch
6. all gone (The money is all gone.) — alle (Das Geld ist alle.)
7. That's none of your business. — Das geht Sie (dich) nichts an.
8. to insist on (He insists on going home.) — darauf bestehen (Er besteht darauf, nach Hause zu gehen.)
9. that consists of (dat.) — das besteht aus . . .
10. That makes no difference. — Das macht nichts aus.

LESSON C-32

Objectives: See Lesson C-30.

Practice:

1.	to pass a test	eine Prüfung bestehen
2.	He flunked.	Er ist durchgefallen.
3.	He passed.	Er ist durchgekommen.
4.	It seems to me that ...	Es ist mir, als ob ... (subjunctive)
5.	the more ... the better	je mehr ... desto besser
6.	to be worth the effort	der Mühe wert sein
	(It's not worth the trouble.)	(Es ist nicht der Mühe wert.)
7.	It's a question of ...	Es handelt sich um ...
8.	to smell like	riechen nach (dative)
9.	to long for	sich sehnen nach (dat.)
	(I'm longing for my mother.)	(Ich sehne mich nach meiner Mutter.)
10.	to remember	sich erinnern an (acc.)
	(I remember the day.)	(Ich erinnere mich an den Tag.)

Deutsch: ZWEITE STUFE
Vocabulary

1. Principal parts of irregular verbs and the plurals of nouns are given in the English-German vocabulary list only.
2. All words in the *Core Text* are repeated in the end vocabularies. All words are not necessarily in both the German-English and English-German lists, but they will be found in one or the other list, depending on the objectives and exercises in the lessons where the words appear.
3. Many, but not all, of the words in the *Complement* are also repeated in the end vocabularies. In any case, the meanings of all new words are given in the text of the *Complement* itself. The same is true of any *Optional Lessons*.
4. Not included in the end vocabularies:
    numbers (Lessons 13, 14)
    time expressions (Lessons 21, 22)
    special idioms (Lessons 30, 31, 32)

VOCABULARY

ENGLISH-GERMAN
Lessons 1-96

A

above über
account/on account of wegen
across from gegenüber
to act so tun (tun, tat, getan)
action (*movement*) die Bewegung, -en
afraid/to be afraid Angst haben
after nach
against gegen
all night die ganze Nacht
allowed/to be allowed, permitted dürfen (darf, durfte, gedurft)
alone allein
along mit; entlang
angry böse
animal das Tier, -e
answer die Antwort, -en
to answer antworten
arm der Arm, -e
to appear (*look*) aussehen (see to see)
apple der Apfel, ⸚
apprentice der Lehrling, -e
apron die Schürze, -n
around um
to arrive ankommen (see to come)
to ask fragen
at (the home of) bei
auto das Auto, -s
auto mechanic der Autoschlosser, -

B

bacon der Speck
bad schlecht; schlimm; böse
baggage claim die Gepäckaufgabe, -n
to bake backen (bäckt, buk, gebacken)
barber der Friseur, -e
basket der Korb, ⸚e
to be sein (ist, war, ist gewesen)
beautiful(ly) schön
because denn
to become, get; will (*future*) werden (wird, wurde, ist geworden)
bed das Bett, -en
beer das Bier, -e
before vor
to begin anfangen (fängt an, fing an, angefangen)
behind hinter
to believe glauben
bell die Klingel, -n
below unten
berry die Beere, -n; **little beeries** = Beerlein
besides außer
between zwischen
beverage das Getränk, -e
bicycle das Rad, ⸚er
bill (*check in a restaurant*) die Rechnung, -en
bird der Vogel, ⸚
birdie das Vöglein, -
bite der Bissen, -
to bite beißen (biß, gebissen)
blacksmith der Schmied, -e **smithy** (*blacksmith shop*) die Schmiede, -n
blade die Klinge, -n
to bloom blühen
to blow wehen

board   das Brett, -er
boat   das Boot, -e
body   der Körper, -; der Leib, -er
bolt   der Riegel, -
bone   der Knochen, -
book   das Buch, ̈-er
bottle   die Flasche, -n
bouquet   der Blumenstrauß, ̈-e
boy   der Junge, -n(s)
bread   das Brot, -e
breaded veal cutlets   das Wienerschnitzel, -
to break   brechen (bricht, brach, gebrochen); zerbrechen
to break out   ausbrechen (see **to break**)
to breathe   atmen
briefcase   die Aktentasche, -n
bright   hell
to bring   bringen (brachte, gebracht)
brother   der Bruder, ̈-
to brush (polish)   putzen; **to brush one's teeth**   sich die Zähne putzen (dative)
to build   bauen; **to build something (for oneself)**   sich etwas bauen (dative)
building   das Gebäude, -
to burn   brennen (brannte, gebrannt)
to bury   begraben (begräbt, begrub, begraben)
button   der Knopf, ̈-e
to buy   kaufen
by the   am

C

cake   der Kuchen, -
calendar   der Kalender, -
calf   das Kalb, ̈-er
to call   rufen (rief, gerufen)
can, to be able   können (kann, konnte, gekonnt)
cap   die Mütze, -n
cape   das Käppchen, -
to capture   einnehmen (see **to take** for principal parts)

car   der Wagen, -; das Auto, -s
care (worry)   die Sorge, -n
to carry   tragen (trägt, trug, getragen)
cat   die Katze, -n; **kitten** das Kätzchen, -
to catch cold   sich erkälten
chair   der Stuhl, ̈-e
to change clothes   sich umziehen (zog um, umgezogen)
cheese   der Käse
chicken   das Hähnchen, -
child   das Kind, -er
chimney   der Schornstein, -e
class   die Klasse, -n
clear   klar
cliff   der Felsen, -
to climb   steigen (stieg, ist gestiegen)
clock   die Uhr, -en
clothing   das Kleid, -er; die Kleidung, -en
cloud   die Wolke, -n
coal   die Kohle, -n
coffee   der Kaffee
cold   kalt
collapse (fall over)   umsinken (sank um, ist umgesunken)
to collect   einsammeln
color   die Farbe, -n
comb   der Kamm, ̈-e; **to comb one's hair**   sich die Haare kämmen (dative)
to come   kommen (kam, ist gekommen)
command   der Befehl, -e
comrade   der Kamerad, -en
conductor   der Schaffner, -
conversation   das Gespräch, -e
corner   die Ecke, -n
to cost   kosten
counter   der Schalter, -; der Ladentisch, -e
country   das Land, ̈-er
to cover   bedecken
crown   die Krone, -n
crumb   das Bröcklein, -
to cry   weinen
cup   die Tasse, -n

Vocabulary

to cut   schneiden (schnitt, geschnitten)
to cut off   abschneiden (see to cut)
cutlet (chop)   das Schnitzel, -

D

to dance   tanzen
dark   dunkel
daughter   die Tochter, ⸚
day   der Tag, -e
death   der Tod
to decide   entscheiden (entschied, entschieden)
to delay   aufhalten (hält auf, hielt auf, aufgehalten)
departure   die Abfahrt, -en
to destroy   zerstören
devout   fromm
to die   sterben (stirbt, starb, ist gestorben)
to do (make)   machen
to do   tun (tat, getan)
dog   der Hund, -e
door   die Tür, -en
down there   da unten
dragon   der Drache, -n
dream   der Traum, ⸚e
to dream   träumen
dress   das Kleid, -er
to drink   trinken (trank, getrunken)
drink   das Getränk, -e
to drive   fahren (fährt, fuhr, ist gefahren)
during   während

E

ear   das Ohr, -en
to eat   essen (ißt, aß, gegessen)
egg   das Ei, -er
to enclose   umschließen (schloß um, umgeschlossen)
end   das Ende, -n
especially   besonders
evening   der Abend, -e
ever   je

everything   alles
except for   außer
expensive   teuer
eye   das Auge, -n

F

face   das Gesicht, -er
falcon   der Falke, -n
to fall   fallen (fällt, fiel, ist gefallen)
to fall asleep   einschlafen (see to sleep)
to fall in love   sich verlieben in
family   die Familie, -n
farmer   der Bauer, -n
fast   schnell
father   der Vater, ⸚
fear   die Angst, ⸚e
to fear   Angst haben; scheuen
to feel   fühlen
festival   das Fest, -e
field   das Feld, -er
to fight   kämpfen
to fill   füllen
to find   finden (fand, gefunden)
to fire   entlassen (entläßt, entließ, entlassen)
to fish   angeln
floor   der Boden, ⸚
flower   die Blume, -n
to fly   fliegen (flog, ist geflogen)
food   die Speise, -n
fool   der Narr, -en
football (soccer ball)   der Fußball, ⸚e
for   für
forest   der Wald, ⸚er
to forget   vergessen (vergißt, vergaß, vergessen)
forget-me-not   das Vergißnichtmein
fork   die Gabel, -n
to freeze   frieren (fror, gefroren)
fresh   frisch
friend   der Freund, -e; die Freundin, -nen
friendly   freundlich

from von
front/in front of vor
fruit die Frucht, ⸚e
fur (pelt, hide) der Pelz, -e

G

to gain zunehmen (see **to take**)
garden der Garten, ⸚
gardener der Gärtner, -
gate (barrier) die Sperre, -n
gentleman der Herr, -en
Germany Deutschland
to get bekommen (see **to come**)
to get (fetch) holen
to get up aufstehen (see **to stand**)
girl das Mädchen, -; das Mädel, -
girl friend die Freundin, -nen
to give geben (gibt, gab, gegeben)
glass das Glas, ⸚er
to go, walk gehen (ging, ist gegangen)
goblet der Becher, -
God; god der Gott, ⸚er
grade (*mark on a report card,* etc.) die Zensur, -en
to grasp packen
grave das Grab, ⸚er
green grün
to grow wachsen (wächst, wuchs, ist gewachsen)
guitar die Gitarre, -n
gun das Gewehr, -e

H

had hatte (see **to have**)
hair das Haar, -e
hairdresser der Friseur, -e
ham der Schinken
hammer der Hammer, ⸚
hand die Hand, ⸚e
to hand reichen
handle (door handle, latch, knob) die Klinke, -n
to happen geschehen (geschieht, geschah, ist geschehen)

happy froh; glücklich; **to be happy** sich freuen
hard hart
to hate hassen
to have haben (hat, hatte, gehabt)
hawk der Habicht, -e
head der Kopf, ⸚e
healthy gesund
to hear hören
heart das Herz, -en
to help helfen (hilft, half, geholfen)
her ihr (poss. adj.)
here hier; hierher; her
hero der Held, -en
hide (skin) die Haut, ⸚e
high hoch
high school (college prep.) das Gymnasium, Gymnasien
to hike wandern
hike die Wanderung, -en
hippie der Gammler, -
his sein
hit (beat) schlagen (schlägt, schlug, geschlagen); treffen (trifft, traf, getroffen)
home das Heim, -e
home/at home zu Hause
home (when going) nach Hause
homework die Hausaufgabe, -n
hood (cape; bonnet) die Haube, -n
hope die Hoffnung, -en; **"hope-green"** hoffnungsgrün
horse das Pferd, -e
hot heiß
hour (class period) die Stunde, -n
house das Haus, ⸚er
human being; man(kind) der Mensch, -en
hunter der Jäger, -
hut; cabin die Hütte, -n

ice das Eis
idea (premonition) die Ahnung, -en

Vocabulary

if only I were wäre ich doch nur
ill krank
immediately gleich
instead of (an)statt
interested/to be interested in sich interessieren für
interesting interessant

J

jazz cellar der Jazzkeller, -
jewel (precious stone) der Edelstein, -e; das Juwel, -en
juice der Saft, ⸚e
to jump springen (sprang, ist gesprungen)

K

keep; hold halten (hält, hielt, gehalten)
kettle der Kessel, -
king der König, -e
kitchen die Küche, -n
knife das Messer, -
knock klopfen
to know (*a fact*) wissen (weiß, wußte, gewußt)
to know (*a language*) können (kann, konnte, gekonnt)

L

lady die Dame, -n; die Frau, -en
lake der See, -n
lamp (light) die Lampe, -n
lap der Schoß, ⸚e
to laugh lachen
lay lag (past of **to lie**)
lazy person die Faulenzerin, -nen
leaf das Blatt, ⸚er
left link-; links
leg das Bein, -e
lend (borrow) leihen (lieh, geliehen)
let (leave) lassen (läßt, ließ, gelassen)
letter der Brief, -e
to lie; to be "down" (*ill in bed,* etc.) liegen (lag, gelegen)

life das Leben
light (lamp) das Licht, -er
to like; may mögen (mag, mochte, gemocht)
to listen zuhören
to live wohnen (*reside*); leben
loaf der Laib, -e
to lock zuschließen (schloß zu, zugeschlossen)
long lang
to look schauen
to look (appear) aussehen (see **to see**)
to look at something sich etwas ansehen (see **to see**)
to look for suchen
lot/a lot viel
loudly laut
love die Liebe
to love lieben
love/to fall in love sich (in jemanden) verlieben

M

mail die Post, -en
to make machen
man der Mann, ⸚er; der Mensch, -en (*the human being*)
marry/to get married sich verheiraten
master ("gentleman," the Lord) der Herr, -en
meanwhile inzwischen
to meet begegnen (dative) (*to meet without planning to*); treffen (trifft, traf, getroffen)
melody die Melodei, -en (old form)
mirror der Spiegel, -
money das Geld, -er
moon der Mond, -e
mother die Mutter, ⸚
mountain der Berg, -e
to move (away) ziehen (zog, ist gezogen); fortziehen
movement die Bewegung, -en

movie   der Film, -e
movie theater   das Kino, -s
music   die Musik   to make music musizieren
must; to have to   müssen (muß, mußte, gemußt)
my   mein

N

name   der Name, -n
to be named, called   heißen (hieß, geheißen)
near   nah
to need   brauchen
need (distress)   die Not, ⸚e
nervous   nervös
never   nie; never ended   nahm kein Ende mehr
new   neu
newspaper   die Zeitung, -en
next to   neben
nice   nett
night   die Nacht, ⸚e
no   kein (adj.)
noon (midday)   der Mittag, -e
to "nose around"   gucken
to notice   merken
nut   der Nuß, Nüsse

O

oak tree   der Eichenbaum, ⸚e
official   der Beamte, -n
often   oft
old   alt
"one"   man
onion   die Zwiebel, -n
onto   auf
to open up   aufmachen
opposite   gegenüber
to order   bestellen
the other (one)   der (die, das) Andere
our   unser
out of   aus
oven   der Backofen, ⸚
over   über
over there   da drüben
to own   besitzen (besaß, besessen)
owner   der Besitzer, -

P

to paint   malen
pancake   der Pfannkuchen, -
paper   das Papier, -e
parents   die Eltern
pass   der Paß, Pässe
to pass (*go by*)   vergehen (see **to go**)
to pay   zahlen
peak (summit)   der Gipfel, -
pearl   die Perle, -n
pebble   der Kieselstein, -e
people   die Leute; die Menschen
to pick   pflücken
to pick up (lift up)   auflesen (see **to read** for principal parts)
picture (photo)   das Bild, -er
piece   das Stück, -e
pig   das Schwein, -e
pill   die Pille, -n
plan   der Plan, ⸚e
plant   die Pflanze, -n
platform   der Bahnsteig, -e
platter   die Platte, -n
to play   spielen
please   bitte
pocket   die Tasche, -n
poem   das Gedicht, -e
policeman   der Polizist, -en
poor   arm
to possess   besitzen (see **to own**)
possible   möglich
post office   die Post, -en
potato   die Kartoffel, -n
precious stone   (see **jewel**)
present (*gift*)   das Geschenk, -e
pretend   so tun (see **to act**)
probably   wohl

Vocabulary

purse   die Handtasche, -n
to put   legen
to put (*stick*)   stecken
to put (*stand*)   stellen
to put on clothes   sich anziehen (zog an, angezogen)

Q

quickly   geschwind; schnell

R

radio   das Radio, -s
to reach   reichen
to read   lesen (liest, las, gelesen)
to receive   bekommen (bekam, bekommen); erhalten (erhält, erhielt, erhalten)
record   die Platte, -n
red   rot
release (fire)   entlassen (see to fire)
to repair   reparieren
repair shop   die Werkstatt, ⸚e
to request (ask for)   bitten um (bat um, um . . . gebeten)
to rest (oneself)   sich ausruhen
restaurant   das Restaurant, -s
Rhine   der Rhein
rich   reich
ride   fahren (see to drive)
ring   der Ring, -e
rock (cliff)   der Felsen, -
roof   das Dach, ⸚er
room   die Stube, -n; das Zimmer, -
rose   die Rose, -n
to rub   reiben (rieb, gerieben)
to run   laufen (läuft, lief, ist gelaufen)
to run to   zulaufen (see to run)

S

saga (legend)   die Sage, -n
salad   der Salat, -e
salesman   der Verkäufer, -
sausage   die Wurst, ⸚e
to save (*keep*)   aufheben (hob auf, aufgehoben)
to save (*rescue*)   retten
saw   sah (see to see)
to say   sagen
school   die Schule, -n
scissors   die Schere, -n
scraps (garbage)   der Abfall, ⸚e
to scream   schreien (schrie, geschrie(e)n)
to see   sehen (sieht, sah, gesehen)
to see again   wiedersehen (see to see)
to sell   verkaufen
to send   schenken
to set (*put*)   setzen
to shave   sich rasieren
ship   das Schiff, -e
shirt   das Hemd, -en
to shoot   schießen (schoß, geschossen)
short   kurz
should; ought to; to be (supposed to)   sollen (soll, sollte, gesollt)
shoulder   die Schulter, -n
to shove in   hineinschieben (schob hinein, hineingeschoben)
to show   zeigen
to shy away from   sich scheuen
silver coin   die Silbermünze, -n
since   seit
to sing   singen (sang, gesungen)
singer   der Sänger, -
to sink   sinken (sank, ist gesunken)
to sit   sitzen (saß, gesessen)
to sit down   sich (hin)setzen
skin (hide)   die Haut, ⸚e
to slam shut   zuschlagen (see to hit)
to sleep   schlafen (schläft, schlief, geschlafen)
slip   das Hemd, -en
small   klein
to smear   schmieren
to sneak   schleichen (schlich, geschlichen)
to snore   schnarchen

soldier   der Soldat, -en
something   was; etwas
son   der Sohn, ̈e
song   das Lied, -er
soul   die Seele, -n
soup   die Suppe, -n
sow (pig)   die Sau, -en (*also* Säue)
to speak   sprechen (spricht, sprach, gesprochen)
spite/in spite of   trotz
spoon   der Löffel, -
spot (place)   die Stelle, -n
stall   der Stall, ̈e
to stand   stehen (stand, gestanden)
star   der Stern, -e
to stare   starren
station (train)   der Bahnhof, ̈e
to stay (remain)   bleiben (blieb, ist geblieben)
steak   das Steak, -s
step   der Schritt, -e
still longer   noch viel mehr
stone (rock)   der Stein, -e
story   die Geschichte, -n
street   die Straße, -n
streetcar   die Straßenbahn, -en
strong   stark
stupid   dumm
suddenly   plötzlich
suitcase   der Koffer, -
summer   der Sommer, -
sun   die Sonne, -n
sunrise   der Sonnenaufgang, ̈e
to swallow   verschlucken
to swim   schwimmen (schwamm, ist geschwommen)
sword   das Schwert, -er

T

table   der Tisch, -e
tail   der Schwanz, ̈e
to take   nehmen (nimmt, nahm, genommen)
to take off   abnehmen (see **to take**)
to take off clothes   sich ausziehen (see **to put on**)
to talk   reden
to taste   schmecken
tea   der Tee
teacher   der Lehrer, -; die Lehrerin, -nen
team   die Mannschaft, -en
tear   die Träne, -n
to tear apart   zerreißen (zerriß, zerrissen)
television   das Fernsehen
to tell   sagen; erzählen
than   als
their   ihr
there   da
there was   es war einmal
thing   das Ding, -e
to think   denken (dachte, gedacht)
through   durch
to throw   werfen (wirft, warf, geworfen)
ticket   die Fahrkarte, -n; das Billet, -te
time   die Zeit, -en; das Mal, -e
tired   müde
to   zu; nach
today   heute
together   zusammen
tomato   die Tomate, -n
tonight   heute nacht
too   zu
took   nahm (see **to take**)
toward   gegen
train   der Zug, ̈e
treasure   der Schatz, ̈e
truth   die Wahrheit, -en
turtle   die Schildkröte, -n

U

umbrella   der Regenschirm, -e
under   unter
to understand   verstehen (verstand, verstanden)

Vocabulary

    to undress   ausziehen (sich) (see **to put on**)
    university   die Universität, -en
    usually   sonst

V

    village   das Dorf, ̈-er
    voice   die Stimme, -n

W

    to wait   warten
    to wait for   warten auf
    to wake up   aufwachen
    to walk   gehen (see **to go**)
    wall   die Wand, ̈-e
    to want   wollen (will, wollte, gewollt)
    war   der Krieg, -e
    to wash   sich waschen (wäscht, wusch, gewaschen)
    to wave   winken
    way   der Weg, -e
    to wear   tragen (trägt, trug, getragen)
    weather   das Wetter
    week   die Woche, -n
    well   gut; wohl
    wheel   das Rad, ̈-er
    while   die Weile, -n; **a little while**   das Weilchen
    white   weiß
    whole   ganz
    whom   wen; wem
    whose   wessen
    wild   wild
    wilderness   die Wildnis
    to win   gewinnen (gewann, gewonnen)
    wind   der Wind, -e
    window   das Fenster, -
    window pane   die Fensterscheibe, -n
    wine   der Wein, -e
    to wish   wünschen
    witch   die Hexe, -n
    with   mit
    without   ohne

wolf   der Wolf, ̈-e
woman (lady; wife)   die Frau, -en
to wonder   (sich) wundern
wonderful/especially wonderful   wunderschön
woodcutter   der Holzhacker, -
woods   der Wald, ̈-er
word   das Wort, -e; ̈-er
work   die Arbeit, -en
worker   der Arbeiter, -
world   die Welt
wrinkle   die Falte, -n
to write   schreiben (schrieb, geschrieben); **to be written**   stehen (see **to stand**)

Y

year   das Jahr, -e
yellow   gelb
yesterday   gestern
your   Ihr, dein, euer
youth   die Jugend

VOCABULARY

GERMAN-ENGLISH

For plural forms or principal parts of verbs, see the English-German vocabulary for the word in question.

A

ab   away; off (of); down
der Abend   evening
abends   evenings
der Abfall   scraps, garbage
abholen   to pick up
abnehmen   to take off
abschneiden   to cut off
abwarten   to wait for
ach   oh!
achtgeben   to pay attention
ade   goodbye
die Ahnung   idea; premonition
die Aktentasche   briefcase
all-   all
alle   everyone; all (of them); all gone
allerfeinsten   the finest of all
als   when; as; than
also   therefore
alt   old
die Alte   the old lady
am   an dem
an   to; at; on   glauben an   to believe in
ander-   other; different
die Andern   the others
anfangen   to begin
angeln   to fish
die Angst   fear
ankommen   to arrive
anrühren   to mix
die Antwort   answer
anziehen   to put on
anzünden   to ignite; light
der Apfel   apple
die Arbeit   work
arm   poor

atmen   to breathe
auf   upon, on, onto; open
auf einmal   suddenly
aufhängen   to hang up
auflesen   to pick up (lift up)
aufmachen   to open up
aufpicken   to pick up (with a beak)
aufstehen   to get up, to stand up
das Auge   eye
aus   out of
aussehen   to appear, look
außer   except (for); besides
ausziehen   to take off
das Auto   the car
der Autoschlosser   auto mechanic

B

backen   to bake
der Backofen   oven
baden   to bathe
bald   soon
basiert   based
bauen   to build
der Bauer   farmer
der Beamte   official
bedecken   to cover
die Beere   berry
das Beerlein   little berries
der Befehl   command
befreien   to free
begegnen   to meet; to come across someone
beginnen   to begin
begraben   to bury
bei   at; at the home of; by

beide   both
das Bein   leg
beiseite   aside
beißen   to bite
bekannt   (well) known
bekommen   to receive
bereiten   to prepare
der Berg   mountain
besitzen   to own, possess
der Besitzer   owner
besonders   especially
besser   better
best-   best
bestellen   to order
bestimmt   certainly
besuchen   to visit
das Bett   bed
bevor   before
die Bewegung   action, movement
bezahlen   to pay
das Bild   picture; photo
das Billet   ticket
der Bissen   bite; morsel
bißchen   little; bit
bitten um   to request; to ask for
blank   shiny
das Blatt   leaf; page
blau   blue
bleiben   to stay, remain
blühen   to bloom
die Blume   flower
das Blut   blood
der Boden   floor
das Boot   boat
böse   wicked; angry
brauchen   to need;   nicht brauchen   not to have to, doesn't need to
brechen   to break
brechen/ausbrechen   to break out
brennen   to burn
das Brett   board
der Brief   letter
bringen   to bring

das Bröcklein   crumb
das Brot   bread
der Bruder   brother
das Buch   book
bücken (sich)   to bend over

D

da-compounds (see page 212)
dabei   in addition; in accompaniment
das Dach   roof
da drüben   over there
die Dame   lady
damit   so that; with it; with that
danach   afterwards; after it (or that)
dann   then
darauf/bald darauf   soon thereafter
darin   in it
davon   away from it; of it; about it
decken   to cover
dein   your
denken   to think
denn   "anyway"; for, because
dennoch   nevertheless
deshalb   for that reason
dessen   whose
dicht   dense; dichtest   densest
das Ding   thing
doch   however; nevertheless
das Dorf   village
dort   there
der Drache   dragon
dran   on it
drinnen   inside
dritt-   third
d'runten   down there
dunkel   dark
die Dunkelheit   darkness
dünn   thin
durch   through
dürfen   to be allowed, permitted

E

eben   just; just now
die Ecke   corner
der Edelstein   jewel, precious stone
ehe   before
ei!   oh!
das Ei   egg
der Eichenbaum   oak tree
eigen   own
eilen   to hurry
einfach   simple, simply
eingeben   to inspire
einmal   once
einmal/Es war einmal . . .   There was once . . . , Once upon a time . . .
einnehmen   to capture
einschlafen   to fall asleep
einwilligen   to agree
das Eis   ice; ice cream
das Eisen   iron
eisern   iron
elend   miserable
elendig   miserably
die Eltern   parents
das Ende   end
endlich   finally
entlang   along; along the length of
entlassen   to release; to fire
erbärmlich   pitifully
die Erde   the ground
erhalten   to receive
erkennen   to recognize
erlauben   to allow
ernähren   to feed; support
erschrecken   to be startled
erst   first
erzählen   to tell
es   there; es folgt   there follows
essen   to eat
das Essen   food
etwas   something; somewhat

F

fahren   to drive; ride
die Fahrkarte   ticket
der Falke   falcon
fallen   to fall
fällen   to fell; chop down
fallen lassen   to drop
die Falte   wrinkle
die Familie   family
fassen   to grasp
fast   almost
die Faulenzerin   lazy person
das Feld   field
der Felsen   rock; cliff
das Fenster   window
das Fernsehen   TV
das Fest   festival
der Festtag   festival; feast day
fett   fat
das Feuer   fire
der Film   movie
finden   to find
finster   dark
die Flasche   bottle
fliegen   to fly
flink   quick, nimble, agile
die Flüßigkeit   liquid
folgen   to follow
fort   away
fortziehen   to move away; to "pull out"
fragen   to ask
die Frau   woman, lady; wife
fremd   strange; foreign
freuen (sich)   to be happy, rejoice
der Freund   friend
die Freundin   girl friend
friedlich   peacefully
frieren   to freeze
frisch   fresh
der Friseur   barber; hairdresser
froh   happy
fröhlich   happily; happy
fromm   pious; religious; devoted
die Frucht   fruit

früh early
fühlen to feel
führen to lead; direct
füllen to fill
für for
furchtbar terrible; frightful(ly)
fürchten to fear
der Fußball football; soccer ball
füttern to feed

G

die Gabel fork
der Gammler hippie
ganz quite; completely
gar nicht not at all
gar nichts nothing at all
der Garten garden
der Gärtner gardener
das Gebäude building
geben to give
geben/es gibt there is; there are
das Gedicht poem
gefallen (*requires dative form of object*) to please; to like
gegen against; toward
gegenüber opposite; across from
gehen to go; walk
gelangen to reach, arrive; to attain
gelb yellow
das Geld money
genau exactly
genug enough
die Gepäckaufgabe baggage claim room
gerade just now
gern gladly
geschehen to happen
das Geschenk present, gift
die Geschichte story
geschwind quickly
das Gesicht face
das Gespräch conversation
gesund healthy; healed; well
das Getränk beverage; drink

getrost with confidence, trust
die Gewalt power
gewaltig violently
das Gewehr gun
gewinnen to win
der Gipfel peak; summit
das Gitter grating
das Glas glass
glauben to believe
gleich right away; same, equal; although
glücklich happy
die Glut heat; glow
der Gott God; god
das Grab grave
grämen to fret; grieve
das Grammophon record player; phonograph
grau gray
groß big
grummeln to grumble
grün green
gucken to look; stare; gawk
das Gymnasium high school (college prep)

H

das Haar hair
haben to have
der Habicht hawk
das Hähnchen chicken
halten keep; hold
halten/aufhalten to delay
der Hammer hammer
die Hand hand
hängen to hang
hart hard
hatte had (*past of* haben)
die Haube hood, cape, bonnet
häufig frequently
das Haus house; nach Hause home (*when going there*); zu Hause at home
die Hausarbeit housework; homework

Vocabulary

die Hausaufgabe homework
die Haut skin, hide
heben/aufheben to save
das Heim home
heimlich secretly
heiß hot
heißen to be named, called
der Held hero
helfen to help
hell light, bright
das Hemd shirt
das Hemdlein blouse, shirt; slip
her here, this way (*toward the speaker*)
herausrufen to call out
herbei to here
herein in(to) here
der Herr master; gentleman; the Lord
das Herz heart
das Herzeleid great sorrow
heute today
heute nacht tonight
die Hexe witch
hier here
hierher here; to this place
die Hilfe help
der Himmel sky; heaven
hin away (from)
hineinschieben to shove in
hinlegen to lie down
hinnehmen to put up with
hinter behind
hinteran behind it (him, her, them, etc.)
hinterher afterwards
hoch high
die Hoffnung hope
hoffnungsgrün hopegreen (*green symbolizing hope*)
holen to get
der Holzhacker woodcutter
hören to hear
hübsch pretty; nice
die Hühnersuppe chicken soup
der Hund dog
der Hunger hunger; **Hungers sterben** to die of hunger, starve
hungrig hungry
der Husar hussar (see page 69)
die Hütte hut, cabin

I

immer always; **immer mehr** more and more; **immer weiter** farther and farther; **immerzu** continually
innen inside
interessieren (sich) to be interested
inzwischen meanwhile

J

ja yes; indeed
der Jäger hunter
das Jahr year
jammern to cry; complain
je ever
jed- each; every one
jetzt now
die Jugend youth
jung young
der Junge boy
das Juwel jewel

K

das Kalb calf
kalt cold
der Kamm comb
das Kämmerchen chamber; little room
kämpfen fight
das Käppchen cap, hood
kaputt broken
die Kartoffel potato
das Kätzchen little cat; kitten
die Katze cat
kaufen to buy
kaum hardly
kein no, none, not any
kein...mehr no more
kennen to know

der Kessel   kettle
der Kieselstein   pebble
das Kind   child
das Kino   movie theater, cinema
die Klasse   class
die Kleidung   clothing
klein   little
die Klinge   blade
die Klingel   bell
die Klinke   door handle, latch, knob
klopfen   to knock
der Knochen   bone
das Knöchlein   little bone
der Knopf   button
kochen   to cook; boil
der Koffer   suitcase
die Kohle   coal
kommandieren   to command
kommen   to come
der König   king
können   can, to be able
der Kopf   head
der Korb   basket
der Körper   body
kosten   to cost
die Kraft   strength
krank   sick
der Krieg   war
die Krone   crown
die Küche   kitchen
kühl   cool
küssen   to kiss

L

lachen   to laugh
der Laib   loaf
die Lampe   lamp; light
das Land   country
lang   long; along (*from* entlang)
lange   a long time
langsam   slow(ly)
lassen   let; leave
lauern/auflauern   to lie in wait for
laufen   to run
laut   loud(ly)
lauter   pure, nothing but
das Leben   life
lebendig   alive, living
der Lebtag   the days of one's life
legen   to lay; put
der Lehrer   teacher
die Lehrerin   (*fem.*) teacher
der Lehrling   apprentice
der Leib   body
das Leibchen   bodice; vest
leicht   light; easy
leihen   lend; borrow
lernen   to learn
lesen   to read
die Leute   people
der Leutnant   lieutenant
das Licht   light; lamp
lieb   dear
die Liebe   love
lieben   to love
lieber   dear; preferably
liebhaben   to love
das Lied   song
liegen   to lie; to be "down" (*ill*; *in the hospital*, etc.)
links   left, to the left
das Linnen (das Leinen *is more common*)   linen
locken   to lure
der Löffel   spoon
das Löffelchen   little spoon(ful)
los werden   to be rid of

M

machen   to do; make
das Mädchen   girl
das Mädel   girl
mager   thin; meager
mal (einmal)   once
das Mal   time
malen   to paint

Vocabulary

man one (*person*)
der Mann man; husband
die Mannschaft team
marschieren to march
mehr more
meinen to mean; be of the opinion, to think, believe
die Melodei melody
der Mensch human being; "man"; people
merken to notice
das Messer knife
die Milch milk
mit with; along (*when used as a prefix with many verbs*)
miteinander together; with one another
mitleidig having pity or compassion
der Mittag noon; midday
die Mitte middle, center
mitten in the middle
mögen may; to like
möglich possible
der Mond moon
morgen früh tomorrow morning
die Müdigkeit fatigue
die Musik music
müssen must; to have to
die Mutter mother
die Mütze cap (*for one's head*)

N

nach after; to
nachdem after (*as conjunction*)
nachdenken to think over; ponder; reflect
nachher afterwards
nachsehen to look over; to check over
die Nacht night
nachts at night; nightly
der Name name
der Narr fool
neben near; next to
nebenan next to it (or someone)
nehmen to take
nett nice

neugeschlagen newly minted
nicht not
nicht mal einen not even one
nichts nothing
nichts mehr nothing else
nicken to nod
nie never
nieder lower
niedersetzen to sit down
niemand no one
noch still; yet
noch immer still
noch nicht not yet
die Not need; distress
null zero
die Null zero
nur only
der Nuß nut

O

ob whether; if
obwohl although
öffnen to open
ohne without
das Ohr ear

P

paar few; pair
packen to grasp; pick
das Papier paper
der Pelz the fur, pelt, hide
die Perle pearl
der Pfannkuchen pancake
das Pferd horse
die Pflanze plant
pflücken to pick; pluck
die Pille pill
der Plan plan
die Platte record; platter
plötzlich suddenly
der Polizist policeman
die Post post office; mail

R

das Rad bicycle; wheel
die Rechnung bill, check (*in a restaurant*)
recht quite
rechts right, to the right
reden to talk
der Regenschirm umbrella
reiben to rub
reich rich
reichen to hand; reach
das Reisig twigs; brush
reparieren to repair
das Restaurant restaurant
retten to save
der Riegel bolt
der Ring ring
das Röcklein skirt
das Rocktäschlein coat pocket
die Rose rose
rot red
rufen to call
die Ruhe rest; peace
ruhen to rest (**Er ruht sich aus.**)
rund round
rundherum all around; round about

S

die Sage saga; legend
sagen to say, tell
das Salz salt
sammeln to collect
der Sänger singer
satt full
die Sau sow, pig
schaffen to do; to provide; to create; to accomplish
der Schaffner conductor
scharf sharp
der Schatz treasure
schauen to look
die Scheibe/Fensterscheibe window pane
scheinen to shine; seem
schenken to give; present; send
die Schere scissors, shears
scheuen to fear, shun
schicken to send
schießen to shoot
das Schiff ship
der Schiffer sailor; skipper
die Schildkröte turtle
schimmern to glimmer
der Schinken ham
schlachten to slaughter
der Schlaf sleep
schlafen to sleep
schlagen hit; beat
schleichen to sneak
schmecken to taste
der Schmied blacksmith
die Schmiede smithy; blacksmith shop
schmieden the art of "blacksmithing" or forging
schmieren to smear
schnarchen to snore
schneiden to cut
schneidig sharp(ly)
das Schnitzel cutlet; chop
schon already
schön beautiful
der Schornstein chimney
der Schoß lap
schreiben to write
schreien to scream
das Schreien screaming
der Schritt step
schritthalten to keep step
die Schule school
die Schulter shoulder
die Schürze apron
schütteln to shake
schwach weak
schwarz black
schweben to float
das Schwein pig
schwer hard; difficult

Vocabulary

das Schwert   sword
die Schwester   sister
das Schwesterchen   little sister
schwimmen   to swim
der See   lake
die Seele   soul
segnen   to bless
sehen   to see
sehr   very
sei   be (*subjunctive*)
sein   to be
sein   his; its; her (*when referring to* das Mädchen)
seit   since
selber   self (myself, himself, etc.)
setzen   to set; put
sich   oneself (himself, herself, etc.)
die Silbermünze   silver coin
singen   to sing
sinken   to sink
sitzen   to sit
so   so; in this manner; like this
sobald   as soon as
sogar   even
der Sohn   son
solch   such
der Soldat   soldier
sollen   ought, to be supposed to, should, to be obliged to
der Sommer   summer
die Sonne   sun
der Sonnenaufgang   sunrise
der Sonnenschein   sunshine
sonst   otherwise
die Sorge   care; worry
soviel   so much
spät(er)   lat(er)
die Speise   food
die Sperre   gate; barrier
der Spiegel   mirror
spielen   to play
der Sport   sport(s)
sprechen   to speak
springen   to jump
der Stall   stall (pen)
stark   strong
starren   to stare
das Steak   steak
stecken   to put; stick
stecken/anstecken   ignite
stehen   to stand; to be written
steigen   to climb
der Stein   stone; rock
steinalt   ancient ("old as the rocks")
die Stelle   spot; place
stellen   to place, put
sterben   to die
der Stern   star
die Stimme   voice
der Stoff   stuff; material
die Straße   street
die Straßenbahn   streetcar
streuen   scatter; strew
die Stube   room
das Stück   piece
das Stückchen   little piece
der Stuhl   chair
stumm   quiet; silent; "dumb"
die Stunde   hour; class period
suchen   to look for; seek
sündhaft   sinful
die Suppe   soup
süß   sweet

T

der Tabak   tobacco
der Tag   day
tagelang   for days
täglich   daily
der Taler   "dollar"
der Tanz   dance
tanzen   to dance
tapfer   brave
die Tasche   pocket
die Tasse   cup
das Täubchen   pigeon

der Teig dough
teilen to share; divide
teilen/einteilen to divide; share
teuer expensive
das Theater theater
tief deep
das Tier animal
der Tingeltangel ding-a-ling (*sound made by a small bell*)
der Tisch table
die Tochter daughter
der Tod death
die Tomate tomato
tot dead
töten to kill
tragen to carry; wear
die Träne tear
der Traum dream
träumen to dream
traurig sad
treffen to meet; hit
treu true; faithful; loyal
trinken to drink
trösten to console; take comfort
tüchtig energetically
tun to do
tun/so tun to act; pretend
die Tür door

U

über over, above; about; left over; **über das Herz bringen** to find it in one's heart
die Uhr watch; clock; ... **Uhr** ... o'clock
um at; around; in order
umher around
umschließen to enclose
umsinken to collapse; fall over
unbegreiflich incomprehensible
unten below
unter below, under
unterwegs underway
uralt ancient
u.s.w. (und so weiter) etc.

V

der Vater father
verbrennen to burn up
verdienen to earn
vereint united
vergehen to pass; go by
vergessen to forget
das Vergißnichtmein forget-me-not
vergnügt happy; pleasurable
verirren (sich) to lose one's way
verkaufen to sell
der Verkäufer salesman
verlangen to demand
verlassen to leave
verschenken to give away
verschlucken to swallow
verstehen to understand
das Vertrauen trust; confidence
verwundbar vulnerable
viel much; **zu viel** too much
vielleicht perhaps
das Vöglein birdie
von from; of (*can also indicate possession*: **von der Mutter** mother's); by
vor because of; in the face of; in front of; before; ago (**vor langer Zeit** = a long time ago)
vor sich in front of her (him, them, etc.)
vorher beforehand
vorig- former; previous
vorsichtig careful
vorwärts forward
der VW (der Volkswagen) VW

W

wach awake
wachsen to grow
wackeln to shake

Vocabulary

der Wagen car; wagon
die Wahrheit truth
der Wald forest, woods
wälzen roll; turn about
die Wand wall
wandern to wander
die Wanderung hike
wann when
wäre were; "if I were," would be
wärmen to warm
warten to wait
warten auf to wait for
warum why
was what; (*also a form of* **etwas** = something)
wecken to awaken
weg away, gone
wegen because of; on account of
wehen to blow
weich soft
Weihnachten Christmas
weil because
das Weilchen a little while
die Weile while
der Wein wine
weinen to cry
weit for
weiter farther
die Welt world
wen whom
wer who
werden to become, get; will (*future*)
werfen to throw
das Wetter weather
wie as, like; **so ... wie** as ... as
wiedersehen to see again
die Wildnis wilderness
willig willing
wimmeln to swarm
winken to wave
wirklich really
wissen to know (*a fact*)
wo where (at)

wo-compounds (see page 212)
die Woche week
wohin where to
wohl probably; well, good
wohnen to live, reside
der Wolf wolf
die Wolke cloud
wollen to want
das Wort word
wunderbar wonderful
wunderhübsch wonderfully beautiful
wundern (sich) to wonder
wundersam strange
wunderschön wonderfully beautiful
wünschen to wish
die Wurst sausage

Z

zahlen to pay
zeigen to show
die Zeit time
die Zeitung newspaper
die Zensur grade, mark (*on a report card*, etc.)
zerbrechen to break
zerbröckeln to crumble
zerreißen to tear apart
ziehen to move (away); to pull
das Zimmer room
zu at; to
der Zucker sugar
zuhören to listen
zulaufen to run to
zünden/anzünden to ignite, light
zunehmen to gain
zusammen together
zuschlagen to slam shut (*see* **schlagen**)
zuschließen to lock
zweimal twice
zweit- second
die Zwiebel onion
zwischen between